MW00387431

The Straits from Troy
to Constantinople

The Straits from Troy to Constantinople

The Ancient History of the Dardanelles, Sea of Marmara and Bosphorus

John D Grainger

PEN & SWORD
HISTORY

First published in Great Britain in 2021 by
Pen & Sword History
An imprint of
Pen & Sword Books Ltd
Yorkshire – Philadelphia

Copyright © John D Grainger 2021

ISBN 978 1 39901 324 6

Typeset by Mac Style
Printed and bound in the UK by CPI Group (UK) Ltd,
Croydon, CR0 4YY

Pen & Sword Books Limited incorporates the imprints of Atlas,
Archaeology, Aviation, Discovery, Family History, Fiction, History,
Maritime, Military, Military Classics, Politics, Select, Transport,
True Crime, Air World, Frontline Publishing, Leo Cooper, Remember
When, Seaforth Publishing, The Praetorian Press, Wharncliffe
Local History, Wharncliffe Transport, Wharncliffe True Crime
and White Owl.

For a complete list of Pen & Sword titles please contact

PEN & SWORD BOOKS LIMITED
47 Church Street, Barnsley, South Yorkshire, S70 2AS, England
E-mail: enquiries@pen-and-sword.co.uk
Website: www.pen-and-sword.co.uk

Or

PEN AND SWORD BOOKS
1950 Lawrence Rd, Havertown, PA 19083, USA
E-mail: Uspen-and-sword@casematepublishers.com
Website: www.penandswordbooks.com

Contents

Maps

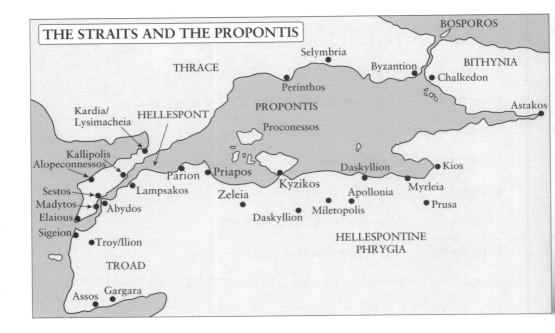

THE STRAITS AND THE PROPONTIS

BOSPOROS

THRACE

Selymbria

Byzantion

BITHYNIA

Chalkedon

Perinthos

PROPONTIS

Kardia/
Lysimacheia

HELLESPONT

Proconessos

Astakos

Kallipolis
Alopeconnessos

Parion

Priapos

Daskyllion

Kios

Sestos

Lampsakos

Kyzikos

Myrleia

Madytos

Zeleia

Apollonia

Elaious

Abydos

Daskyllion

Miletopolis

Prusa

Sigeion

Troy/Ilion

HELLESPONTINE
PHRYGIA

TROAD

Assos

Gargara

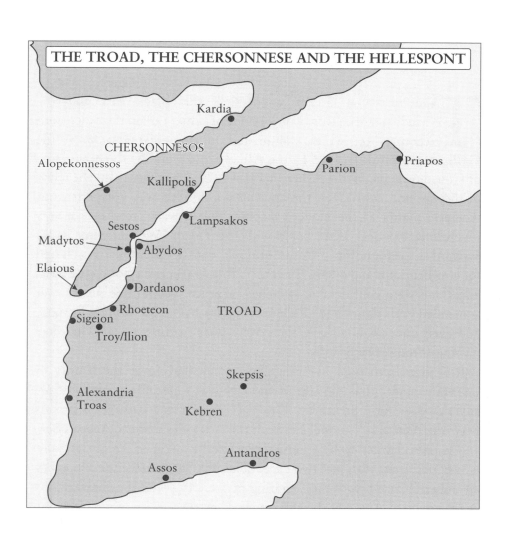

THE TROAD, THE CHERSONNESE AND THE HELLESPONT

Kardia

CHERSONNESOS

Alopekonnessos

Parion

Priapos

Kallipolis

Lampsakos

Sestos

Madytos

Abydos

Elaious

Dardanos

Rhoeteon

TROAD

Sigeion

Troy/Ilion

Skepsis

Alexandria
Troas

Kebren

Antandros

Assos

Introduction

The maritime Straits connecting the Black Sea and the Mediterranean were a major bone of contention in the nineteenth century AD, which culminated in the great assault on the Gallipoli Peninsula in 1915 by the Allied armies, and by the occupation of Constantinople by the Allies in 1918–1922. They were also the scene of dispute and conflict in the ancient world. This was not perhaps as violent a matter as the modern disputes, but it was spread over a very much longer period. If we begin with the Trojan War and come as far forward as the founding of Constantinople, conflict over the region lasted for a millennium and a half. Of course, this conflict was not continuous, and there were considerable stretches of peace, but no one power ever controlled both shores and all the settlements before the Roman Empire, and even under Roman rule there were wars in the area, and invaders passing through the Straits.

It is often remarked in discussions, particularly over the history of Constantinople, that the site of the city was especially geographically advantageous for a great city. The place is seen as a natural crossroads between 'Asia' and 'Europe', between the Black Sea and the Aegean Sea, and is thus claimed to be a natural place to be a seat of empire. If so, it is very odd that, with just two exceptions, the Straits never developed as an imperial base before the founding of the city – and those exceptions were very brief. Again, if the city is such a perfect setting for a capital city, it is equally odd that it was in fact the last place the imperialists chose for their imperial seat – at least four other imperial cities had been tried or considered in the Straits area before Constantinople was chosen and founded. Not that the region has been ignored, for states had been founded and developed all round the Straits since Troy and perhaps before. But it is remarkable that such successful military men as Alexander the Great, Diocletian, and Constantine the Great largely ignored the site, choosing to build elsewhere, until Constantine finally, after considering a dozen other sites, opted for Byzantium. That is to say, it was not the geography of the area which determined the history of the Straits, but man, and particularly colonising, political, and military man.

A little geography is needed, therefore, to begin with. There are three maritime elements in the Straits. Moving as the current flows, in the north is the Bosporos, a waterway flowing out of the Black Sea southwards. This is a little over thirty kilometres long, reaching the Propontis (the Sea of Marmara) at Constantinople (Istanbul, originally Byzantion). The Propontis is, in effect, an inland sea, or even a large lake, with one river – the Bosporos – feeding it, and another river, the Hellespont (the Dardanelles) draining it. The sea is 280 kilometres long, from Izmit to Gelibolu, and seventy-three kilometres wide at its widest, though in shape it is more or less oval, with a tail and a beak (its shape is reminiscent of the profile of a duck-billed platypus). The Hellespont is almost as devious in its course as the Bosporos, and at about sixty kilometres it is almost twice as long; certainly it is more than twice as difficult to navigate. It reaches the Aegean near to the site of Troy.

It was the land which interested most of the inhabitants, rather than the sea, unless they were merchants or sailors or fishermen. It is therefore the lands on either side of the Straits which will particularly concern this account. Reversing course, and moving from the Hellespont north-eastwards towards the Balkans, on the west and north is 'Europe', and on the right, east and south, is 'Asia', though these concepts are generally meaningless in such a restricted geographical area; and it is the way the lands on either side are linked which is one of the elements of this study. The more useful names, at least when dealing with ancient history, are Thrace to the north and west, and Mysia and the Troad on the south, and Bithynia to the east.

Thrace is a name which covers all the western shores, but must be divided into sections for greater convenience. At the southern extreme, beside the Hellespont, is the Thracian Chersonese, better known since 1915 as the Gallipoli Peninsula; it is a hilly strip of land, a little over eighty kilometres long and about twenty kilometres wide at the most, and is connected to the rest of Thrace by a narrow neck of land only six kilometres wide. North of this and west and north of the Propontis, is the main part of Thrace, generally poorly watered and poorly cultivated in that section close to the sea but more productive further inland. The northern part is a range of hills, the Istranca Hills, parallel to the Black Sea coast, and in effect making another peninsula, at the end of which Constantinople is built; much of this peninsula is in fact now covered by the urban sprawl of the successor city to Constantinople, Istanbul; it faces a similar peninsula on the east across the Bosporos, also now much built over.

The eastern and southern coast is more complicated, with several inlets digging deep into the mainland, and so subdividing it. Across from Constantinople the similar peninsula, a continuation of the Istranca range, is the Bithynian region. To the south, another peninsula juts out between the coasts of Izmit and Gemlik, and both of these inlets lead on to lowland valleys stretching east between mountain ranges; these were formerly much longer inlets of the sea, and even now they hold lakes and marshland. A mountainous area – one mountain is an Olympos – is to the south. The mountain ranges sink into the sea, their higher parts standing as islands and peninsulas, notably the Princes' Islands (Prinkipe) south of Constantinople, and the Marmara or Prokonnesos Islands, and the Kyzikos peninsula in the southern part of the sea. The eastern coast of the Hellespont is the Troad, technically part of Mysia; here another mountain is Mount Ida. The land behind this Marmara coast is thus more generally subdivided than that of the Thracian shore, thanks to strong rivers and mountain ranges and lakes which have created a more varied, better watered, and more fertile land.

Greater detail in all this geography will appear as we go along, but two particular extra items need to be mentioned from the start. This is an active land tectonically, which is to say that earthquakes are frequent. In particular, a major earthquake fault runs east and west through the Istranca mountain range south of the Black Sea coast, and this fault covers Bithynia and Constantinople, the Sea of Marmara, and the Hellespont. It produces powerful quakes at irregular intervals (at least six major ones in the past six decades). This is a most fearsome earthquake zone, and the whole Straits area is liable to be shaken.

The two Straits themselves, which can be likened best to rivers, have strong currents, on average two and a half knots in the Bosporos and one and a half in the Hellespont – though in the Bosporos especially a strong northerly wind can double that rate and more, while, as Strabo noted two thousand years ago, at times a southerly wind can virtually halt the current. These winds and currents can be strong enough to prevent powerful steamers from docking at some places, notably at Canakkale in the Hellespont; in a wind-driven sailing ship, making progress against such a current was very difficult; in an oared vessel it would be even worse. This is one of the elements to bear in mind while considering any sea war in these waters, or any mercantile enterprise.

A point about names: I shall use the ancient names as much as possible, which in turn means that the modern terms Bosphorus and Dardanelles will not usually appear. But then I am dealing with the Ancient Straits.

Chapter 1

The Early Settlers (before c.3000 BC)

The initial human occupation of the Straits region came after the ending of the Ice Age, during which the form and geography of the land and waters had been altered and changed repeatedly. Since this affected the human process of occupation it is necessary to delve into that geological and aquatic history first, somewhat awkward and technical though it is.

The crooked form of both the Bosporos and the Hellespont shows that both originated as rivers, a factor emphasised by the powerful currents flowing through them, which generally erode their valleys by swinging from one bank to another. This original form the Greeks appreciated,[1] but other forces were also involved in their formation. Geologically both sides of both straits are similar, and it seems very probable that the rivers eroded their way along lines of least resistance. The banks of both straits show considerable and frequent fault lines,[2] and it seems likely that the erosion process was further assisted by the shattering effect of earthquakes – both straits are along or close to the major North Anatolian fault, a very active earthquake zone. But the major continuous erosion was caused by seawater.

The Black Sea, originally a smaller, lower lake with no outlet to the south, was filled up by meltwater from the northern icecap at the end of the Ice Age, until it overflowed to the south, possibly at first by way of the wide valley now occupied by the lower course of the Sakarya River, to the east of the Bosporos, flowing along that valley and into the Gulf of Izmit. There is also the later possibility that it was also drained by the present Bosporos, which, as its course shows, clearly began as a river. But this supply of eroding water ceased soon after the Ice Age, when the meltwater was redirected westwards into the pre-Baltic Yoldia Sea instead of south along the great Russian rivers, and later for a second time when a dry climatic period reduced the flow of the great rivers. The drainage pattern thereby repeatedly changed.

In each of these periods the freshwater Black Sea shrank by evaporation, or as a result of its supply from the north being held up in the ice cap from about 10,000 BC, and again probably about 3000 BC. The level of the sea was lowered until its surface was considerably below the present level; it was also lower than the level of the Propontis and any outflow along the Sakarya River and the Bosporos stopped. There are remains of human habitation in what are now water-covered parts of the Black Sea, notably along the coast of modern Bulgaria. The two outlets from the Black Sea therefore ceased to flow, and when the Black Sea filled up again, only the Bosporos was used, perhaps because earth movements and earthquakes had opened it up, and blocked the Sakarya route.

The Propontis was similarly at a low level in these periods, lower than today, and it formed a lake unconnected to either the Black or the Aegean Seas, and with little water inflowing from the land; it was probably half its present size. As the level of the Mediterranean rose with the melting of the ice and the general rise in the world ocean levels, however, the Propontis was reinforced by saltwater flowing upstream through the Hellespont from the Aegean. This caused a deepening and widening of the channel by erosion. The force imposed was considerable, and this flow of saline water eventually brought the Propontis to a level above that of the Black Sea, with only the narrow trans-Bosporos mountain range separating the two seas. There, a small river (the 'Bosporos River') had begun eroding a valley, no doubt assisted by the freezing action of the ice on the damaged rock during the preceding Ice Age, and perhaps also by the effect of earthquakes, until the saline waters broke through, and the flow of water from the Propontis to the Black Sea began – that is, in the reverse direction of today. The force of the overflowing seawater powerfully worked to erode further the size and depth of the minor river valley, in much the same way as the Hellespont had been eroded. In addition, the sea water flowing into the formerly freshwater Black Sea changed that sea's nature, killing off much of the freshwater aquatic life, which is the source of the toxic lower levels of the sea, and possibly driving the shoreline-living human inhabitants away. The force of the water increased the erosion effect at the 'Bosporos River', assisted by the heavily faulted land, and very quickly, at least in geological terms, the inflowing water, from both the Mediterranean and the Russian rivers, released by the melting of the ice, 'filled' the Black Sea.[3]

One of the effects of the high level of the Mediterranean waters had been to flood the plains surrounding the old, much reduced and smaller, Propontis, and this now happened also in the Black Sea, though to a much greater degree. (It has been theorised that this set off migrations of people displaced by the floods, in many directions; something like this is quite possible, though it seems unlikely that the effect was as rapid and widespread as has been supposed, or even that it necessarily happened – the population was hardly very large.) In time, of course, the sea levels on both sides equalised. The Black Sea continued to receive freshwater from the many rivers flowing into it from central and Eastern Europe – the Danube, the Bug, the Dniester, the Dnieper, and others, and overflowed through the Bosporos – but it also continued to receive seawater from the Mediterranean. Seawater being denser than fresh, the seawater flows northwards beneath the southward-flowing surface freshwater current, the two flowing in opposite directions, a singularly curious effect, which was always known to the local fishermen, who exploited it in their methods, but also was utilised by submarines in the Great War.[4]

Locally, in the Straits area, the effects of these geological and aquatic changes were no doubt dramatic, but were essentially marginal for any inhabitants, as the rise in the level drove them away from the old shores to the present dry land. Archaeological surveys have suggested that the region was essentially uninhabited until after all these major events had run their courses,[5] and when the Bosporos ceased to flow the inhabitants left. Hunters of the Ice Age had, of course, moved through the area, and a string of sites has been located, identified by the finds of Palaeolithic and Mesolithic flints, along the present coast of the Black Sea and on either side of the Bosporos, and they spread into the Propontis shores.[6] A substantial population has been suggested (unless, of course, this was the remains of a small population which moved about often). This would not be a particularly useful series of sites for hunters while the Black Sea level was lower than at present; perhaps these are the refugees that may have been displaced by the floods.

It was not until perhaps 5000 BC or later that any permanent settlement by human beings was established on the shores, and this was some centuries after the overflow of the Propontis into the Black Sea began, when the disturbances of the waters had ended, and the relative sea levels had probably stabilised. By this time, the melting of the Russian ice cap had increased the flow of the rivers, so that the flow of the sea's surface water had reversed, and it now ran from the Black Sea into the Propontis, and from the Propontis into the Mediterranean, which is the process as it is now.

That the earliest known permanent settlements on the Straits date from the time following the decline of the obvious turbulence of the waters is hardly a coincidence. For one thing the changes in the sea levels in both the Propontis and the Black Sea involved substantial rises; if any settlement existed on the old shores, whenever and wherever they had been fixed, it quickly became drowned, and the remains are largely buried by the sediment which now covers the old sea floor. Those submerged off the Bulgarian coast were probably replicated in the Marmara.

The earliest known permanent settlement in any of the shores of the Straits is at Fikirtepe, on the north shore of the Gulf of Izmit in Kadikoy, the suburb of Istanbul east of the Bosporos, with another similar settlement of the same group of people at Pendik, a few miles to the east.[7] The culture was at first identified at Fikirtepe, provoking considerable puzzlement as to its origins and affiliations, but it is now clear that it was actually derived from a longer-lasting set of settlements further east, of which the most important site is probably Ilipinar, on the shore of Lake Isnik, between that lake and the long Gednik Bay.[8] This in turn is derived from, or at least influenced by, earlier settlements which had developed in the south centre of Anatolia, notably the well-known site at Hacilar. That is, the people of Fikirtepe – and Pendik – were migrants, or descendants of migrants, originating from the centre of Anatolia.

The economy of these settlements was still largely that of hunter-gatherers. In fairly typical Mesolithic style, they settled at places which were particularly rich in foods which could be collected without too much effort, particularly on sea bays and lakes, where shellfish could be collected, supplemented by fruits and vegetables acquired on the land. The earliest strata at Ilipinar are dated to about 5200 BC, and the latest are of about 4800; at Fikirtepe the settlement is dated to about 5000 BC. Across the Propontis on the western side there are two or three other sites: the cave at Yarimburgaz just west of Istanbul, Toptepe halfway along the Marmara coast, and Hoca Cesme near the mouth of the Maritza River west of the Thracian Chersonese on the Aegean coast. Other evidence has emerged in the course of the excavations connected with the extensive building activity in Istanbul in recent years.[9] All of these sites from Ilipinar to Hoca Cesme are situated close to the sea, or on a bay or at a river mouth, or, at Ilipinar, between the sea and the Iznik Lake. They show much the same characteristics of lifestyle as Fikirtepe and Ilipinar, with the exception of the architecture of the houses. These western examples rather extend the timescale originally determined, with the site at Ilipinar commencing about 5200 BC and that at Toptepe lasting to about 4200 BC. (The cave at Yarimburgaz had also been used earlier in the Palaeolithic period.) There is some indication that the culture penetrated south into the Thracian Chersonese, at Kaynarca Mevkii; this is well inland, but it is suggested that the stream the site overlooks had originally been an inlet of the sea; and nowhere on that peninsula is far from the sea.[10]

These discoveries all show a slow progression from hunter-gatherers through to pastoral farming, to which was eventually added some arable farming, and the last phase at Ilipinar is on the verge of the Chalcolithic. And all of these sites come to an end well before 4000 BC.[11] There were connections with Balkan cultures further inland, particularly at the Thracian sites, but only in the later phases. On the other hand, the 'Fikirtepe'-type pottery which appears in later phases is found in southern Thrace and as far west as Thessaly; the people were mobile still and liable to shift to new sites; this may be the explanation of the desertion of their original sites, from Thrace on into Greece and north into the Balkans.[12]

This implication of mobility and wide trading connections is emphasised by the presence of obsidian being used in the place of, or as a supplement to, flint at several sites. The obsidian must have arrived from some distance, perhaps – again – from central Anatolia (where a centre of production sent its goods even further afield into Syria), though the island of Melos in the Aegean is perhaps as likely a source – which would imply seagoing capability by the miners or their customers. This was a continuation of the connection which had already existed before the development of the settled society, for obsidian is also found in some of the Palaeolithic pre-Fikirtepe sites along the Black Sea coast.[13]

In the southern part of the Straits region, on either side of the Hellespont, the story is much the same, but begins later. The fluctuations of the sea levels in the Hellespont area were even more dramatic than in the Bosporos region, and it is probable that this accounts for the rather later settlement of this southern area. The key site here is Kumtepe on the

Asian coast, overlooking the entrance to the Hellespont, though it was not actually the first place a permanent settlement was made. The first village on the site had a similar economy to that which operated in much the same way at the Fikirtepe coastal site, where the inhabitants gathered shellfish to provide much of their diet – oysters were the preferred diet here – or perhaps only the easiest to gather. But this early settlement is only dated to about 3200 BC, a good millennium after the end of the Fikirtepe sites to the north.

A slightly earlier settlement is suggested at two other sites, Bezik Tepe, overlooking Bezik Bay on the Troad coast facing the Aegean, and Hanay Tepe, close to the valley of the Scamander River. The earliest layer at Kumtepe is labelled 'Ia', and it is thought these two sites show signs that their pottery was even earlier than Kumtepe Ia. However, the differences appear slight, and it is perhaps best to regard the settlements of the three places as originating at much the same time.[14] The date of these settlements is well before 3000 BC, perhaps as early as 3300 BC.[15] The economy of the earliest inhabitants was similar to that of the Fikirtepe inhabitants: some pastoral herding, hunting, and a strong bias towards shellfish, but they also rapidly adopted, or applied, agriculture, and in Kumtepe Ib the site had access to copper and the wealth to acquire small pieces of it.

The site of Kumtepe is a prime one: close to the sea, with freshwater in the river, at a fairly low level but clear of the sea and occupying a small fertile plain on a long narrow peninsula between the sea and the bay. That plain has since been formed by alluvium filling the bay, brought down by the Scamander River, partly as a result of deforestation in the pursuit of agriculture. Yet its first inhabitants settled there two millennia after the development of a similar society at Ilipinar, and the Fikirtepe sites had been abandoned for a millennium before the Kumtepe sites were settled.

Across the Hellespont, on the peninsula of the Thracian Chersonesos, the earliest site, apart from Kynarca Mevkii, was Karaagactepe (also known as 'the grave of Protesilaos'), more or less contemporary with a settlement at Kumtepe, from which it was separated only by the mouth of the Hellespont. It is near the southern tip of the Thracian Chersonese, a substantial mound ('tepe' in Turkish is equivalent to the Arabic 'tell') and was first excavated in his usual brutal fashion by Schliemann and then by a team from the French military occupation forces in 1921–1922; a clear and accurate result can hardly be expected under the circumstances. The occupation layers are up to eleven metres thick, so not a great deal of the earliest material was reached – and neither excavation reached bedrock. The lowest finds were contemporary with the second level at Kumtepe (Kumtepe Ib), and there was still lower, that is, earlier, material.[16]

Occupation of this period appears at several sites in the peninsula, while on the opposite shore it is found only at Kumtepe; the early sites at Bezik Tepe and Hanay Tepe were abandoned after their early occupation and 'Kumtepe Ib' appears only at that site.[17] But across the Hellespont there are at least seven sites, besides Karaagactepe, where pottery of that date and style has been found during surface surveys conducted by Ozdogan in the 1990s. These are all along the coast of the Strait, with none apparently either inland or on the western, Aegean, coast. It looks as though the early inhabitants of Kumtepe were particularly interested in this side of the Strait.[18] We thus have clear evidence of contacts across the Strait, just as the Fikirtepe pottery indicates the same to the north, in the opposite direction, at a much earlier period. (This is relevant to a theory concerning the flow of water in the Straits at this time, to be considered later in this chapter.)

Not much more than the basic occupation of the various sites by the people can be deduced from the scattered finds, most of which were only located in surveys. These find and collect whatever can be seen on the surface, usually no more than fragments of pottery, and can never come to any final conclusions, particularly about the earliest occupation, which requires excavation. But we can assume that these gatherers and early farmers were as much sea-goers as they were landsmen – a major part of their diet was marine – so we can also assume that the waters of the Straits were familiar to them. Their ships were, again making an assumption, open boats, possibly with a single sail, more likely purely oar-driven, but they were good enough for their purposes.

The first settlement at Kumtepe was in what is now known as the Chalcolithic period when copper began to be used and available. It was largely employed initially for jewellery, because of its colour and shine, which can have displayed individual wealth. This developed, of course, into the Early Bronze Age, as copper became more plentiful, and a more useful metal was devised. The general culture of the Straits sites in this period is linked both with inland Anatolia and the eastern Aegean islands, and ultimately with Minoan Crete. For quite some time very little bronze was available to the inhabitants of these places, who were initially only peasants living at subsistence level, but they developed greater wealth, and their diet of food from the sea soon became merely a supplement to what they produced themselves from the land, either by farming or by hunting. They had settled in a fertile corner, so presumably agriculture was one of their first considerations, and the positions of their settlements along the Hellespont coast also imply a busy marine economy, fishing, gathering shellfish, and maritime contacts across the Strait and presumably elsewhere in the region; their acquisition of copper and bronze goods also implies that they had trading contacts with central Anatolia.

The village at Kumtepe lasted for several generations, certainly for two centuries, perhaps three. The accumulated deposits of occupation debris, of which three successive substantial layers could be distinguished, implies as much. About 3000 BC the village was destroyed by fire; it was a small settlement, and this could have been accidental – or a deliberate act of hostility. Since this also happened, at more or less the same time, to many other places in the wider vicinity, in both Anatolia and in the Aegean islands, a violent convulsion may be postulated.[19] If the people of the Straits could sail the seas, so could others, so the further suggestion is that the destroyers came from the sea, and by sea; but then there are always also the earthquakes.

There is nothing in all this to suggest that the Straits were of any particular importance in themselves. It would be reasonable to conclude that their general geography from the Aegean Sea to the Black Sea was known to those who lived at Kumtepe or Karaagactepe or even Fikirtepe, though the peculiarities of that geography were perhaps not fully appreciated. The strength of the current flowing through from the Black Sea has always been an ongoing problem for the seamen, but they may not have had much of a standard of comparison, and it may be that the Bosporos was not open at the time, or that the current through the Bosporos did not flow with any strength. The less turbulent Aegean was no doubt preferred for a sail, but the Propontis was hardly a difficult sea. On the other hand, it is clear that the Fikirtepe culture was spread over a wide area from Western Anatolia to Thessaly, and communication between communities on either side of both of the Straits is to be presumed.

The occupation of the northerly parts of the Straits region was abandoned after the Fikirtepe villages. The inland (western) area of Thrace, notably in the valley of the Maritza River, was certainly occupied by farmers, whose cultural products were connected with those further west in the Balkans, while in Anatolia the successors of the Fikirtepe culture remained inland, away from the sea. Essentially the Straits region was either abandoned or, with the advent of the Kumtepe settlers, independently occupied, and only alongside the Hellespont.[20]

The culture of Kumtepe Ic had been copied on the western coast of the Hellespont (or this area had been colonised from Kumtepe – or Kumtepe had been colonised from the west) and this connection continued into the next cultural period. The destruction of Kumtepe in about 3000 BC was followed by the decisive occupation of the mound which became Troy. There was perhaps an earlier occupation of the site, called by the latest excavators 'older-than-Troy-I'), which is contemporary with the earliest Kumtepe (though little is made of it in the report) but it was the arrival about 2950 BC or thereabouts of the new settlers, quite possibly refugees, or including refugees, from burnt Kumtepe, which began the continuous occupation of the site of Troy.

In support of the theory that Kumtepe's destruction was the result of widespread disturbances in the region is the fact that these first Trojans at once constructed fortifications around their new home. This is 'Troy I'. Whereas Kumtepe had been low down and actually close to the shore, Troy was located on a low hill at a little distance from the coast, across 'Trojan Bay' from Kumtepe. The circuit of the walls was roughly circular, about eighty metres in diameter, and the wall was clearly defensive, not simply designed to keep out wild animals – this excuse for walls has not been required in the preceding unfortified villages. And yet a settlement of this size cannot be considered as anything more than a village. The excavations have located at least six houses within the circuit; there is room for about as many again; ten inhabitants per house – a very generous estimate – would give a population of less than 200 people; there were also no doubt others living in the surrounding area, outside the walls, but even so we are looking at only a very small place.[21] The amount of work needed to build their wall by such a small population is a good indication of the dangers they felt they faced.

This first Trojan settlement lasted about five centuries without being expanded significantly, but its culture (that is, the style of pottery the people used) was shared with people in other villages in the immediate area and, more importantly – once again – with those living across the Hellespont in the Thracian Chersonese. Several of those villages in the Troad, the area around Troy, had been first occupied in the last phase of Kumtepe (Ic), like Troy itself. Some, like Kumtepe, ceased to be occupied when Kumtepe died. There was thus a considerable alteration in the human geography of the region about 3000 BC, and yet the overall situation roughly replicated that before the destruction took place.

Contemporary with 'Early Troy I' was Bezik Burnu not far from Bezik Tepe (which had been abandoned in Kumtepe Ib), Coban Tepe on the Hellespont coast, and Han Tepe south of Bezik Bay facing the Aegean. Across the Strait, in the Chersonese, it is the Ic period remains which are missing. Since these are survey results it is possible that they could have been mixed with or confused with Ib pottery. At any rate the implication of much of the findings is that at all the sites which had produced Kumtepe Ib pottery, occupation was continuous into Troy I: perhaps the people mainly went on with the Ib style of pottery through Ic and then took up the later Troy I type. The original settlements along the Hellespont coast were now also supplemented by new villages on the Aegean coast to the west, and some others well inland. That is, the region was not affected at all seriously by whatever had damaged Kumtepe and its fellows, but the people were able to expand into new territories rather than being merely relocated; by the appearance of inland villages they were clearly emancipated from their earlier apparent dependence on the sea and its products.[22]

Troy and its satellites in both the Troad and the Gallipoli Peninsula – assuming that Troy was the local 'metropolis' – show the occupation of the region during the Bronze Age, but the rest of the region is a problem. There are significant Early Bronze Age occupation sites along both shores of the Sea of Marmara as far as the Gulf of Iznik and almost to the Istanbul peninsula, but they do not reach the Istranca range and its fellows across the Bosporos in Bithynia, and they fade away by the end of that period – before the end of Troy I, that is, about 2500 BC. Troy and its companion sites in the southern area continue through the third and into the second millennium BC, but on both sides of the Propontis there continues to be little sign of any occupation in the northern part of the region in that period.

This is a problem, or a 'predicament', as the scholar Mehmet Ozdogan, who has studied and surveyed the region most intensively, puts it.[23] The question is why should a fertile well-watered region on both sides of the Sea of Marmara be ignored by the Bronze Age population, when to the south, in the Troad, to the south-east in inland Anatolia, and to the north-west in the Balkans from the Maritza Valley westwards, there are clear indications of occupation, and that all three regions were well populated. It is all the more curious in that these areas were the most heavily occupied in the Neolithic.

One possible solution is that the surveys have not located the occupation sites of the Later Bronze Age. One site, Kanlijesit, produced only Early Bronze Age finds on being surveyed, but when it was excavated it was found to be a fortified village similar to, but rather smaller than, Troy, as if the people of Anatolia had colonised the area. That it was fortified might mean that there were enemies in the area, or it could be that this was now how the colonists preferred to live. This is a Middle Bronze Age population which was not found by the survey and it could be that there were other similar sites in the region. But it does seem that even if there were such settlements, the population was thin and poor. Further, a second problem has also appeared, in that there have been found clear indications of Bronze Age settlements along the Black Sea coast of Bulgaria, but they were situated in places where the land is now flooded by the sea.

These submerged Bulgarian settlements indicate that the sea level since they were occupied – or rather abandoned – has risen by perhaps twelve metres. They were thus established on dry land in the Early Bronze Age (the time of Kumtepe Ic and Troy I, and the well-occupied Marmara coast), so it is clear that the Black Sea level has risen since the Bronze Age to flood them. This suggests that further investigations into the history of the outlet of the Black Sea waters into the Sea of Marmara and the Mediterranean is needed. Ozdogan has suggested that the outlet was blocked for the period of the Middle and Late Bronze Age, say until the time of Troy VI, the mid-second millennium BC, and that the Bosporos outlet was only fully established as it is today from about 1000 BC.

This would help explain the initial connections across the Hellespont of Kumtepe and its contemporaries in the Thracian Chersonese, and the similar connection between the Troy I settlements on both sides. And it fits with the curious history of the 'Trojan Bay', the inlet from the Hellespont which has apparently been filled by alluvium brought down by the Scamander (Karamenderes) River. This is not a particularly powerful or lengthy stream, and the quantity of alluvium seems hugely disproportionate. The bay was originally (4000 BC) six kilometres long and more than three kilometres wide, yet it was filled with alluvium in no more than 1,000 years, and its present coastline was reached by the beginning of the first millennium AD; this is a tremendous process of deposition, which it was unlikely that the contributory streams could produce.[24] It is possible that some eustatic movements, raising the level of the land, may be involved, just as it is possible that tectonic movement along the North Anatolian Fault was partly responsible for the closing and reopening of the Bosporos Strait.[25]

None of this is, it must be admitted, more than educated guesswork, but the curious behaviour and distribution and fate of the Bronze Age settlements demand some explanation, and the behaviour of the sea levels must have some relevance. (For example, the deposition of the alluvium in 'Trojan Bay' could have been accelerated if there was no current to remove it or interfere with the process.) The destruction of the Troy VI/VII cities (two destructions in a fairly short time) about the end of the second millennium BC has long been another problem. They do not in fact fit any acceptable chronology for the 'Trojan War', and a rather strong case has been made that at the time of the war the Bosporos was blocked, and so the Hellespont would then be a relatively peaceful sea-inlet. The two Trojan cities may have been destroyed by earthquakes.[26] There is also a longstanding argument between scholars over the problem of Mycenaean access to the Black Sea during the late second millennium BC – that is, whether their ships could actually reach it. The quantity of archaeological evidence of Mycenaean origin in the Black Sea regions is small and they could as easily reach the region by land as by sea.[27] So, if the Mycenaeans did not sail to the Black Sea, maybe it was because they could not, because the way was blocked, either by the closure of the passage, or because the current was too strong – or, of course, maybe they did not choose to go there.

Chapter 2

Troy and its War (c.3000–c.1000 BC)

The previous chapter considered the overall condition of the Straits and their human inhabitants for the long period from the end of the Ice Age to about 1000 BC; in this chapter I shall turn back to consider in more detail the history of one of the two most famous sites in the region. The other, Byzantion/Constantinople/Istanbul, will be discussed later; here the subject is Troy and its famous war – if there was one.

Troy had a long history, of course, one which the archaeologists have traced from a little before 3000 BC to its end about 1200 BC or later, and then from its resumption as a Greek town till it faded away in the late Roman period. The original village ('Troy I') lasted for about five centuries and was part of a culture which can be found in various settlements in Anatolia, in the Mediterranean area, and around the Sea of Marmara – in effect it was a successor to the fishing village at Kumtepe. It formed a fairly undistinguished Neolithic agricultural village, its people made and used handmade pottery, very like that at Kumtepe, but with less reliance on fish. Its size, about one hectare, implies a population within the walls of 200 to 300 people at the most.[1]

Troy II, whose commencement was about 2500 BC, is distinguished from its predecessor not by any obvious sudden change but by a certain expansion in population and in material possessions, and the acquisition of better tools: it was better off and better equipped. The walls of this place enclosed an area roughly double that of Troy I, that is, about two hectares (or five acres), and it may be supposed that the population was also bigger, up to 500 approximately at the most, though in all cases we must also assume that there was an extra-mural agricultural peasant population, which might or might not have gone to Troy for refuge in times of danger. The place, from the start of Troy I, had serious fortifications with just two well-guarded gates; these were approached by narrow ramps leading up to equally narrow 'entrance chambers', which were roofed and enclosed, in effect short tunnels, and were thus eminently defensible by being blocked, or by a small force. It might also imply that the outside rural population was being denied entry.

The material culture of this community gradually improved with the introduction of the new technology which had been developed further east. Pots were now made on a potter's wheel – a substantial time-saver over the handmade variety, and probably now made by specialist professionals. Bronze metallurgy was available, and had expanded from making minor items of jewellery to producing axes, spearheads, arrowheads, and other useful tools – again this was a more specialised activity than the previous versions made of stone or wood. There are signs of widespread commerce, and this larger village acquired imported goods from as far off as Central Asia, the Persian Gulf, and the Caucasus region to the east, from the Eastern European steppes to the north, and from the Aegean to the west and south. This is not to say that the people of Troy were in direct contact with these far-flung places, but the presence of such imports, which presumably in many cases arrived after passing through several hands, is evidence that the place was part of a wide commercial system covering much of the Middle East, a system which developed during the relatively peaceful period of three centuries during the later part of the third millennium.

The succeeding archaeological period, Troy III, was not really very different from I and II, except that it seems to have been poorer, and it lasted only a brief time, perhaps a century (c. 2400–2300 bc). It came to a sudden end by destruction; as with Kumtepe seven centuries before, this was not an isolated destruction, but one which affected other places, especially in the Aegean, but also places in Anatolia, though what agency caused it, human or natural, is not known. The sheer extent of the damage is wider than is likely to be caused by an earthquake, which would normally be fairly local, so human action seems most likely.

This is also, of course, the period when the Indo-European migration may have taken place,[2] and this, and associated disturbances, have been adduced as a possible cause of the destruction of Troy III. The date is about right, give or take a century or so, but no evidence exists to connect the two events, or even that the Indo-Europeans were migrating into this area. It would have taken a fairly substantial effort to capture Troy III behind its high and solid walls, and there is no sign that any migrating peoples were of sufficient strength to achieve the task. Internal disturbances, perhaps an uprising of the rural population – possibly excluded from the village even in emergencies – seems as likely an explanation as any.

Whatever the cause, the village was immediately re-inhabited (Troy IV), quite possibly by the survivors of Troy III, but the cultural connections from now on are mainly with Anatolia to the east rather than with the Aegean. Troy IV continued to be a poorer community than Troy II, though perhaps it was not really worse off than Troy I or III. The difference in prosperity was hardly very great, given the basically peasant lifestyle of most of the people at all these sites; these are, after all, technical archaeological terms, which do not directly describe the life of the people.

The village was essentially part of the wider Anatolian culture, developed by the time Troy V ended (about 1750 BC), into the time of the Hittite kingdom. It slid from Troy IV into the period called Troy V without any real change, though Troy V has been difficult to find archaeologically. General poverty and perhaps some depopulation may be to blame for this. It may be significant that it seems that hunting for food was much more important than before, which may suggest a reduced population and a reduction in agricultural production or productivity, but it may also be the mark of a society which emphasises the possession of horses and a pastoral lifestyle above that of farm work. Horses arrived sometime during Troy IV–V, quite possibly along with those putative Indo-European migrants.

In all this there is nothing exceptional about the village of Troy except perhaps the size of its walls, which by the end of Troy V had been in existence on the same lines without more than repairs for seven centuries, since the expansion at the start of Troy II. The history of the place was not really any different from that of other villages around the eastern Mediterranean. The identification of the different archaeological periods depends on recognising relatively small differences in pottery shape and decoration, and on locating different building layers – nine of these have been recognised in Troy IV–V, but in none of these developments did the layout or size of the village materially change, nor did the lifestyle and culture of its inhabitants. The size of the place at the end of Troy V was much the same as it had been in Troy II – it used the same walls and gates – though it has been described as a 'town' during Troy II, and it had reverted to a 'village' by Troy III. The difference is minimal, and 'village' is still the best term for the size of the place during the whole period from Troy I to Troy VI; the population of Troy II to V (3000–1750 BC) was perhaps never more than a few hundred at the most; the buildings on the hilltop were crowded, but it held large structures which might be public buildings or which belonged to a wealthy layer of society, who could afford more space – larger buildings imply a smaller population – but they can have been no more than a few people. The cultural connections of the whole period since the end of Troy II remained primarily with the Anatolian interior rather than with the Aegean or the Balkans.

Troy VI was different. Troy V ended in a fire in the mid-eighteenth century BC, but again the cause, human or natural, deliberate or accidental, earthquake or conquest, or something else, cannot be determined. It may have been followed by a period of desertion, or at best it now had only an even thinner population. In the following period of Troy VI the population was clearly stratified into different classes. This had possibly been the case for a time during Troy II, but the indications then are ambiguous; in each case it is clear that it is the increasing communal wealth that lies at the base of the social development which distinguished the wealthy and ruling group from the rest. In Troy V the possession of horses and the development of the larger building inside the walls may well be signs of such a process, thus beginning a differentiation which has lasted into the twentieth-first century AD.

As an archaeological period, Troy VI began about 1740 BC and lasted until about 1190/80 BC (including Troy VIIa), and was therefore longer in duration as a developing and continuing culture than any one of the earlier periods (though non-archaeological eyes, not distinguishing the minutiae of changes, might suggest that Troy I to V were all essentially much the same). The longevity of VI/VII suggests that it was a more stable society with a more certain and well-founded development, and perhaps that it had a more powerful state apparatus both for conducting war and for controlling its population. Certainly by about 1500 BC it was a kingdom, and therefore with a king and a surrounding and supporting aristocracy. The place grew in size and in wealth, and it might now be called perhaps a 'city', though it was still a very small one.

The old walled village was much expanded with new walls to an area four times the original size – double that of Troy II to V – and the old village inside the walls became the acropolis of the new city, with some large palatial buildings occupying the whole of the original village space (so anticipating what would later happen at the transition from Byzantion to Constantinople). The rest of the population lived in the Lower Town below, and on the plain between the acropolis and the river – there is now evidence for this population, where before it had been presumed. The architecture therefore implies that there was a king and a ruling group living in some luxury on the acropolis, with a lower class outside, probably of artisans and servants, in the Lower Town, and a rural peasantry in the surrounding lands – an architectural interpretation tending to confirm the archaeological interpretation, though both use the same evidence.

Let us be clear, however. To call Troy VI a 'city' is not to imply any great size, nor any real importance. The population of the acropolis, filled as far as can be seen with large houses and a temple, cannot have been more than a few dozens, no doubt rather fewer than in the smaller houses and narrow lanes which occupied the same area in Troy V. The Lower Town is reckoned to be about three or four hectares inside the walls, which would contain possibly a population of several hundreds (the excavators have supposed an extravagant 7,000 for the whole site, inside and outside the walls).[3] A fairly substantial rural population may be assumed, giving a total population of a few thousand.

This is not a great and powerful city, and in modern times it would be no more than a small town; while it was wealthier than the preceding settlements on the site, it was not especially so. There were no doubt more subjects of the king in the surrounding country, and even in other villages, for the kingdom seems to have extended over the whole Troad. But even that only makes him a minor ruler in a world of great empires, and the 'city' a small town.

The interpretation of Troy VI as a kingdom, with a clearly stratified population separated into upper and lower classes inside the walls and a peasantry outside, is partly the result of the interpretation of the archaeological findings, but also, at last, of some written evidence. The basis of this social development was slowly increasing wealth, of course, which in turn appears to be due, as in Troy II, to widespread trade contacts as well as to the increase in the population and to increased agricultural production.

It is during this long period, Troy I to Troy VI/VII (c.3000–c.1190 BC), that the theory that the Bosporos was closed applies. It is also, more definitely, the period when the occupation of the territories north of Troy, on either side of the Sea of Marmara, was very thin, and that the area to the north of the sea, on both sides of what would become the Bosporos, the two blunt peninsulas of Bithynia and the Istranja Hilla, was effectively unoccupied by humans.[4]

If the Bosporos was closed, the Sea of Marmara would have shrunk, and the Hellespont would have been no more than a stream, even perhaps an inlet of the Aegean. The isolation of the Marmara, which is almost 1400 metres (about 5,000 feet) deep at its deepest, would have, by evaporation, reduced it in volume and size, and it would not take a great reduction to end the flow of water from the Propontis into the Hellespont. Once properly isolated the Sea would shrink even more quickly and in the process will have become steadily more saline. This would render it, like the lower depths of the Black Sea, inimical to life. The removal of the human population of the area would have followed.

Even if the theory of the closed-Bosporos is not accepted, the lack of human occupation beyond about a hundred kilometres north and north-east of Troy is clearly significant. It fits well enough with the fact that during this period, from the mid or early third millennium to the mid or late second millennium (Troy II to Troy VI), Troy remained a fairly poor village, declining from the end of Troy II but rising once more in Troy VI. During the Bronze Age, therefore, which here ran from the middle of Troy I to the end of Troy VI, Troy was a frontier society, with unoccupied lands not very far away. Indeed, in the Gallipoli Peninsula, so well occupied in the Troy I period, occupation from Troy II onward gradually faded away – which helps explain the pastoral period in Troy V, since the land would be satisfactory for raising horses. In the Gallipoli survey which reported the relative density of population in the Troy I period, only two sites, both on the Hellespont coast, produced Troy VI pottery. No site produced any Mycenaean pottery, and the peninsula seems to have been deserted until well into the Iron Age.[5]

The apparent comparative wealth of Troy VI is usually thought to be due to its participation in international trade. There are certainly goods from Mycenaean Greece found in the excavations, but a considered judgement points out that the Mycenaean pottery found at Troy is only a fraction of the total pottery used in the town.[6] Wider contacts are not evident. Its own pottery shares characteristics, as before since Troy I, with a wide variety of places in Anatolia,[7] but none with those in the Aegean.

The increasing wealth of Troy VI has also been explained by the situation of the place at the mouth of the Hellespont, with the implication – actually explicit at times, and even stated as a fact in some accounts[8] – that its geographical position made it an obvious trading centre, and that this was the source of its suggested wealth and supposed power. This theory was at times elaborated into describing the 'city' as an entrepot, or as a place to which ships resorted to await a fair wind; certainly they did in the 'sailing-ship' era, waiting west of the Gallipoli peninsula or in Bezik Bay (as it was known), but the ships of the Bronze Age were by no means as seaworthy or as tractable to the wind as the sailing ships of the early modern period, and their capability was not sufficient to get them through the Straits with any ease – if the Straits existed, of course. It was even supposed that Troy could have forced the ships to pay dues, even compelled them to discharge their cargoes and sell them in Troy itself, to the financial benefit of the Trojans, of course. All these are certainly ploys to which cities and states in other periods have resorted, but it has to be said that there is no evidence whatever for any of this at Troy, and given the small size both of the town and of its population these ploys are highly unlikely to have been developed or used.

The question of the difficulty in passing through the Hellespont is usually held to be relevant. For sailing ships the strong current and the frequently adverse winds are certainly a problem, but only if the ship is aiming to pass beyond Troy. The existence of at least two places on the Gallipoli coast which used pottery of Troy VI date indicates that cross-channel traffic did exist, but there was no point in going further, since the thin population along the Sea of Marmara coasts provided little commercial incentive. Further, the data respecting the practice of ships waiting in shelter on the Trojan shore for a favourable wind relates above all to sailing ships trying to reach Constantinople; but ancient ships had the option of rowing, which can be done, wearyingly no doubt, by keeping close to the shore where the current's force is lessened – and no worthwhile centre, it bears repeating, existed beyond the Hellespont.

Certainly one of the main engines of economic growth in the second millennium BC was the wealth accumulated in the greater civilised states in the Near East – Egypt, Babylonia, Syria, central Anatolia – whose economic reach expanded throughout the first half of the second millennium. Into this system, Minoan Crete and then Mycenaean Greece were successively drawn, and with its Mycenaean contacts Troy was thus part of this wide international trading system (once again, it may be pointed out, as in Troy II). Yet by its geographical position and small size, Troy VI cannot have been more than a minor fortified market on the edge of the trading system.

In Troy VI a steadily increasing volume of evidence does show that the city was a part of the Aegean commercial world. At Bezik Bay, a cemetery which appears to be contemporary with Troy VIIb – right at the very end of the existence of Bronze Age Troy – has been identified as being used primarily by Mycenaeans,[9] though this can hardly be used to prove contacts centuries before that time. In political as in cultural matters, Troy was much more closely connected with the Anatolian hinterland. It has been identified as Wilusa, a small state which was brought under Hittite suzerainty during the fifteenth century BC,[10] and of which the names of four kings are known from Hittite sources. Wilusa tried to escape from the Hittite grip, distant though it was, by participating in a widespread rising (the 'Twenty-Two Cities' rebellion) in the mid-fifteenth century BC, but was then re-incorporated into the Hittite system after the defeat of the rebellion. This is the first written record which can identify the kingdom of which Troy was a part.[11]

There is, of course, no reason to believe that the cultural and commercial orientation towards the Mycenaean Aegean and the cultural and political orientation towards the Hittite interior of Anatolia were necessarily antagonistic attitudes for the Trojans to hold. Hittite sources do show that the Hittite state was concerned for some time before its own destruction at the activities of Mycenaean kings who raided into western Asia Minor.[12] Yet Wilusa is not mentioned in connection with any of these events, which took place further south and inland.

In terms of its geographical situation, therefore, the city of Troy VI had no connection with the lands to the north, including the Black Sea, nor even, probably, with the Sea of Marmara; it was not involved in the intermittent Mycenaean/Hittite warfare, according to the (undoubtedly exiguous) written sources from the Hittite archives; it is probable that the Hellespont was not used as a seaway during the existence of Troy, at least not since the end of Troy I, except for boats crossing from one shore to the other, since, whether or not the Bosporos was open, there was no destination worth the effort beyond Troy itself. If there was no flow of water through the Bosporos, there would be no strong current in the Hellespont, and therefore there was no need for any ship to take shelter except on especially windy days, and the lack of a current would make the passage, whatever it amounted to, much less difficult. There were only a few settlements in the Gallipoli Peninsula contemporary with Troy VI; the lack of human occupation in the northern Marmara region is an effective refutation of the notion of the Hellespont as a trade artery – for if there were few settlements, there would be no trade and so there was no reason to go there. The only settlement worth a merchant's attention was therefore the town of Troy, situated inland, not on the coast, with only a few thousand potential customers, the vast majority of whom were peasants living at the edge of subsistence, in a state of poverty which would ensure that they had no surplus to use to buy exotic goods.

Troy therefore was a semi-isolated town of a few thousand people, which was of marginal concern to its Hittite overlord, but of some minor commercial interest to the Mycenaean traders in the Aegean Sea. It was marginal to both, and this general marginality is indicated by the fact that the city had not yet adopted any form of writing.[13] It therefore had no archives, nor did it have a sufficiently complex economy to require records to be kept; taxes will have been paid in kind, if at all. The major Mycenaean kingdoms, by contrast – Mycenae, Thebes, Pylos, Knossos, and others – all had a bureaucratic system of record keeping, reputedly counting every sheep and every slave; the Hittites had a well-arranged and systematic archive, and the kings conducted a continuous diplomatic relationship by written messages with every kingdom within reach – but hardly with Wilusa, where it seems that no-one could read. Such records were the marks of rich, organised kingdoms, which had relations with others of the same type. Troy has been sufficiently well excavated that we can be certain that it had no such records.

Troy VI ended about 1300 BC in another catastrophe, but once again the cause is unclear. Carl Blegen was certain that an earthquake was responsible, and pointed to some collapsed buildings as evidence.[14] This is now fairly generally accepted. The site was at once reoccupied and the cultural continuity indicates that the survivors of the catastrophe had emerged from the ruins, or had returned – such immediate returns are a characteristic of destroyed settlements after earthquakes. Blegen thought it was now a city under siege, because the large houses on the acropolis had been re-divided into smaller sections, and so housed a larger and poorer population during Troy VIIa. It could, of course, also be that the survivors did not include the original ruling group, for whatever reason, and that their houses had been taken over by others (often referred to as 'squatters').

A re-dating of the pottery has pushed the date of the end of this phase towards the late thirteenth century – 1230 to 1190/80 BC – which some have refined, or summarised, to c.1200 BC, though occupation of the place ended distinctly later than that. This settlement was burnt, and a large area of the lower town also shows evidence of this destruction. It also appears to have been militarily prepared – heaps of sling bullets were found, and some skeletons – but this does not necessarily make the city one under siege, or even under attack, though it can be interpreted in that way.[15]

None of this archaeological evidence seems to connect in any precise or convincing way with the story of the Trojan War as imagined by the poet Homer in the eighth century BC – four centuries after the supposed occurrence. The destruction of Troy VI took place, according to the archaeologists, about 1300 BC, and of Troy VIIa between 1230 BC and 1190 BC or 1180 BC. Its successor, Troy VIIb/1 lasted until about 1150 BC, and the next settlement was destroyed about fifty years later, perhaps about 1100 BC (Troy VIIb/2), either by another earthquake or by another enemy attack. The round figures of the suggested dates betray, of course, their very approximate nature.[16]

According to the Hittite archives (which are, no doubt, incomplete, and whose datings are dependent on chronological calculations of a fairly abstruse nature), Troy came under attack by an enemy before c.1280 BC. There are three references to Wilusa in thirteenth century BC Hittite documents. The first reference reports an expedition by a Hittite force against Wilusa, sent by the Hittite Emperor Muwatalli II, first to assist their ally Alexandu, the Wilusa king, but later to defeat him after some other trouble;[17] the second is a treaty of alliance between the same two kings. It is this treaty which is dated about c.1280 BC, so the violent events had already taken place. In the next Hittite reign, of Hattusili III, and so between c.1267 BC and c.1237 BC, the country may have been a bone of contention in a war between the Hittites and the Ahhiyawa, who are usually identified as the Akhaians – that is, the Mycenaeans. Wilusa is, however, mentioned only as an afterthought, and the report is that the problem there had been settled; no details are given of what was wrong or what had happened, so what did happen had done so before 1237 BC, and probably years earlier.[18] In the next Hittite reign, the Wilusa king Walmu was deposed by an enemy, but then reinstalled by the Hittite king; this was at some point in the reign to Tudhaliya IV, and so between c.1237 BC and c.1209 BC.[19]

It will be seen that the archive dates are usually almost as approximate as are those of the archaeologists, in that they can only be dated by the reign of the Hittite king, but at no point, except perhaps once, do the two chronological schemes coincide in any meaningful way. Only in the problem of King Walmu's deposition and restoration can it be said that the dating of the political problem overlaps with the archaeological dating evidence for the destruction of one of the Troy cities – that is, Troy VIIa, in the period 1230–1190/80 BC – but this is hardly precise. The letter in which Walmu was referred to only deals with Walmu himself; he had been driven out by an enemy, and was to be reinstated by Hittite forces; there is no reference to the city – Wilusa was the kingdom – nor to its destruction, though Walmu's restoration evidently did mean his return to Wilusa/Troy.

The *Iliad* of Homer has been the basis for attempts to reconstruct the history of Troy, and these attempts have all failed. This is hardly surprising, for Homer lived perhaps four centuries after the events he sets his story around, in a completely different society, when living elsewhere, and he was writing a poem, not a history. A sort of excavation process based on his poem has been indulged in, to find fragments and details and references which might 'prove' that he was basing himself on factual events at the city. No such detail can possibly 'prove' anything, and for every detail which seems to be an authentic reference back to the Bronze Age, there are others which are a denial of it. It has even been claimed that the 'catalogue of ships' which is included is an authentic, detailed, and accurate memory of the fleet which set out from Greece to go to the war, preserved in some way by human minds, through several centuries of illiteracy and with complete accuracy. We are asked to believe that it is a catalogue drawn up by the Greek invaders, recording the details of places involved, numbers of ships and men, and so on. Yet it is a catalogue which omits some places which should be included by the poet's own account. The process of remembering and passing on the knowledge is simply not believable, and the 'catalogue' is best seen as an invention of a much later time, perhaps even by Homer himself. To use this as historical evidence is desperation masquerading as scholarship.

What needs to be remembered is that Homer's poem is in fact an historical novel, and furthermore it is set in verse. It is no more accurate than Homer himself could discover by any type of historical research, though how he would have set about it is not known, especially in the absence – I repeat – of any relevant written records, either from the Mycenaean kingdoms or from (illiterate) Troy. In fact, it is a product of his own imagination, and probably that of other poets; he was not seriously interested in 'authenticity'. To show that minstrel poets in primitive parts of Europe could memorise and recite large chunks of apparently ancient poetry, as has been done,[20] cannot be used as a means of demonstrating that Homer's memory was similarly accurate, and that he had received elements of the poem from equally memorising predecessors, through at least a dozen generations. This is the real message of the archaeological findings: it is simply not possible to link the 'city' as revealed on the ground with the city as described by Homer. The very claim that the war lasted ten years should be enough to relegate Homer to the realms of fiction. It was not logistically possible for a war of that period to have lasted more than a single campaigning season, if that.

This, of course, is not to say that the city of Troy did not suffer the adverse attentions of the Mycenaeans, but it is to say that there is no evidence that any Trojan-Mycenaean War took place. The Hittite archives show that until late in the thirteenth century the city – if such it still was by that time – was under Hittite protection, as recorded more than once by the Hittite royal letters. In only one reference might the city be thought to have been involved in an Ahhiyawan war; the last reference shows that an enemy drove out King Walmu from Wilusa, but he was about to be reinstated by the Hittite military when the letter referring to the event was written (whose date is anywhere between c.1237 BC and c.1209 BC), and there is no indication of who the enemy was – it is not legitimate to link this event with the Mycenaeans. The fighting took place during the archaeological period Troy VIIa, which was the poverty-stricken place which Carl Blegen thought might have been under siege. This is also the period of the Bezik Bay cemetery, one grave of which contained Mycenaean pottery sherds. Troy VIIa imported Mycenaean pottery, and its own potters made imitations of it. This was the city which was probably destroyed by an enemy, in so far as archaeology can identify such an event. The excavator found evidence of fire, remains of weapons (arrowheads especially), and bodies left in the streets – in some cases, portions of bodies. On the other hand, there was no evidence of who had been the attackers and the destroyers of the place, or who the victims were. Putting these details into a discussion of the Trojan War and claiming proof of the latter is not an acceptable process.

In fact, of course, the question should not be to seek for evidence of the Trojan War in the poem, but to discover the history of Troy by excavation first. It has taken a century and a half for the latter to bring us to that ordering of the issue, and it is decisive in relegating the Trojan War to fiction. It is high time this was recognised in classics as well as archaeology; the two need to be separated.

This period of desertion was followed by the occupation of the site by people of a very different culture; this is level Troy VIIb/1, which lasted less than half a century, until about 1150 BC. Since the bodies had been left in the streets to decompose, and be scavenged by wild animals, at the end of VIIa, it seems probable that the new occupants did not take up residence for some time, and that the burnt city had been left abandoned, perhaps for a generation – at least long enough for the bodies to have been reduced to skeletons, and the skeletons then covered over by debris. But the last two phases VIIb/1 and the following VIIb/2 (c.1150–1100 BC) were deep in poverty, and neither would have been able to resist any serious attack for very long. A final Bronze Age phase (VIIb/3) was detected in the latest excavations, but this occupation simply faded away; by 1000 BC, and probably well before that date, the site was deserted.

It has been tempting, of course, to identify the enemy which sacked Troy VIIa as the Mycenaeans, and then to claim that Homer's poem refers to this moment. The problem is that by the time of the sack the Mycenaean homeland was itself under attack, with its political centres falling to enemies in the same way as Troy did; most of them had already gone down to destruction by c.1200 BC, before the usually suggested dates of the 'Trojan War'. Another possible destroyer of Troy has been identified as the 'Sea Peoples', whose mass migration along the Levant coast and their attack on Egypt is to be dated to the last years of the thirteenth century or the first quarter of the twelfth.[21] But these Sea Peoples are only recorded in Syria. In Anatolia, sometime after the Sea Peoples had arrived in Syria, the Hittite kingdom fell to invaders, but this was not due to actions by the Sea Peoples,[22] so there is no reason to find the Sea Peoples active in north-west Anatolia while they were in Syria, any more than they can be found in Greece.

The conclusion must be that whatever lies at the root of Homer's poem, it is not the great siege of the wealthy city of Troy ruled by a king called Priam during a war lasting for ten years. No such long war was possible given the culture and technology of the time; second, the city of Troy was not great and rich at any time during which the attack could have taken place. It was instead only a moderately sized town within an agricultural region. Nor can it be accepted that whatever power the city wielded was based on the control of the passage of the Hellespont, for which no evidence exists.

Troy was a small city on the edge of the civilised world of its time. It was subject to distant control and occasional protection by the Hittite kings, but by the end of the thirteenth century that protection would have disappeared along with the Hittite Empire, just as at the same time any political Aegean enemy was eliminated. If the greater powers of Mycenae and Hattusas were overthrown by invading barbarians, Troy, small, unimportant, peripheral, on one of the civilised world's barbarian borders, could never have survived, particularly after the earthquake destruction; it does not need a Trojan War to account for the destruction of the city; but one may all the more admire Homer's rich imagination, conjuring a great war out of nothing.

In the history of the Straits and the Sea of Marmara, Troy is marginal, just as it was marginal with regard to both the Mycenaeans and the Hittites. Its geographical position put it on the very edge of the Straits region, and the direction of its people's attention was rarely towards the Sea, still less towards the Bosporos – they looked continually, partly to the Aegean, but mainly to the Anatolian interior, whence came their protection. During the two thousand years of Troy's existence the Straits and the Sea were of little or no concern, either to the Trojans or to their neighbours and enemies.

Chapter 3

Thracians and Greeks (c.1000–546 BC)

T he final phase of occupation at Troy at the end of the Bronze Age saw the brief presence of a new population whose culture, such as it was, indicates that they came from the European side of the Straits.[1] It is clearly possible that they were the people in the hamlets on the Gallipoli Peninsula who had earlier connections with Troy, in that they used pottery of a similar style to that of Troy VI. More likely, however, they were from further afield. They were, in that case, probably Thracians, though Strabo says they were Mysians.[2]

This population had vanished from Troy by about 1050 BC. The next centuries, from the end of Troy VII to the beginning of Greek settlement at the site (c.1100–800 BC), are effectively blank in our knowledge, both historically and archaeologically, except for the existence of a shrine called by the excavator the West Sanctuary. The surveys conducted in Thrace and in the Gallipoli Peninsula by Ozdogan and his students have produced no evidence for this period, which elsewhere is the Early Iron Age. This is perhaps in part because it is difficult to recognise material of that period, but Ozdogan on the Gallipoli survey is quite certain that no Early Iron Age stuff was found.[3] In that time also, Troy remained deserted. The conclusion to be reached is that the region seems to have been largely empty of human population, at least as far as archaeology is concerned. It is as though the area of thin or nil population to the north of Troy in the Late Bronze Age had spread southwards. Given the small size of Troy at all periods, it would not take much to remove the whole population, urban and rural.

However, the historical evidence is rather different. In many cases, when the Greek colonists arrived in the region, they settled in places which were already occupied by Thracians. This is the case at Ainos, on the north Aegean coast at the mouth of the Maritza River, where there was a well-established Thracian town when the Greeks arrived;[4] at

Abydos on the Asian side of the Hellespont, a king is said to have ruled; at Sestos on the other side of the Strait,[5] at several places on the European side of the Sea of Marmara; at Kyzikos on the Asian side, there was another Thracian king.[6] There is also the mythological attribution of the original Byzantion being ruled by the Thracian king called Byzas before the Greeks arrived; the word Byzantion is apparently at base Thracian.[7] There is therefore plenty of evidence of Thracians in occupation both along the Marmara and Straits coasts and at other places in the region. Since they are certainly known to have crossed the Straits (as at Abydos and perhaps at Kyzikos) it is reasonable to accept that Thracian colonists had traversed the Straits during the Early Iron Age, before the Greeks reached the coast. It is tempting to suggest that the way had been opened by the twelfth-century destruction of Troy, but it is difficult to accept that Troy was ever powerful enough to deny anyone passage of the Straits, and absence of any population after 1000 BC on both sides of the Straits and Marmara is conclusive: the repopulation originated from elsewhere.

It may be noted that when the Thracians arrived, which seems to be dated to the tenth or ninth centuries BC,[8] they certainly found the Straits and the Sea of Marmara flowing with water out of the Black Sea. Whether or not one can accept that the flow had been blocked in a period 3000–1000 BC (very approximately), it is clear that this condition had changed by 1000 BC or so, and that from then the Straits and the Sea existed more or less at their present size, shape, and condition. Why the flow re-started at that time is not clear, but it was perhaps due to a combination of rising water level in the Black Sea and earth movements, which opened the passage of the Bosporos.

The movement of Thracians into the lands along the now wet Straits is partly shown by the encounters of the Greeks with them when the latter arrived to form their colonies (but not until the seventh or sixth centuries), but is also part of the general movement of peoples which accompanied, followed, and maybe caused the upheavals of the end of the Bronze Age. Dorians moved into Greece to take advantage of the destruction of the Mycenaean kingdoms, and then across the Aegean into Karia and Crete. The Kaska in northern Anatolia moved against the Hittite kingdom, destroyed it, and took over some of its northern territories. The Sea Peoples moved along the Levant coast and twice vainly attacked Egypt, then settled in southern Palestine. It is not clear how, or if, these various movements of peoples were connected, but that they all occurred within a short space of time is certainly suggestive.

There was also another movement, one which has been regarded with some scepticism. The Phrygians are reported, very much later, to have migrated from the Balkans to the north centre of Anatolia, where they formed their kingdom in part of the former territory of the Hittite kingdom. This new kingdom is not really heard of until about 800 BC, but it is clear that the movement of the people to the region where they formed the kingdom would have taken place some time previous to that. The archaeological evidence, such as it is, does not provide any confident information. The scepticism is mainly at the idea of a migration of the whole people, which is no longer an idea which is regarded with any favour by any archaeologist anywhere, despite continuing migrations of people over the last several thousand years – though recent studies have largely rehabilitated the migratory notion.[9]

There are, indeed, certain indications which tend to support the notion that Phrygians arrived from outside, and from Europe. There was certainly a movement of Thracians into the Straits' lands. The evidence, apart from the Greeks' encounters with Thracians at their colonies, is in part Homer, who set down his poems late in the eighth century and whose notions of the political geography of the lands he was writing about were those of his own time – thus he comments that Sestos and Abydos were occupied by Thracians, even though he puts that situation in the time of his Trojan war, the date of which he did not particularise. Strabo reports that the Thracian word for a town or city was *bria*,[10] and this ending appears in several places from Ainos, whose original name was Poltyobria, to Selymbria on the Propontis, and Mesambria on the western Pontic coast; along with the myths of Byzas of Byzantion and the Thracian 'King of Kyzikos', this would seem to be pretty good evidence of the Thracian occupation of all these shores. Given that in the Bronze Age the lands of the Straits and Marmara were very thinly occupied, or not at all, it seems reasonable to suggest that this movement was slow and gradual, an occupation of largely vacant lands.

The Phrygian language, from the few indications there are, principally personal names,[11] is reckoned by linguistic historians to be more closely related to Greek than to any other language. Strabo several times refers to the Phrygian migration and to the Phrygian connection with Europe.[12]

The coast east of Kyzikos was thus probably inhabited by a Phrygian group called the Dolionoi when Kyzikos was founded.[13] The region inland of this had the name Hellespontine Phrygia under the Akhaimenids and in the Hellenistic period.

Given the generally disturbed condition of Anatolia – and its partial desertion – after the collapse of the Hittite state, movements of populations are to be expected – the Kaskas certainly moved south to take over some of the Hittite lands – and if Thracians could cross from Europe to Asia, so could Phrygians. Their numbers are not necessarily to be thought large, nor was the migration necessarily all at one time, but by 800 BC the Phrygian presence was strong enough in north-central Anatolia for them to constitute themselves into a kingdom. The kings, apparently usually named Gordion or Midas, were wealthy, according to the tombs excavated at Gordion (and according to Greek stories linking Midas and gold), and they were strong enough to attract the negative attention of the paranoid and aggressive Assyrians.[14] The kingdom was destroyed in the first quarter of the seventh century by an invasion of nomad Kimmerians,[15] just at the time when the Greeks were beginning to venture into the Straits and towards the Black Sea.

This series of migrations saw Dorian Greeks moving into Greece, Phrygians into Anatolia, and Thracians into the Straits/Marmara area. These peoples all came originally from the southern Balkans. It is a nice question to wonder what it was that thus impelled, or compelled, them to move. There seems to be no tradition of disturbances in their original homeland; probably therefore it was the attraction of moving into lands which were either empty (for the Thracians) or into the lands of formerly rich societies (Phrygians into Hittite Anatolia, Dorians into Mycenaean Greece) when these imperial societies collapsed. It was their misfortune to find that the collapse had in effect also wiped out much of the wealth – though the Phrygians prospered for a time, of course.

The centuries between the end of Troy VII and the fall of the Phrygian state (c.1100–700 BC) were therefore fairly busy, and probably increasingly so in the Straits. We must envisage, in the decades after perhaps 1000 BC, small parties of Phrygians and Thracians occupying the northern and western shores, perhaps the Phrygians first, having separated off from the early-Greek speakers in the Balkans (who, as Dorians, went south), then the Thracians coming along and pushing the Phrygians onwards.

More likely they were mixed together, and those who became the Phrygians moved directly into central Anatolia with a view to exploiting the confusion there. The Thracians, less adventurous but more persistent, took over the shores of the Straits and stayed there.

When the Greeks in their ships ventured into the Straits, therefore, they were latecomers. They met Thracians already established on many of the shores on both sides, Phrygians and others elsewhere, and then more Thracians on the western coast of the Black Sea. Thracians had already also moved into the northern part of the Asian shore, where the Bithynians were reckoned to be Thracians who were originally related to others, a group called the Thyni, who still lived on the European side. The Bithynians' eastern neighbours, the Mariandyni, could also be thought to be Thracian later, though this might be because they were included within the Bithynian kingdom when it was formed. The Greeks' reception by all these Thracian peoples, already in occupation as they were, varied, but eventually mutual hostility between the two became general (and lasted well into the much later Hellenistic period).

The Greek penetration into the Propontis would seem to have been part of a determination to reach the Black Sea and its rumoured trading opportunities. The collapse of the Phrygian kingdom between c.700 BC and c.675 BC as a result of the invasion of the Kimmerians and attacked by the Assyrians, seems to have disrupted the trans-Anatolian trade routes which had brought such goods as gold from Colchis in the Caucasus and ironwork from the Chalybes of north-east Anatolia to the Greek market. It was this trade (and the gold) which had brought wealth to the golden King Midas (the name of several Phrygian kings). These kings had facilitated trade through to the Greek cities of the western Asia Minor coast, principally, it seems, through the city of Kyme,[16] but no doubt other Greek cities in Ionia and Aiolis, such as Miletos and Ephesos, participated. The origin of the goods was hardly a secret, but so long as they arrived in sufficient quantities to be bought at the Greek cities of the Asia Minor coast there was no need to go hunting for their precise source. The destruction of the trading system which had been organised by the Phrygian kings broke up the organization which generated the supply.

This break was one element which stimulated the Greek explorations northwards. But it was not the only agent of change in this region. The Aegean had been a busy water world since well before the end of the

Mycenaean period, but the main target of its trading had been to east and west, to the eastern Mediterranean where the luxury goods which rich men coveted were available in the markets of Cyprus and the Levant, and westwards where raw materials could be acquired. The sea was being continually crossed by migrations of Ionians and Dorians from Greece to Asia. The Aegean was also, according to the later Greek historians, a region into which the ships and merchants of the Levant – 'Phoenicians' – came. There is credible evidence, both written (later) and archaeological, for a Phoenician presence in Thasos in the northern Aegean, where gold was mined.[17] One of their legacies to the Greeks was writing, using alphabetic script, in which Homer's poems were ultimately published.

Beyond this commercial activity, there was also a wider Greek impulse to colonise other areas. This had already been linked with the trading expansion in the western lands, but a new trading base of the Italian coast at Pithekoussai on Ischia Island, in existence by the mid-eighth century BC, was soon followed by Greek colonisations in southern Italy and Sicily; and the traders foraged still further afield, to southern Gaul and Spain, again in the sea-tracks of the Phoenicians.

The lands north of Greece inevitably attracted the same attention, but it seems to have happened in the reverse order to what was happening in the west. Troy, for example, was colonised by a small Greek population late in the eighth century, even before the collapse of the Phrygian monarchy, though perhaps not before some exploratory voyages had been made into the Black Sea. There was a tradition, incorporated in the *Chronographia* of Eusebios in the fourth century AD, that Greek colonies were established at some of the Black Sea sites as early as the middle of the eighth century BC. No confirmatory archaeological evidence has been found, which has led to Eusebios' evidence being dismissed, or his dates argued downwards, but it may actually be a memory of the preliminary exploratory voyages by Greek traders who hoped to cut out the Phrygian middlemen and tap into the supply of gold and ironwork at their sources. (If they did, the plan seems to have failed: no doubt the Phrygian connection would be too valuable to the producers to be jeopardised – while it lasted.) Such explorations would be dangerous, and it is these voyages which may well be the original factual bases for the romance of *Jason and the Argonauts*, which, like the *Iliad*, is essentially an elaborated tale of much imagination (and formalised by Apollonios in the Hellenistic period). It is just possibly based on old stories, but quite unacceptable as an historical source.

The very idea of these exploratory voyages is not widely accepted, but some information about the Black Sea clearly existed before the first colonies were planted – the first voyagers and colonists clearly knew that the sea existed and that there were places where they knew it would be possible for them to settle.[18] In any case, such early explorations seem to have led nowhere in the immediate term, though perhaps they were not forgotten. Meanwhile, in the lands around the mouth of the Hellespont, there was a different quiet process of colonisation going on. The reoccupation of Troy (Troy VIII) is to be dated to the 720s BC, or perhaps a little earlier.[19] And it was about this time that several other places in the Troad received Greek settlers.[20] These came from two nearby islands, Lesbos and Tenedos.

Mytilenians from Lesbos planted small settlements at half a dozen places along the coast of the Troad: Hamaxitos, Larisa, and Kolonai along the western-facing coast, Sigeion, Rhoetion, and Ophryteion further north on the Hellespont coast, and at Ilion (Troy) somewhat inland. The islanders of Tenedos, very close to this coast, probably planted colonies at places called Achilleion and Achaiion, names which, if original to the late eighth century BC, may imply that Homer's stories were already well-known. It was, of course, just at this time that Homer is supposed to have composed his great poems; probably the colonisation of the Troad was one of the triggers for their composition.

Mytilenians also settled along the Troad's southern shores, founding the cities at Assos and Antandros and Gargara. From these various coastal sites, some of which always remained small and have the appearance of being little more than beachheads, the Mytilenians spread inland, founding more prosperous and bigger colonies at Neandria and Kebren and Skepsis, where land for farming was available, as it was not on the coast. This work was a manpower-expensive business, and the Mytilenians had Kymaians with them in founding Kebren; their fellow Lesbians from Methymna founded some of the places on the southern Troad coast. The overall effect of their infiltration was that at least one existing local 'native' community, Gergis, adopted a city-state model for itself, either in emulation or in self-defence; Skepsis may have been similarly 'native' in origin, but was soon gobbled up by Greeks.

This activity emanating from Lesbos and Tenedos has nothing of the overtly commercial about it, nor is it an obvious attempt to gain 'control' of the Hellespont. The new settlements were all small, at least to begin with, and the settlers quickly pushed inland in search of new and more productive land. This was what they were clearly after: to possess and cultivate, and the inland cities eventually had control of fairly wide territories. The question of motive is clinched by the only other Mytilenian foundation in the region; this was Alopekonessos, on the Thracian Chersonese, established on the western side of the peninsula, less hilly and with more cultivable land than the Hellespont side. The city's later coins show grapes and wheat, indicating its priorities. This, therefore, was a colonisation movement which had little or no commercial motivation; the reason was a search for land and for a means of exporting the population which was felt to be too great for the home islands' resources.

Most of this Lesbian colonisation had been achieved by about 700 BC, though this is based on rather thin archaeological findings, which are not entirely agreed, and the foundation of Alopekonnesos in particular is only conjectural,[21] the suggested date being based on those of other Mytilenian colonies. It is, of course, likely that the process of colonisation took some time. The coastal towns were no doubt planted in fairly quick succession, and were no more than small villages at first. The gap in the line of Lesbian settlements along the coast between Kolonai and Sigeion is where Tenedos planted its colonies – the coast became the Tenedian *peraia* – which suggests that Lesbos and Tenedos were actively laying out claims on these lands on the mainland at much the same time: in such a competition it would be worthwhile planting a whole series of small communities at the start of the process in order to reserve for oneself a particular stretch of coast so as to be able to move inland: we may thus assume that the whole of the Troadic coast from Gargara to Ophryteion was occupied very quickly; the movement inland would then follow at leisure.

These foundations were all small in their origins, and most of them stayed small. The distances involved in moving from Lesbos to the mainland were short – a voyage of no more than a day – and the home island in most cases remained visible and accessible. The number of people involved was clearly small. It seems probable that this was a peasant movement, perhaps an overflow from inland colonisation within the islands of Lesbos and Tenedos. It is only later that some of these places can be regarded as cities: indeed, they may have been self-governing, but in size they were, in most cases, no more than villages. There seems to be no indication of opposition to the settlers, though the Troadic interior was clearly occupied.

The Phrygian collapse took place while the secondary interior colonisation from Lesbos was going on. In the west of Asia Minor a new kingdom, Lydia, seceded from Phrygia (its first dynasty was soon overthrown by Gyges, who ruled from about 680 BC). By defeating Kimmerian raids the Lydian kings secured a sizeable territory, much of which had formerly been Phrygian, and in effect this became the principal successor state of the Phrygian kingdom, though based rather farther to the west, at Sardis, rather than at sacked Gordion.[22]

Some of the Greek cities perhaps took advantage of the chaos and expanded their mainland territories, and so provoked Gyges and his Lydian successors to retaliate, though as wealthy places perhaps in sympathy with Phrygia they may also have been seen as worth securing for their wealth and their enmity. As a result, some of the cities fell under Lydian control, some were destroyed, and others survived, though under constant threat.[23] These latter were the ones who became the main colonisers, their motivation being thus rather different from that of the earlier colonies around the mouth of the Hellespont. Of these colonisers the greatest, most active, and prolific, was Miletos. Others which took part in the movement to the north were Erythrai, Phokaia and Teos: across the Aegean the prime operator was Megara; all of these gathered participants from other cities, acting as colonising entrepreneurs.

For Megara the issue was that it was blocked from any expansion by the presence on two sides by the seas, the Aegean and the Gulf of Corinth, and on the land sides by two more powerful states, Corinth to the south and Athens to the north. Megara had to go through a process of unification and a war of independence to escape from Corinthian control.[24] In the process a large fraction of the city's fertile land was lost to Corinth, just as most of Miletos' land was lost to Lydia; the emigration of a part of the population was an answer to the pressure on resources. But these cities were not so fertile in people as to be the sole sources of the emigrants who were numerous enough to have founded several dozens of cities which later claimed to have Megara and Miletos as their home cities. They collected emigrants from other places because they became the experts in transporting the people, selecting the site, and supporting them in their first difficult years. The Milesians were joined by Klazomenians, Phokaians, Teians in jointly founding colonies, and Megara's manpower sources included parties of Boiotians, Argives, and Arkadians.

The dates of the foundations of the Greek colonies have been a long-continuing game played by historians and archaeologists, each claiming primacy for the evidence on his side of the contest. It is only by excavation that some approximation to the dates of the first settlement can be found, but as it happens those sites where proper excavation has taken place and clear early evidence has been secured do tend to confirm many of the dates which have been sorted out from the written sources. Yet it is not always possible to be sure that an excavation has reached the lowest level or the earliest remains, which by definition is the most difficult to reach; on the other hand, in the evidence used by historians it is not always positive that the written dates are accurate; there is still plenty of room for dispute.

The archaeological evidence, of course, only exists if it is found, and can only be found if it was deposited. It is quite possible to believe that early Greek colonies left no physical evidence to be discovered: that is, that there is no archaeological evidence for the first Greek expeditions, though archaeologists are sufficiently skilled to detect even ephemeral evidence in the ground. The dates of the colonial foundations are recorded in late – sometimes very late – documents, and all seem to have been calculated by working back to a probable time. Some colonies have no record at all, the first arrivals having better things to do than write down their reminiscences. So both the sources of dating evidence are essentially approximate, and both could be out by decades.

Large numbers of the colony cities, therefore, have neither a recorded foundation date, nor have they been excavated. So the only means of proceeding is to take the established dates of cities where this has been worked out, and then fit other colonies around them. This is not by any means a satisfactory proceeding, but it will do for now. Precision is never likely to be achieved.

In reference to the Black Sea coast, a three-stage process of colonisation has been suggested: first, a reconnaissance, which probably has left no evidence on the ground; second, an establishment of several new cities on a fairly small scale; third, an elaboration of secondary settlements, including new cities, sometimes founded from existing colonies, and in some cases an expansion of the original settlements into the nearby countryside.[25] This is essentially also the process which is likely for the small Lesbian settlements discussed above.

For the Straits and the Sea of Marmara this sequence would suggest that the first stage was one in which the colonisers would explore the shores of the Hellespont and Propontis, and locate the best places at which to establish a post for trading and for prospecting other possible sites for a new city. Once the possibilities of the Black Sea were appreciated, the Straits could be seen only as a way-station on the voyage.

The first exploratory stage has been dated to the mid-seventh century, and so almost half a century after the Lesbian colonisation of the Troadic coast began, but almost at the time that Miletos came under serious and final pressure from the Lydians. The first places to be founded in the Black Sea – at Beresan, Istros, and Apollonia – were clearly pushed out well in advance, so it would be reasonable to suggest that the Milesians had been exploring the possibilities of the sea for some time in order to find such places before direct colonisation began. The pattern of settlement may be seen as similar, though on a much larger scale to that employed by the Lesbians in the Troad: marking out Milesian claims by a spread of secured positions. But in the Straits the Milesians and others were also establishing themselves and had clearly been doing so for some time before serious settlement began in the Black Sea. Whether this was planting colonies to mark out a claim, or to seize land for the city's surplus population, or was a process of seizing control of useful way-stations on the route north, depends on the site, the date, and the background. That is, the early foundations were probably not directly aimed at the Black Sea, but at the Propontis, though it may well be that the aim was to secure some control over the routes towards the Black Sea.

One of the earliest of Miletos' ventures was to plant a post at Kyzikos, in the first quarter of the seventh century, i.e., between 700 BC and 675 BC, which is exactly the time the Phrygian state collapsed. Eusebios gives two dates for the foundation of the colony, 756 BC and 676 BC, the second being accepted as the more likely,[26] though a preliminary expedition may well be likely – a small quantity of Greek pottery dated to about 700 BC has been found inland of the city's site, suggesting earlier contacts, perhaps in trade, perhaps exploration, probably both. The city was established on a large island separated from the mainland by a narrow strait, so providing both a sheltered port and a large territory for farmland. From there, quite possibly following a pre-concerted plan, subsidiary posts were established on the island of Prokonnesos, next door to Kyzikos' own island (separated from the mainland by only a narrow strait), and on the main island at Artake. The Argonaut legend claims that Kyzikos was ruled at the time by a Thracian king, and since Artake was a Thracian name, even if the existence of the king is not necessarily accepted, the Thracian name of Artake does indicate that the area was occupied by Thracian people before the Greeks arrived.[27]

This element in the story is generally ignored, but it is clear that the Greeks were in many cases following Thracian pioneers in their colonising activities. It is necessary to understand that the Greeks were not themselves pioneers in the Straits and the Propontis and the Black Sea, but that in many cases they took over control of Thracian (and other) foundations which already existed, and they had come into the Propontis as into a sea already well understood by its peripheral inhabitants. That is, the preliminary investigations located the Thracian settlements which the Milesians and Megarians judged worth seizing. The process was that they could either arrive in overwhelming strength to subdue the occupants, or they could infiltrate their own pioneers into existing settlements to gain control by encouraging others. In either case the land was already under cultivation and the town was already habitable. No doubt after an initial fight the Greeks enslaved the defeated Thracians, seized their wealth and their women, and instantly became prosperous; such conflicts are repeatedly recorded, often in romantic terms, at the Greek cities in their foundation myths.

For ships sailing from the Hellespont to the Bosporos there were two obvious routes to follow, sailing along the north or south coasts of the Propontis, so that wherever possible voyagers could stop for the night, land, make a meal, and sleep ashore. It is thought that the south coast route was the most favoured, in part because it included several bays and harbours in which the ships could shelter in times of storms, or overnight, in part because the north coast was less fertile and food to buy or steal was less plentiful or available; Kyzikos' site was on a narrow strait between its island and the mainland, where traffic could be intercepted, or could halt for the night. The early Milesian posts on the islands and the mainland neatly seized control of that southern route. This may well be the preliminary move in a Milesian campaign to gain control of the whole of the Black Sea, which becomes clearer when the pattern of Milesian posts there is considered. It is, of course, exactly what the Lesbian towns had done already in the Troad on a much greater scale.

Another early plantation was at Abydos, at the crucial choke-point, with Sestos on the opposite side of the Hellespont, Abydos on the east, Sestos on the west. Again one source, Homer, claims that Abydos was subject to a Thracian king, along with Sestos,[28] and here his information may well be accurate, for the events took place not long before his own lifetime. Another source, however, claims that it was subject to the Lydian king Gyges, who encouraged Miletos to take over the post,[29] as part of a peace agreement with that city. (The two stories were not incompatible, of course, if Gyges had established his supremacy over the original Thracian settlers.) This will have happened therefore in the second quarter of the seventh century, during Gyges' reign (c.680–c.650 BC). It was a Thracian place at the time, and presumably Gyges' aim was to dislodge the Thracians, by using the equally troublesome Greeks of Miletos as his instruments; if the Milesians succeeded it would be as his agents.

These two Milesian colonies illustrate two different colonising purposes. The capture of Abydos was clearly for a strategic purpose; Gyges was aiming to extend his kingdom, and the place was a fortified post at the narrowest part of the Hellespont, a place like Kyzikos where traffic could be monitored and controlled – and taxed. This may well also have appealed to the Milesians, if one of their purposes was to dominate, if not control, access to the Propontis and the Black Sea. (It is also noticeable that the earlier Lesbian colonies stopped well short of Abydos. Dardanos, between Mytilenian Ophyteion and Milesian Abydos, is not claimed for any founding city, but there is seventh century material found there.)[30]

By contrast, while Kyzikos seems to have been planted originally to dominate the seaway along the southern Propontis coast, the city rapidly became avid for land. It controlled its own island, and had Thracian Artake also on the island, apparently peacefully annexed; it gained control of 'New' Prokonnesos, an island rich in marble deposits close to the 'Old' Prokonnesos; fairly soon it had penetrated inland into the continent and founded two places at either end of a large lake: Apollonia-on-the-

Rhyndakos and Miletopolis, whose names indicate that the people of Kyzikos still held to their Milesian origins – Apollonia later enquired of Miletos if it had been a colony of that city, and received an affirmative reply; perhaps reinforcements came from the homeland to expand the city. By expanding in this way, of course, Kyzikos was establishing itself more as a prosperous agricultural city with a wide territory (*chora*) – Apollonia is seventy-five kilometres from Kyzikos – than as merely a way station on the seaway.[31]

The attempt of Miletos to control the route along the southern Marmara coast – if that is what was intended – was only partly successful and led to conflict. At the Hellespont both shores were colonised from other cities. At Lampsakos the arrival of a group from Phokaia soon developed into a contest with the resident Thracians which the Greeks won. This was, however, later claimed to be a Milesian success, though the evidence (of the names of months used by the city, for example) supports the alternative foundation for the city by Phokaians. The date is about the middle of the seventh century, a generation after the Milesians at Abydos and Kyzikos, but about the same time as the first settlements in the Black Sea region. The later claim of a Milesian foundation suggests that one aspect of the fighting involved the Milesians seizing the place after the initial Phokaian settlement, though it seems that the Phokaians ultimately succeeded.[32]

Such a conflict would certainly fit with the notion that the Milesians were keen to monopolise access to the seas of the north. A series of small places along the southern Marmara coast, together with the substantial penetration inland from Kyzikos, seems to show much the same intention. On the European coast of the Hellespont, the later Kallipolis, was reckoned to be part of Lampsakos' *peraia*, and the city thus controlled parts of both shores.[33] Small Milesian settlements are also known at Limnai and Kardia, also on the Chersonese – the latter in concert with Klazomenai[34] – and at Praisos and Priapos on the Asian shore.[35] Around Kyzikos, Kios at the head of Gemlik Bay was also Milesian;[36] its suggested foundation date makes it the last of Miletos' foundations in the Propontis.

By this time other cities had succeeded in muscling in. Miletos at times joined with a neighbouring city in founding a colony. Some of those partners also operated alone; Myrleia, not far from Kios, was founded from Kolophon.[37] This may well have been one of the Lydians' ploys, for the city of Kolophon was overrun by a Lydian attack, and the Lydian king could well have included an offer of a city-site on the Propontis as part of the subsequent peace terms, in the same way that the Milesians had been induced to colonise Abydos. Not far from Myrleia was Daskylion, named for King Gyges' father,[38] and so presumably a place he or a successor of his had founded or occupied and fortified with the intention of expanding their territories at the expense of, or over, the local Thracians and Phrygians, and of overseeing the activities of the Greeks along the shore. Miletos and its partners were thus generally successful in gaining control over much of the southern coast of the Propontis, quite probably in alliance with the Lydian kings – the Thracian tribe of the Kyzikos area, the Trieres, are known to have fought against the Lydians after the Milesian colonisation of their lands.

The major competitor in the Propontis – apart from the Thracians – was Megara, which necessarily concentrated on colonising where the Milesians did not. The aim of the Megarians was apparently not to pioneer a wide commercial sphere, which was clearly a major part of Milesian intention, but to find land on which to settle the colonists – the same motivation as the Lesbians along the Troad coast, and eventually of the Kyzikans in their foundation of subsidiary colonies on their islands and their hinterland. The Megarians had no relationship with the Lydian kings, so their choice of sites was dictated in part by the availability of land for agriculture, and by the need to maintain a careful distance from the Lydian lands. This brought them first to Chalkedon, at the mouth of the Bosporos, where they secured a generous portion of the nearby territory at the expense of the local Thracian tribe. Selymbria – note the Thracian ending to the name – on the northern coast, was a second site acquired at Thracian expense. Then, about 630 – the date is disputed – they planted a colony at Byzantion. Again, this city acquired a considerable extent of territory, opposite Chalkedon. The name Byzas was either that of the Thracian king or the name for the place, but it is firm evidence in either case for Thracian occupation before the Greeks arrived. At some later point Chalkedon planted a colony of its own at Astakos at the inner end of Izmit Bay, which gave access to the well-watered valley of Lake Sapanka and the Sakarya (Sangarius) River beyond.[39]

The Milesians also penetrated into the Black Sea, and it is tempting to see the Straits and Propontis settlements as deliberate preliminaries for the Black Sea colonies. In fact, the two movements overlapped, and the Black Sea settlements began to be founded even as the Propontis settlements were still being found and exploited. The early places seized in the Black Sea, however, were often islands or capes on or close to the mainland where there was commercial access to the interior – the Bay of Burgas, for example, where Apollonia, on an island, was well placed to open trade with the established Thracian settlements nearby, and further afield into the Balkan interior. Such settlements are different in character to those on the Propontis, which were often less commercial in intention and more aimed at exploiting the land around them.

By c.600 BC the coasts of both Straits and the Propontis were occupied by Greek settlements, some no more than villages, others capable of growing to considerable sizes. Although founded mainly by Megarian and Milesian expeditions, no serious attempt seems to have been made – or if it was made it was unsuccessful – to maintain control of the colonies by the originating cities, no doubt in part because the initial populations were usually mixed, but also because of distance. (The involvement of the Lydians may also have discouraged empire building.) The new foundations were independent cities from the start. And yet there were significant differences in the several geographical areas involved.

The geography of the region as a whole was a decisive factor in the placing and development of the majority of the cities. The north Propontis coast was dry and inhospitable to agriculture in large parts, so the cities along that coast were small and well spread, and generally founded later than those on the south coast; on the southern coast, the land was more agriculturally friendly, more fertile, and the cities therefore became larger and more numerous, and were founded first, but on both coasts, the settlers had chosen bays and harbours and headlands for their new homes, for they were also to some extent commercially minded, and looked to defences.

The Straits themselves were more difficult to settle. The Bosporos coasts were largely steep, if not cliffs, and only the two cities of Byzantion and Chalkedon could find a decent site, though along the neighbouring coasts wherever the cliffs gave way, or a stream came down, villages were established – very likely Thracian in origin. The danger of the passage, from the current, the weather, and from intermittent piracy, prompted the establishment of several temples and shrines at which sailors who had survived paid thanks.

The Hellespont was not so hostile to settlers, as the Lesbians had found. Both coasts became lined with Greek towns, villages, and cities, and its strategic situation made it a crucial centre for activity involving both Miletos and its neighbours and Megara. Miletos only participated in settlements at two places, at Limnai and Kardia, at the latter city along with Klazomenai; both were probably founded during the seventh century and both were small. Neither place looks to have been part of the city's apparent original plan, though once Kardia was founded on the narrow neck of the peninsula, the city took on a considerable strategic importance for the defence of the whole peninsula against Thracian attack.[40] The colonisation of the Greeks on the coasts is emphasised by the continued existence of a Thracian tribe, the Dolonchoi, in the peninsular interior for the next two centuries.

Elsewhere in the Hellespont area there were already some Lesbian plantations, and others from the same source were in this area established at Madytos and Sestos, both of these more or less opposite Abydos at the Narrows.[41] Perhaps these were seized as a means of ensuring Lesbian ability to reach into the Propontis, or to be able to reach the Lesbian colonies along the north Troadic coast, for Sestos had been Thracian (as had Abydos) and could have posed a blockage. At some point also the Mytilenians joined with their colonists at Alopekonnesos and a party from Kyme to establish a colony on the Thracian mainland at Ainos.[42]

This plantation is a different matter from other Lesbian colonies. Their early colonies along the Asian coast were clearly aimed at securing land for small groups of the surplus population of the island, and this would seem to apply as well to the colonies they had planted on the western coast of the Chersonese. But the Lesbians were also, probably considerably later than Miletos and others, caught up in the commercial possibilities of access to the Propontis and the Black Sea. Hence the settlements at Madytos and Sestos, which acted to protect their settlements both to the west and to the east.

Ainos, however, was more overtly commercial, and had developed as a Thracian trading town before the Greeks infiltrated, then seized, the city. The site is at the mouth of the Maritza River, whose valley provided access to the interior of Thrace, but also to the Thracian settlements at the Bay of Burgas (where Apollonia was founded by Miletos in about 610 BC). This was an old trade route which had provided a well-used connection between the Black Sea and the Aegean during the Bronze Age, when the Straits do not seem to have been in use, either because of the difficulty of the passage or because the Bosporos was blocked. The Maritza (the ancient Hebros) was navigable for a considerable distance inland, and a substantial Thracian settlement of the Apsinthian tribe, called Poltyobria, existed, and had probably been there for centuries.

The well-established Thracian town was no pushover. The Alopekonnesians were the first Greeks to attempt to gain access. What methods were used we do not know, but the small city of Alopekonnesos was hardly strong enough by itself to launch a serious attack on a Thracian town which was probably larger, wealthier and more populous. A smallish colony of the commercial sort infiltrated by individual merchants may thus be expected, with some Greeks moving across the Gulf of Melas to settle individually in the Thracian town. Reinforcements came from Mytilene and from Kyme, with the result that Poltyobria ultimately became the Greek city of Ainos, probably in the end by *coup d'état* and conquest. No doubt it acquired a controlling Greek population and an underclass of disfranchised, even enslaved, Thracians. Whatever permanent enmity was generated between the new citizens and the neighbouring Absinthians, it did not stop trade, and the Greek town took up the Thracian town's role as a port giving access to the interior and to the Thracians at the Bay of Burgas, and as an outlet for the continuing trade in Thracian slaves, sold down the river by other Thracians.

The result of this colonising activity was to change the Straits and the Sea of Marmara from a Thracian region to one dominated by Greeks. Politically also the Thracian kings were replaced by Greek republics, probably in most cases ruled by oligarchies. Yet the Thracians were not wholly displaced. There were probably some Thracian villages close to the coasts which survived, and there are some instances of Greeks and Thracians cooperating. But generally, the Greeks dominated the coasts, and the Thracians retreated to the interior; on the Asian side the Phrygians were also forced away from the coast but had a larger and more fertile region to which to retreat in Hellespontine Phrygia. But the victims did not forget, and the pattern of hostility between Greeks and 'natives' endured for centuries.

Chapter 4

Persians and Greeks (546–478 BC)

T he last of the Greek colonies to be established in the Propontis was Perinthos, planted on the north coast west of Selymbria by an expedition from Samos, and about halfway between the two Straits. This foundation, according to Eusebios, whose dates are curious, came in 602 BC, while Synkellos gives 599 BC – so let us say about 600 BC. The foundation was challenged at once by Byzantion and Chalkedon, who joined forces to send a fleet to suppress the new city. With armed help from their homeland Megara, they laid siege to it, which in turn was assisted by a relief force from Samos, the founding city. This was in the event decisive. Perinthos was thus founded with a victory.[1] The new city was later attacked by Paionians, whose homeland lay next to Macedon, a considerable way to the west. This is an isolated item of information with no context, but since the Paionians were later seriously damaged by the Persians, the raid probably happened well before 513 BC.[2] One is tempted to surmise that the attackers might have been called in by the other Perinthian enemies.

The site is a headland protruding into the Propontis, fortifiable and with harbours on each side.[3] It is something of a surprise that the site had not already been taken; possibly, though this is not mentioned, it was a Thracian site before the Samians arrived, and, in that case, given its natural strength, only a well-armed expedition could have taken it.[4] Its neighbours to the east, Selymbria and Byzantion, had Thracian names, and Thracians were long active against the cities of the Thracian Chersonese to the east. Thracian occupation of the Perinthos site seems therefore to be highly probable before the Greeks arrived. The reaction of the Megarians, Byzantines, and Chalkedonians to the Samian arrival was no doubt due to their potential loss of control of the northern sea route at this point; if a friendly Thracian king had been in residence before the Samians arrived this would help explain their annoyance and their joint reaction.

This episode of violence is a suitable introduction to the region in the sixth century. The Greek cities of the Straits came under steadily increasing pressure from outside the region throughout that century, which ended with many of them damaged, others sacked and burnt and abandoned to enemy forces; these events did lead on to their eventual rehabilitation but then to their eventual subjugation. The agents of enmity were not the traditional local forces, the Thracians, Phrygians, and other local non-Greeks, but first the kingdom of Lydia, based in west central Asia Minor with its royal seat at Sardis, then the empire of Persia, based even farther off in Iran, and finally, and most successfully, the city of Athens. In this chapter only the first and second of these will be considered, though there were Athenian intrusions into the area contemporary with them.

The Lydian kingdom pressed hard on the Greeks in Ionia, where relations varied between open warfare and tacit alliances, each Greek city adopting a different policy. It was with Lydian encouragement, for instance, that several of the Milesian colonies had been founded, notably Abydos on the Hellespont, founded 'by permission of Gyges', Strabo says.[5] This city's position enabled its controller to dominate the passage of the Strait, at a particularly awkward point where the current forced ships from one coast to the other, but where there was also a helpful harbour. Strabo also notes that the Troad was ruled by Gyges.[6] The Lydian city of Daskyleion on the southern coast of Lake Daskylitis (now the Rus Golu), was named after the father of Gyges (and sometimes thought to have been from there), and it was a major centre of Lydian, and later Persian, power in the north-east. A second Daskyleion lay on the Propontis coast between Kyzikos and Myrleia; it may be presumed that Kyzikos, a particularly wealthy and locally powerful city, was thus deliberately hemmed in on at least two land sides by Lydian power.[7] The position of the main Daskyleion, south of the lake, implies that it stood as a threat to Kyzikos, though no hostilities are known. The city on the coast was maybe only a small outpost, planted by Gyges as a signal of possible later advances. It is therefore likely that Kyzikos, as so often in its history, rapidly came to terms with the Lydian king, as indeed did its home city more than once.

In the Persian period which succeeded that of the Lydians, the territory inland of the coastal cities – Priapos, Kyzikos and its local colonies – was divided into a series of *paradeisoi*, according to Xenophon, who passed through the region in 401 BC. These were hunting parks, but there was also a number of large estates. This was a region which fell under Persian control easily, and where they chose to plant their government centre at Daskyleion – a clear element of continuity with the preceding Lydian place. The estates are marked, at least in the Granikos valley, by a series of tombs. Some of these have been excavated, and it is contended that though the Persians ruled from the mid sixth until the early fourth centuries, the whole region actually remained under the occupation of the local aristocracy. These were either Lydians, or were just as likely of Phrygian descent, and the absence of any indication of disturbances earlier than that period (not a good argument, of course) would suggest that the resident lords of the land had been in occupation during the Lydian period and probably before.[8]

Lydia was often involved in war on its eastern frontier, against the Kimmerians, against Media, and eventually against Persia. It was also repeatedly involved in attempts to gain control of the Greek cities of Ionia. In all this it seems that the early ambition of Gyges to expand into the Northwest was successful, but neither he nor his successors seem to have looked to expand farther; domination of the Greek cities was perhaps sufficient here; the area Mysia was thinly populated until the arrival of the Persians.[9] The colonial cities therefore were left largely to themselves, no doubt paying over a tribute, a relationship certainly to be expected in the circumstances.

Lydia's warfare on its eastern frontier finally brought defeat at the Persians' hands. In 546 BC Cyrus the Persian defeated Kroisos, the sixth and last Lydian king of Gyges' dynasty, and his royal regime collapsed. After the military defeat, Cyrus' army rapidly captured Sardis, the Lydian capital; Kroisos died, probably by suicide,[10] and suddenly the Greeks all along the coast of Asia Minor were faced with the greatest military power ever seen.

One of the purposes of Miletos and Megara in founding their many colonies was probably to secure preferential access to supplies of food. Megara had only a small home territory and was quite unable to expand, being bounded by the more powerful states of Corinth and Athens;[11] Miletos was repeatedly pressed by Lydia, which seems to have gained control of part of its home territory, and whose repeated military campaigns were mainly directed at destroying the crops in the remaining lands.[12] The traffic through the Straits was thus not merely bringing gold from Colchis and iron from the Chalybes, but more basic supplies imported from the Black Sea lands and the cities of the Propontis.

During the sixth century, while Lydia was first pressing on the Greek cities of Ionia and Aiolis, and then struggling to fend off the Medians and the Persians, other cities in Greece also found that their home production was becoming less than adequate for their needs. The islands perhaps suffered first, because of their strictly limited territories – and Tenedos and Lesbos had been the first to send out colonies to the Asian coast – but then the greater cities were also feeling the pinch. Some, such as Corinth, could rely on their wide networks of colonies and well-established trading systems to acquire the necessary supplies; others, notably Athens, whose territory was large, but stony and dry – dry, even for Greece – had to develop a trading system from new. This is probably the origin of an early Athenian attempt to gain control of Sigeion, one of the Mytilenean posts on the coast of the Troad and close to the entrance to the Hellespont. The attempt, made about the same time as the Samian seizure of Perinthos (about 600 BC, that is – which may have had the same policy) produced a war between Mytilene and Athens, which the Athenians could not win; after an arbitration by the tyrant Periander of Corinth Sigeion was adjudged to Athens, but the terms were such that any Athenian expansion in the area was blocked. Sigeion in fact soon returned to the Mytilenean sphere for another half-century or so.[13] But the intrusion of Samos and Athens into the Straits region, two particularly, and potentially, powerful Aegean cities both new to colonising, was a harbinger for later events.

The success of Samos contrasted with the failure of Athens. In founding Perinthos, the island seems to have been making an attempt at cutting out a Samian area in the Sea of Marmara which could dominate not just the route along the north coast of the Sea, but also across the sea itself. Apart from Perinthos other Samian settlements were made at Bisanthe and Heraion Teichos to the west, on the north coast, and across the sea in Prokonnesos Island. Samos' success was partly due to the fact that the government of the city was in the hands of a family of tyrants, whose most important member was Polykrates, and to the Samian development of a powerful navy. In 600 the Athenian polity were still indeterminate and unformed, but by the middle of the sixth century, Athens had also succumbed to its strong man, Peisistratos, who ruled as tyrant between 561 BC and 528 BC, and gave a firm direction to the external policy.[14]

In Lydia, Cyrus' conquest of the kingdom in 546 BC was too easy, and as soon as he had marched off to return to the east, a rebellion broke out. This was hardly unexpected, and Cyrus was not far away. It did not need the full Persian force to suppress it. The rebel, Paktyas, a Lydian who had been made satrapal treasurer by Cyrus, was soon in flight. The result was that the Lydians were disarmed, which in effect meant disenfranchising the military aristocracy – any survivors among the rebels were no doubt forcibly conscripted into the Persian army – and a relatively small force garrisoned in Lydia with the aim of mopping up any remaining opposition.[15]

This meant mainly dealing with the Greek cities along the coast, at least according to the main Greek source, Herodotos – for there were surely other groups within the kingdom who had to be persuaded or forced to submit, such as Thracians, Phrygians, Karians, Lykians, who, like the Greeks, would look on the change of regime as a chance for throwing off an alien supremacy. The Persians expected the Greek cities, most of which had been subjected in some way to Lydia, to accept the new regime, regarding the Persian victory as in some way a liberation. They had in fact been contacted by Persian agents before the Persian invasion and this might have created expectations of generous treatment; Cyrus, however, had not received their submission before the fighting and was not in a generous mood, especially after Paktyas' rebellion. The change of masters was not to the Greek cities' taste, but it did not take long for them to be subdued. Two cities – Teos and Phokaia[16] – decided to evacuate their populations, but most of the rest surrendered. This process took time, but the Persian advance was inexorable, and several of the cities were taken by assault. Miletos came to terms, gaining the same conditions as with the Lydian kings.[17] Well before Cyrus died in 530 BC, the fighting was over, and the Greeks, like the Lydians, reluctantly settled down as Persian subjects.

For the cities along the Straits, the crucial result was the choice of the inland Daskyleion as the governing centre for the northern part of the former Lydian kingdom, now called the satrapy of Hellespontine Phrygia (at least by the Greeks). The governor was confronted by a line of cities along the coast from Troy to Chalkedon, but away from the coast the country was one of Lydian/Phrygian landowners, a feudal country of lords and peasants. The lords were fully in sympathy with such men as were to rule at Daskyleion, and no doubt accepted the change of king easily. The reaction of the cities is not known, but they may be assumed to have submitted fairly readily; the home city of several of them, Miletos, had quickly made terms, and those who did not were equally quickly captured by the Persian forces. There was clearly no percentage in individual resistance; they may be supposed to have equally quickly submitted. The form of government in the cities at this time is not known, but is likely to have been oligarchic; the Persian preference, also at this time, was for single-man rule – monarchy or tyranny. A city which voluntarily surrendered would be likely to retain the political form it had then for some time, but tyranny was very likely to develop.[18]

There was also in this time of Persian advance and Lydian power a new power coming out of Greece, specifically. Peisistratos' intermittent career as a tyrant between c.561 BC and 528 BC, more or less contemporary with the Persian conquest of Lydia and its aftermath, had included a spell in Macedon where he had developed gold mines at Mount Pangaion. This gold had financed his eventual seizure of power in Athens in 556 BC, and it lubricated his continued control. He maintained a hold on this useful source of wealth while in power in Athens, but he also expanded into Naxos, where he installed a fellow tyrant, Lygdamis, and which he used as a prison camp for his Athenian enemies – those, that is, who had not escaped quickly enough when he seized power. He also returned to the former Athenian ambition of gaining power at the Hellespont, and seized control once more of Sigeion.[19]

The date of this expedition is unknown, and the brief account in Herodotos is included in an explanatory aside in a story of later events. The town was on the coast of the Troad, land that had been Lydian until the Persian conquest in 546 BC, and was then Persian.

In fact, it seems best to conclude that the seizure of the town occurred in coordination with an expedition commanded by Miltiades to the Thracian Chersonese, which took place during Peisistratos' first period as tyrant in Athens, between 561 BC and 556 BC.

The only possible purpose for this move on the part of the Athenian tyrant was to establish his, and Athens', power at the mouth of the Hellespont; no doubt it was one of Peisistratos' aims to make Sigeion a base from which to expand. He installed his son Hegesistratos as ruler of the little city, but at once, as before, the Athenian position was militarily challenged, at first certainly by Mytilene, within whose region Sigeion fell, but also probably by others of the colonial cities in the Troad, who were in no doubt as to Athenian intentions. The Mytilenean base of operations was in fact Achilleion, a short distance south of Sigeion, which had originally been a colony of Tenedos. This place was fortified by the Mytileneans, which might imply that it had been deserted by that time or that Tenedos was sympathetic to the Mytilenean anti-Athenian cause. The threat from Athens probably frightened the small colonies in the region. This time, however, the Athenian aggression succeeded, and Peisistratos could claim a victory. But by the time success was clear, it was also clear that the possibility of further Athenian expansion in the Troad was blocked.

Peisistratos, however, was fertile in expedients and, perhaps simultaneously he had come up with an even better alternative. One of his associates – and potential Athenian rivals and enemies – was a distant kinsman, Miltiades. Peisistratos agreed that Miltiades should lead the expedition to the Thracian Chersonese, to which he had been invited by a group of Dolonkoi, Thracians who still lived in the peninsula. They were apparently at peace with the several small Greek cities along the coasts, though they were threatened by another Thracian tribe, the Apsinthii, who were based in the mainland to the north of the peninsula. From Peisistratos' point of view, of course, all was gain: Miltiades' jealousy and energy and potential enmity were directed elsewhere, while Athenian power would be established at the crucial Hellespont, alongside his post at Sigeion.

Miltiades took a band of volunteers with him (so more enemies of Peisistratos were drained from Athens) and had some success for a time. He began, of course, with local support from the Dolonkoi, and the settlement of his Athenians was established at Elaious at the southern tip of the peninsula, a former Lesbian colony, and directly across the mouth of the Hellespont from Sigeion; there is some suggestion that archaeological evidence for the Athenian presence there has been found.[20] No doubt the alliance with the Dolonkoi alienated others, perhaps especially the Greek cities, while Mytilene would be confirmed in its enmity. He also had friendly contact with Kroisos of Lydia, who intervened at one point to secure his release when he had been captured by the Lampsakenes[21] – again the Athenian presence seems to have provoked a fairly wide local alliance in opposition. Lydian acquiescence in Miltiades' efforts may also be presumed for Sigeion since the Troad was Lydian territory until 546 BC, as well as Kroisos' situation at Lampsakos.

With Lydian and Athenian support, Miltiades prospered. Control over the whole peninsula seems to have been gained fairly quickly, since he had a defensive wall built across the narrowest part of the peninsula in the north, aimed at preventing Thracian raids, and so fulfilling his alliance with the Dolonkoi.[22] Of the Greek cities, most of which were small, it must be supposed that Miltiades either crushed or conciliated them. Any Lesbian foundations may well have showed fight, on the pattern of Sigeion, but Miltiades was clearly sufficiently powerful to ensure his ultimate control. He was sent to the area in the early 550s BC, and remained there even while Peisistratos was exiled from Athens between 556 BC and 546 BC. He was thus both independent of Peisistratos and perhaps in good graces with his Athenian opponents.

Miltiades died in about 520 BC. His cousin Stesagoras succeeded him in his Chersonesian tyranny, though he had to fight to enforce his authority, suggesting that Miltiades' regime had been less than popular. Stesagoras was murdered, apparently at the instigation of Hippias, Peisistratos' successor as joint tyrant at Athens, then his half-brother, Miltiades son of Kimon, was installed by the two of them.[23] Presumably he succeeded in re-establishing full control which would have been damaged by the political events. This brings the adventure to after 520 BC, so the family had been campaigning and ruling in the area for perhaps thirty years. By the time of the second Miltiades's regime, however, the Persian power was approaching.

The Persian Empire collapsed into civil war in 522–521 BC, which ended with Dareios emerging as the new Great King. The government of the empire, which had perhaps been left by Cyrus in an unformed state, was instituted by the Dareios (if not before) in the form of a series of large provinces ('satrapies', to the Greeks). Each satrapy was under a governor and assorted officials, who were appointed directly by the king.[24] Within the satrapies in Asia Minor the Greek cities were mainly controlled by tyrants, who also in many cases owed their posts to the Persian rulers; if such rulers had not existed in the 540s BC, they were very common twenty years later. This neatly established Persian control without much expense on the empire's part, and blocked off, it was hoped, the Greek tendency to rebellion. There were two satrapies which controlled the majority of the Greek cities – Ionia and Hellespontine Phrygia, the latter covering the Straits, from the Troad to the Black Sea.

Dareios' first priority was the eastern frontier, as had been Cyrus', and he campaigned to secure full control over Central Asia, and then invaded India. He came to the west in 513 BC, and instigated a campaign into Skythia, north of the Black Sea. The Greek cities of the Straits became involved in this campaign by providing ships, by seeing their own men conscripted into the army and the fleet, and by having to provide supplies for the army.

Tyrants are recorded at several of the Straits cities in this period. Kyzikos was ruled by Aristagoras, and its neighbour Prokonessos by Metrodoros, Byzantion had Ariston.[25] Several of the islands at the approaches to the Hellespont, Lemnos, Lesbos, and Chios, were seized by the Persian fleet, and after Polykrates of Samos had been captured by a trick in 522 BC, his brother Syloson was installed as a compliant tyrant in the island. Tyrants were acceptable to the Persians but only if they were relatively weak, and Polykrates had not been weak. The same would presumably apply to Peisistratos and his sons had the Persians needed to pay them any attention. Miltiades fitted into this scheme well enough, though one would have thought him closer to Polykrates in power, and so difficult for Dareios to accept. A preliminary campaign into the region under the command of satrap Otanes had secured these cities and islands and when the king arrived he was able, with no difficulty, to summon a fleet of ships from the cities. With these he established control at the Straits and in the Propontis, and then sent a fleet into the Black Sea.[26] An engineer from Samos, Mandrokles, constructed a bridge of boats across the Bosporos, and the army marched into Thrace dryshod and speedily.[27]

The campaign which followed took the Persian forces to and beyond the Danube River, which was crossed by another bridge of boats.[28] The campaign has sometimes been regarded as a failure, though since we do not know either what Dareios' aim was, or what occurred during the campaign – Herodotos' account is unbelievable, which suggests that he did not have any accurate information – it is best to suspend judgment. Several of the city tyrants were left to guard the Danube bridge, a gesture by Dareios of some confidence. Herodotos has a story that Miltiades, or one of the others, suggested destroying the bridge and marooning Dareios and his army on the north side, but the other tyrants demurred, though this has the air of a story made up later. Some of the tyrants had been Persian nominees, others had been readily confirmed, but all knew well enough that they depended on the Great King for their positions at home. Miltiades himself was an example of those who had accepted Persian suzerainty, even though he had reached his control of the Chersonese principality by himself, and surely had more self-confidence than the others. It seems clear that even if the idea of destroying the bridge originated amongst the Greeks at the Danube, Miltiades was not the originator; he probably invented the story later, or perhaps elaborated it, for the benefit of an Athenian jury and his own reputation.[29]

Dareios' expedition was successful in deterring any Skythian intervention south of the Danube while his forces campaigned to gain control of Thrace. He took immediate measures to avoid trouble on his return. He left the bulk of his army in Thrace under the command of his general Megabazos. He himself crossed the Hellespont at the Sestos/Abydos crossing, and headed straight for Sardis.[30] Dareios' arrival at Sardis, his main base for the campaign, and a major garrison, would have demonstrated that he was alive and in charge, if there had been a doubt, and would have calmed any jangled nerves. He distributed rewards and ordered Megabazos to campaign to conquer Thrace. This sort of activity was clearly necessary, for other revolts were being planned besides those by Ariston and his co-tyrant at Chalkedon – no doubt the origin of Miltiades' story. Megabazos had already had to conquer Perinthos.[31] It would evidently be dangerous to pull the army out of Thrace, and while it was there it might as well campaign to enlarge Dareios' territories, though it is likely that Dareios would have put Megabazos' tasks the other way about.

Dareios, still seized of the need to stabilise affairs within the empire, and to deal with accumulated business in the rest of the empire, now returned all the way to Susa,[32] thereby demonstrating that he felt that his task in the north had been largely completed. Before going off he appointed two new satraps, Artaphernes, his own brother, went to Lydia, and Otanes son of Sisamnes was appointed to Hellespontine Phrygia. Otanes also now took over Megabazos' command in Thrace and removed the danger from Byzantion and Chalkedon by occupying, and perhaps destroying, their cities and presumably removing their tyrants. The cities of Antandros and Lamponion in the Troad were also taken over, though a revolt by these small places seems unlikely; perhaps he was simply filling in the gaps in Persian control.[33] Lemnos and Imbros were seized once more.[34] There had evidently been considerable unrest in the whole region, though it had not proceeded very far. Most of the tyrants stayed in office, or were easily replaced, and the Persian Great King's authority was well confirmed.

At the Danube bridge there were tyrants from at least six cities of the Straits. Daphnis of Abydos and Hippoklos of Lampsakos held cities dominating the crossing of the Hellespont, along with Miltiades in the Chersonese. The south coast of the Propontis was controlled by Herophantos of Parion and Aristagoras of Kyzikos, while Metrodoros of Prokonnesos held that strategic island in the middle of the Sea. At the Bosporos was Ariston of Byzantion; it is possible that there was also a tyrant in office at Chalkedon, though he is not named, probably because he remained in the city guarding the Bosporos bridge.[35]

It is noticeable that apart from Miltiades and Ariston, at the ends of the sequence, none of the cities of the north Propontis coast were mentioned, though they were closest to the Danube and its bridge; Perinthos, Bisanthe and Selymbria were unrepresented. Either they had no tyrants, or their tyrants had been left at home, like the Chalkedonians, to guard the rear – but Perinthos was later attacked by Megabazos soon after Dareios returned from his expedition, so it seems that the city, tyrant or no, was, or had become, actively hostile.[36] This was part of his campaign to subdue Thrace, beginning with the towns and villages near Byzantion, after dealing with that city and Chalkedon.[37] But all this fits well with the later Persian disposition of power after the conquest of Thrace.

One of the further sources of trouble was a plot by Ariston of Byzantion and the tyrant of Chalkedon to break the Bosporos bridge (probably the ultimate source of the story annexed later by Miltiades). It is possible that it was news of this which persuaded Dareios to cross by the Hellespont, avoiding the need to deal with the plot – an unlikely reaction by this king – but in fact crossing at Sestos would have been the quickest way to get to Sardis, whether or not Dareios was in a hurry. But Ariston and his fellow tyrant were certainly punished later for their plot, whatever it amounted to; Ariston probably died, and part of Chalkedon was wrecked by Persian troops.[38]

The Persian king's authority stretched through Thrace as far as the border of Macedon – King Alexander of Macedon had staved off an invasion by accepting Persian suzerainty.[39] Part of the Paionian people had been transplanted into Asia by Megabazos, allegedly because Dareios was impressed by the ingenious industry of a Paionian woman, in reality because Megabyzos had faced serious opposition from that people.[40] The Greek cities of the Straits and the Sea of Marmara had all been, like those of the Asia Minor coast and nearby islands, reduced to subjection. Some had been disloyal (Chalkedon, Byzantion, Perinthos) and had suffered accordingly, but most had succumbed to the overwhelming might and numbers of the Persian army and remained loyal to the Persian king throughout the Skythian adventure.

There followed a decade of relative peace. Persia controlled both of the Straits, and both sides, and dominated the Propontis from the cities he controlled along the coasts. Thrace was in theory a Persian province, which therefore included the Greek cities of that area. The Persian conquest of Thrace may have appeared a convincing display of power and resolve, but without detailed attention to the government of the region Persian authority soon decayed. Similarly, the expedition into the lands north of the Danube may have been intended to warn off the Skythians – it is hardly an expedition of conquest – but its effect was only temporary, and the Skythians were able to raid deep into Thrace. Exactly what was the relation of Miltiades in the Chersonese to the Persians is not clear; he may have remained in power for a time, but in Persian eyes he was clearly too powerful to be allowed to continue for long, and was put to rout by a Skythian raid and driven into exile, leaving the Chersonese to its Thracian and Greek communities.[41] The raid, of course, presupposes an absence of Persian power, and it is probable that Persian forces had been withdrawn (unless the Skythians were a force operating under Persian authority). Bisanthe was recorded as being subject to the Thracian King Sitalkes in 494 BC.[42] The best interpretation of all this is that the Persians, having been withdrawn in large part from Skythia and Thrace, had set up subject allies in the region, as in Macedon, and Sitalkes was one of these. The Skythians spotted the opportunity to make a revenge raid, which reached the Chersonese, drove out Miltiades (a Persian subject) and then withdrew.

The wrecked cities were at least partially repopulated and in part rebuilt, though any city wall dismantled by the Persians was hardly going to be revived. In the event, of course, it would not have taken much effort by the Persians to regain control, if they had wanted to. It would seem that, after the conquest, the actual Persian frontier line was the Straits and the Sea, Thrace being an area left to the Greeks and the barbarians to fight each other; the threatened Persian suzerainty could easily be reactivated if necessary. The Persians had adopted the same practice as the Lydians who had also extended their power to the Straits and the Sea, and had made the water their frontier as a means of insulating themselves from the Thracians in Thrace proper; it is, of course, a mistake to see narrow waterways as useful frontier lines.

Tensions clearly therefore existed in the area, between the Greek cities and the Thracians, between Persians and Greeks, and amongst the Greeks themselves. It must be supposed that the tyrants or their successors who were imposed or supported by the Persians remained in office, unless, like Ariston at Byzantion, they were detected in disloyalty. To those tyrants already noted we may add Hippias of Athens after 510 BC. Peisistratos died in 528 BC, and his two sons then shared the tyranny, until one, Hipparchos, was murdered; the survivor Hippias tightened his grip on the regime in self-defence, and so was eventually expelled by the Athenians, with Spartan help. Sigeion was still an Athenian post, and, rejecting several offers of other cities of refuge, Hippias went there. This can only have been done by permission of the Persian regime.[43] It was an early sign Persia and Athens were potential enemies, and Hippias was aiming, with Persian help, to return to his Athenian tyranny.

Tyrants remained Persia's favoured means of ensuring control over the Greek cities all through this period of peace. They were therefore disliked by the Greeks, not because they were tyrants necessarily, though no doubt some made themselves obnoxious, but because they were Persia's instruments. Tyranny in mainland Greece was a system which was fading away fast as an acceptable means of government, notably at Athens, which was regarded as the original homeland of the Ionians in Asia, where tyranny remained the norm. The Persians were also aiming to expand, and a new expedition against Naxos was sent in 499 BC, planned by Aristagoras of Miletos, an associate of Histiaios, that city's tyrant, along with a group of Naxian political exiles. He persuaded the local Persian commander Megabates to assist, with permission from King Dareios. But the expedition failed, and the Naxians, forewarned and prepared, succeeded in outlasting a Persian siege.[44] The Persian fleet, composed mainly of Greeks of Asia, returned to Ionia, but then was kept together by the Persian commander Megabates, evidently with the intention of returning to the attack after restocking with supplies of food and weaponry; by this time money to pay the sailors was short, and this may have been given as the reason to keep the fleet in being, so that the pay could be found and then distributed.

This appears to have been the trigger for the beginning of what is known as the 'Ionian Revolt'. Its precise and larger and longer causes are unclear, and economic issues have been suggested.[45] The Persian conquest of Thrace may have appeared a convincing display of power and resolve, but without detailed continuing attention to the region it soon decayed. Similarly, the expedition into the lands north of the Danube may have been intended to warn off the Skythians, but its effect was only temporary, and the Skythian raid into the Thracian Chersonese was the most obvious result. Such evidence as there is, however, shows that the domination of the Persians was the main issue for the rebels. There were also no doubt other and perhaps local issues involved, but the unifying slogan was 'freedom', and one of the earliest measures taken by the rebels was to drive out their tyrants. The presence of the defeated fleet at Myous, near Miletos, provided a useful pretext for those organising the revolt. The leader of the revolt, Aristagoras, was in trouble with the Persians because of the failure of the Naxian expedition, and supposedly on the orders of his master Histiaios, who was held in captivity at Persepolis, he organised the arrest of five ships' captains who were known to be antagonistic, and the rest of the fleet then joined, or perhaps made, the revolt.[46]

The original target of the fleet's expedition, Naxos, was at the centre of the Aegean Sea, halfway from Miletos to Athens. Had the Persians won control of the island, they would undoubtedly have gone on to other islands, of which the most strategically sensitive was Euboia. This would place Persian power firmly in the centre of the Aegean, dominating the Kyklades, and next door to two Greek cities who were already at enmity, Thebes and Athens. The potential for extended Persian expansion by diplomacy and alliances, and small helpful expeditions to assist one or other of the contenders on the Greek mainland was unending. Those who thus came under threat, or pressure, would have seen that. It is thus not unlikely that some mainland Greeks would have helped the Naxians (and Athens had an old interest in Naxos), and contacted disaffected Ionians, perhaps in the fleet at Naxos, and perhaps Aristagoras himself. The action of Aristagoras in locating and arresting the five captains suggests also that the plot was well laid and well advanced when the fleet returned to Myous.

The revolt was limited to Ionia at first, but it spread quickly as far as Cyprus, and then up to the Straits, but the cities along the Straits and the Propontis were not initially affected. The Ionian fleet was the main military power in the rebels' hands and it campaigned to extend the revolt by sailing along the Asian coast north and south. Athens and Eretria (one of the Euboian cities) sent help, partly as a result of the fright they had received in the Persian attack on Naxos. They took part in a land raid as far as Sardis, which was burnt. (The participation of these two cities rather confirms the supposition that they had been likely later targets of the Naxos fleet, had it won there.) The raid on Sardis brought a large and determined Persian response, one of whose results was the rapid withdrawal of the Athenian and Eretrian help.

The fleet expanded its range by a cruise through the Hellespont and into the Propontis, where Byzantion was singled out by being taken under control;[47] the city may well have had to be forcibly persuaded. In other cases it is not clear how the local cities reacted to this Ionian incursion. The anti-tyrant moves in Ionia were evidently not repeated. Abydos is known to have joined the revolt, as did Chalkedon, because the Persians had to retake them later. The participation of Kyzikos appears to have been compelled; that of Perinthos is not known.

The Persians concentrated at first on recovering control of the Ionian cities, the centre of the revolt, but two subsidiary forces operated in the north. One of these, under the command of Daurises, marched north along the coast, taking Abydos, and then a series of four small coastal towns, Dardanos in the Troad, and Perkote, Lampsakos, and Praisos eastwards, none of which put up any resistance.[48] From this it may be assumed that their participation in the revolt had been under compulsion, and that Persian domination had not been oppressive – at least so far. Daurises was then ordered south to Karia, and was replaced by Hymaies, the commander of the northern force which had moved against the northern cities. He had taken Kios when he was in turn ordered south to replace Daurises. He took control of the Troad, but died of disease, though he had done his work.[49] The opposition of the Greeks everywhere was scarcely determined, and the smaller cities did not resist at all. Hippias at Sigeion does not seem to have been involved; no doubt he welcomed the Persian reconquest.

The revolt had begun in 499 BC, and the cities of the Straits region had become involved during the next year. They were recovered by the Persian forces during 497 and perhaps 496. It is about that time, when the revolt in the north was effectively over, that Miltiades son of Kimon returned to the Chersonese.[50] Where he had been in the previous fifteen or so years is not known, but he was not in either Athens or the Chersonese. He may have been living with his father-in-law, Oloros, a Thracian king.[51] That he chose to return, by request again of the Dolonkoi, just at the moment of the local Persian victories, suggests that he was doing so in concert with them. At the same time, however, he was renewing his Athenian contacts, and he used his revived power in the peninsula to seize control of the islands of Lemnos and Imbros, which had received a Persian conquest and tyrants during Dareios' expedition, but had presumably freed themselves at the time of the revolt, either by their own efforts are at the behest of the Ionian fleet. Now Miltiades took control of them, drove out the native population of Lemnos, and at once invited Athenian settlers to come to occupy the emptied lands.[52]

Miltiades' return took place probably in 495 BC, by which time the Persians had secured control of the main posts and cities of the region, and were at the stage of mopping up the remnants of the rebellion. The Persian fleet – 'Phoenicians' in Herodotos – moved steadily north through the whole region, beginning with the islands of Chios, Lesbos, and Tenedos, a sequence which implies that Lemnos and Imbros were being left to Miltiades. In Miltiades' Chersonese Kardia was not attacked – no doubt Miltiades intervened. The other shore of the Hellespont had already been recovered by Daurises and Hymaies. Kyzikos prudently made terms of surrender with the satrap of Daskylion next door, thus avoiding any unpleasant dealings with the Phoenician fleet. As the fleet approached Byzantion and Chalkedon the populations of both cities fled to take refuge at Mesambria in the Black Sea.[53] All this strongly implies that Miltiades' return, contemporary with the Phoenician fleet's advance, was coordinated with it; he was organising it as an agent of Persia.

But the troubles of the north were not yet over. The former tyrant of Miletos, Histiaios, had been allowed to return to his home city, but then was shut out by his former subjects. He persuaded eight ships of Lesbos to join him and sailed to Byzantion. After its history of the past twenty years, and the fleeing of the population from the prospect of Persian retaliation, it seems likely that this was a deserted site, the buildings in ruins. Histiaios spent the next four years based in the city, operating as a pirate, intercepting the ships and fleets which came through the Bosporos, and extracting protection money from them. His aim, other than to get rich and pay the crews of his ships, is not known, but a man like that, always ambitious, clever, deceitful, no doubt had some political plans, or at least intentions, in mind. These were, it seems, frustrated by the success of the Persians. As the Persian fleet came into the Aegean and defeated the Ionians in battle at Lade, Histiaios came out of the Marmara and campaigned among the Ionian islands, though to little effect.[54]

At the other end of the region, Miltiades' double dealing came to light. Evidently in concert with the Persians and at the same time in contact with the Athenians, he was apparently playing for both sides, as a Persian surrogate, and yet a friend of Athens. But he was not needed by the Persians and in 493 he was driven out.[55] He and Histiaios were suppressed at almost the same time, the final details. The Persians had re-established full control over the islands the Straits and the Sea of Marmara.

The war, however, was not over. Dareios was determined to scotch the threat from Greece, as he might have put it, focusing on the two cities which had participated in the raid on Sardis and that city's ruin. The connection between Ionia and Athens was understood, the strong interest in Athens in the Straits as a route along which its supplies of food came was also appreciated, and it seems that, having gained political control of that route, the Persians enforced a blockade. Athens had to open up new sources of food for its increasing population.[56]

Miltiades was chased away from the Chersonese in 493 BC, and Histiaios was killed at much the same time. Next year a new Persian commander, Mardonios, arrived with a fleet and an army. He had a wide-ranging authority which he used to remove many of the tyrants, especially in Ionia, and replace them with democracies, which were, of course, just as fully under Persian control as the tyrants had been.[57] At the Hellespont he crossed the strait and moved his army across to Europe, establishing a base camp at Doriskos, near the mouth of the Hebros River.[58] This was the first result of the control of the Straits which the Persians had re-established, and might have been threatened if Miltiades, who was clearly less than reliable, had remained in control of the Chersonese. Mardonios contacted King Alexander of Macedon, who submitted once more, and married his sister to the son of that Megabazos who had originally received the Macedonian submission in 512 BC.[59] But then the Persian fleet was damaged by a storm rounding Mount Athos, and its advanced camp was attacked at night by a Thracian band, the Brygi, and suffered considerable casualties. Combined with the damage to the fleet, this was enough to make Mardonios turn back.[60]

The Thracians had apparently kept out of Mardonios' way until the Persian army reached the Macedonian border, and until the storm which had so damaged his fleet. There may be more to it, however, than opportunism. During the Ionian revolt one of the minor incidents had been the arrival at the Ionian coast of a number of Paionians, refugees from the deportees who had been taken by Megabazos into Asia. These had been returned by the rebels to their homeland, which was somewhere inland of the area where the Brygian raid took place.[61] It seems likely that the experience of deportation had been related widely in the region, and that one result was that the Thracians between the Hellespont and Macedon had simply drawn back to let Mardonios' army pass, and another result was that the Brygi took fright. The army stopped advancing when the fleet was wrecked, and maybe the Brygi decided that they were under the threat of a Paionia-type deportation and decided to get their retaliation in first. If so, they suffered from Mardonios' own retaliation after the raid, and his army crushed them.[62] No doubt the opportunity was taken with some pleasure – any insolent attacks on the imperial army had to be shown to be pointless.

Nevertheless, Mardonios withdrew his army, though it seems probable that some garrisons remained in Thrace along the coastal road, and the relationship with Macedon was not severed. Herodotos remarks that governors had been appointed by Dareios or by Xerxes in Thrace and the Hellespont;[63] since we know that Byzantion was held by the Persians until 478 BC, this clearly included the Marmara cities. It is, however, a vague statement geographically, and in particular 'Thrace' was a large country, not all of which was ever under Persian rule. The attempt to march on Greece, if that was what Mardonius intended, had been thwarted. The new Persian plan was to mount a naval expedition along the lines of the failed Naxos expedition. It came to grief, rather unexpectedly for both sides, at Marathon, but only after most of the Aegean islands and many of the mainland cities had symbolically submitted to Persian demands that they render 'earth and water' (the traditional tokens of submission demanded by Persian kings).

As a result, Persian power recoiled from Greece, but not in the north. The Straits and the coasts of the Sea of Marmara continued to be held, and while many of the earth and water submissions were soon in effect abrogated unilaterally by many of the Greek states – or simply forgotten – the Persian military occupation of Ionia and the Straits and the Thracian coast continued, and these positions were available ten years later when a new Great King, Xerxes, and the former Persian commander Mardonios revived the latter's plan of a joint army and fleet expedition along the north Aegean coast with the object of conquering Athens and so dominating Greece.

Xerxes had to cope with the succession to his father in 486 BC, and rebellions in Egypt and Babylon, before he could begin the extensive preparations for an assault on the Greeks. The several campaigns and expeditions in the Aegean area after 499 BC had shown the difficulties involved, and this time there were to be no disasters, no intervention by storms or Thracian raids. The Greek expertise in warfare was to be countered by Persian numbers.

At some point the Greek cities all the way from Pamphylia round to the Bosporos were ordered to contribute ships to the fleet. Of the 320 ships tabulated by Herodotos, the towns of the Hellespont and the Bosporos produced 100; the Greeks of Thrace and the islands added about 120 more.[64] Abydos provided no ships, but like Chalkedon in the previous war, it was charged with guarding the bridges, this time over the Hellespont. Herodotos' numbers for the fleet are regarded as exaggerated, but these contingent numbers could well be more or less correct – Kyzikos alone had a fleet numbered in dozens of ships. How many of these survived the Salamis fight is unknown. They were probably counted as part of the 'Ionian' contingent at that battle; two thirds of the Greek contribution to the Persian fleet came from these northern cities in the Straits and the Propontis.

The Hellespont was bridged,[65] supply dumps were established along the coast of Thrace, at Tyrodiza, in Perinthian territory but at the root of the Chersonese, at Doriskos (again), and at Eion at the mouth of the Strymon River, which was also to be bridged.[66] A canal was cut through the root of the Athos peninsula for the fleet to pass, avoiding the dangers of its rocky coast.[67] If King Alexander of Macedon had considered breaking his Persian connections he did not dare to carry it out. The organization involved in all this, the quantities of supplies, food, weapons, ships for the fleet, cables, collecting ships for the bridges and their construction, recruiting labour and soldiers, was immense, and it is a tribute to the wealth of the empire, and to Persian powers of organization, that it was carried out – the king's abilities and resolve above all.

As the army marched from Abydos, at the eastern end of the Hellespont bridges, to the first supply post and refreshment camp at Doriskos, the Thracian chieftains – listed as of the Paeti, Cicones, Bistones, Sapaei, Dersaei, Edoni, and Satrai – had to decide their attitude. Most of them, especially those located in the coastal areas, prudently paid homage, but then saw many of their young men conscripted as auxiliaries–cum–hostages into the Persian forces as a result.[68] Further on and inland, there were different reactions: the king of the Bisaltai refused homage and took to the hills, though his sons joined the Persians; this could have been a deliberate survival strategy; the king is said to have blinded his sons when they returned, but this may be a story put out by the king.[69] The Satrai of the forested hills above Mount Pangaion held aloof, protected by their difficult country.[70]

From Thrace the great army passed through Macedon with King Alexander's assistance, and into Greece, occupying Thessaly and Boiotia and Attika. The fleet was badly damaged in passing Thessaly, and in the defeat of Salamis, but the army remained in control of the conquered territory for another year. Xerxes handed over command to Mardonios and returned to Asia, travelling back along the road made by the army, though he found that the bridges at Sestos/Abydos had been broken by the rough weather.[71] The Persian grip on Thrace, Macedon, Thessaly, and the Straits was not finally damaged for another year or more. And

Mardonios brought the Persian army forward again next year to occupy Athens once more.

But this provoked the Spartans into sending decisive military help to Athens and her allies. The joint Greek army defeated Mardonios' army later in 479 BC at Plataia, and this time there was to be no early Persian recovery. The army had been broken and had suffered massive casualties; the survivors retreated northwards, following Xerxes' route of retirement. Xerxes had ordered the fleet after the battle of Salamis to head for the Hellespont to guard the bridges[72] – before he had learnt that they had been broken – and this had probably been done, but the ships had then moved south and the fleet was now stationed at Samos during 479 BC, much reduced in numbers. It is probable that many of the Greek ships from the northern cities had deserted or had been dismissed, since they were no longer regarded as loyal.

This was the fleet which was defeated and destroyed at and after the battle of Mykale, which began the process of removing Persian authority from the Ionian cities. But it was the bridges at the Hellespont which now became the new targets of the Greek fleet. When the Greek fleet got to the Strait, they found, of course, as had Xerxes, that the bridges were gone. The Persian forces in the area had collected the cables of the bridge and had concentrated into the well-fortified city of Sestos and stood siege there – but their numbers cannot have been very great if they could all get into one city. The Greek fleet began to break up, for the Spartans, seeing that the bridges had gone and were no longer a threat, went home, leaving the fighting to the Athenians and the Ionians. These latter were now no doubt at least in part men and ships which had survived Salamis on the Persian side: they were joined by ships sent by the Hellespontine cities, who were also presumably survivors from the Persian fleet. This would suggest that their home cities had now escaped from Persian control. Both of these groups had deftly switched sides, and by joining in the final fight, they were laying out their new loyalties in public, at least for the moment.

Sestos was finally taken after a gruesome siege, when the Persians escaped through a gap in the siege lines. This conveniently allowed the Greeks to chase, capture, and kill the Persian survivors. The ships then sailed off to their homes, the Athenians towing the great cables captured at Sestos.[73] The fighting had lasted into the winter, and it had been a long and hard year, but in 478 BC, after instigating a revolt in Cyprus, the allied fleet, a mixture of Athenian, Peloponnesian, and Ionian ships, which after Mykale had the freedom of the Aegean, went to Byzantion and expelled the Persian garrison. This accomplished what had no doubt now become one of the Greeks' main war aims, opening up the Straits once more. Food supplies could flow again.

Chapter 5

Under Another Empire – Athens (478–405 BC)

When in 479 BC the Greek allies drove the Persians out of Sestos, then next year out of Byzantion, the Straits area was cleared of Persian power. The commander of the allied forces at Byzantion was Pausanias, a Spartan and the commanding general at Plataia, who evidently felt that only once he was out of Sparta would his true potential be released. His precise position in Byzantion is unclear, though he was later accused of setting up a tyranny. He was recalled to Sparta during 478 BC, but then returned voluntarily later in the year to Byzantion once more.[1]

But how much of a 'city' – that is, what quantity of the people – were present at the site while Pausanias was there is a problem, as is also the condition of the city itself. Byzantion had been through a bad time in the wars. It had certainly been damaged by Megabazos in 512 BC, when its tyrant had been removed. It was retaken by the Persians in 498 BC, when the population fled for refuge to Mesambria, along with the Chalkedonians, who had been similarly attacked, and the site was used by Histiaios in his piratical-cum-political activities after that, an episode lasting four years. How much of the expelled population had returned during these difficulties is not known, but it seems very likely that the city only began to revive in Pausanias' time.[2] The flight of expelled refugees rarely results in their wholesale return; many will have settled elsewhere – they were out of their home city, after all, for a dozen years or more.

This might therefore supply a context for Pausanias' own position in the city when he returned to it. The allies – not the Byzantines – specifically the Athenians, organised his expulsion later, by force. The date is disputed, usually stated to be between 476 BC and 471 BC, but not the event, and whichever date is accepted he had been living in the city for some years. This would suggest that his rule – if that was his actual position – was generally acceptable to the Byzantines, perhaps as a calming influence, suppressing internal disputation. The stability thus postulated would permit, even encourage, the return of Byzantine refugees from Mesambria and from other refuges. The expulsion of Pausanias at Athenian behest, would, in accordance with Athenian current political ideology, probably require the installation of a democratic regime in the city.[3]

The revival of Byzantion would no doubt be accompanied by the same result at Chalkedon, whose population had also fled from Persian vengeance to Mesambria. Elsewhere, other cities may or may not have been affected, though the Persians are said to have established governors over the whole region, and the Greek fleet is said to have burnt the cities of Perinthos, Selymbria, Byzantion and Chalkedon.[4] The practice of employing tyrants as Persian agents to control the cities is not to be ruled out as late as 480 BC – the expulsion of tyrants carried out by Mardonios in 481 BC seems to have applied only in Ionia.[5] It will have been at the orders, therefore, of the governors or the tyrants that the 'Hellespontines' contributed 100 warships to Xerxes' fleet.[6] The contributors would have been every city (except Abydos, guarding the bridges), but Byzantion and Chalkedon can probably be ruled out, their populations having fled; maybe Perinthos also, after being destroyed by Megabazos in 512 BC. The one city which may have retained a substantial navy was Kyzikos, with its two harbours and its long seacoast and extensive land territory, and its political tradition of submitting to whoever threatened it. Other cities were no doubt expected – instructed – to supply small naval contingents, since one of the reasons for having Greek Asian naval contingents with Xerxes' fleet was that they would serve as hostages for the continued loyalty of their home cities.

One result of the overthrow of the Persian regime in the Straits and the Sea of Marmara was the increase in the potential use of the seaway for maritime trade. In 480 BC Xerxes saw ships sailing through carrying grain to Aegina from the Black Sea,[7] though it is suggested that their cargoes were small. The producers in the Black Sea (the territories beyond the north coast) were apparently disturbed at the time, and unlikely to be able to supply larger cargoes.[8] Histiaios' exactions in the 480s were directed at Ionian merchant vessels.[9] It is certain that the Persian regime would not permit ships heading for its enemies with vital supplies to pass through, though Xerxes explicitly allowed an Aeginetan ship to pass, so advertising his confidence in the war's outcome, and incidentally showing that normally such ships would be stopped. (Having bridges across both the Bosporos and the Hellespont would enable him to institute any interruptions. Quite possibly Histiaios was simply operating the same regime of 'taxation', but for his own benefit; that he was allowed to do so for four years, using only his little squadron of eight Lesbian ships, might suggest that the Persians were quite happy to see him interrupting the trade.[10]

If the interpretation of the direction of Athenian trade before 480 BC is correct (summarised in the previous chapter), together with the evidence of widespread disturbance in the north, there might not have been much trade to interrupt after Dareios' Skythian expedition. Archaeological investigations in South Russia/Ukraine/Crimea could find little evidence of trade with Greece before the late sixth century and the early fifth. That is, the trade appears to have developed mainly during the Persian period, and therefore most likely with the Ionian and other cities under Persian rule in Asia, and since the trade was thus new it would be on a small scale for a time.[11] After 480 BC, however, with the elimination of Persian naval power from the Aegean and the Straits, and the removal of Persian authority from the coastal cities, the whole region was available as a market for Black Sea products. It is in the period after 480 BC, therefore, that the transport of large quantities of grain to, amongst other places, Athens, grew in importance. Histiaios was one of the early beneficiaries.

The removal of the Persian rearguard from Sestos opened the Hellespont; the participation of men and ships of the Hellespontine cities, once they had joined the Greek side, guaranteed the Sea of Marmara's clearance of Persian forces; the expulsion of Persian strength from Byzantion opened up the Bosporos. In this last exploit Ionian ships participated, so some of the cities which had freed themselves of Persian authority after Mykale, had, after a year, become sufficiently organised to send squadrons of ships to the Propontis, and their self-interest was probably in securing access to supplies from the north.[12] For Persian power had not retired very far, and it dominated the inland regions close to the coastwise cities. From Byzantion, Pausanias, in power or influence in the city soon after its capture, contacted the satrap of Hellespontine Phrygia, Artabazos, at Daskyleion;[13] in Lydia, Sardis was the seat of another satrap, and even if these men were for the moment short of troops and without ships, they would not be so for very long.

That is, the Persian power was still great, potentially overwhelming, and close by; the Ionians would be one of the first targets for the Persian counter-attack. Not only that, but there were still Persian forces in Thrace and these would need to be removed. For the Greek cities facing Artabazos in Daskyleion, the danger was just as real. He is said to have intrigued with Pausanias when the latter released some Persian relations of Xerxes who had been captured at Byzantion,[14] and the temptation to slide back into Persian protection was probably strong amongst parts of the population in every city.

The two continuing Persian bases in Thrace, at Eion at the crossing of the Strymon, and at the base at Doriskos, had to be dealt with. They were both in control of important trade routes leading into the Balkan interior, and their presence was a promise of the Persian return which kept the Thracian kings and the nearby Greek cities on edge, and kept Macedon under threat and therefore neutral. Further, in Greece many communities from Thessaly to Boiotia had 'Medized'; after the Greek victories they were being persuaded to change their views, but sometimes reluctantly. There were also many cities along the Asian coast which were still under Persian control and which could be bases for the empire's naval recovery. Having only half-finished the essential tasks, therefore, it became clear to the Greek allies in the winter of 478–477 BC that the war would continue and, further, that the cities of the Asian coast, from Chalkedon on the Bosporos to and beyond Halikarnassos in Karia, would need continuing protection. Suddenly the war was seen to be potentially unending.

At Byzantion the alliance which historians call the Delian League began with a meeting between the Athenian general Aristeides and the commanders of the ships provided by Lesbos, Chios, and Samos, the three largest island states. This took place after the return of Pausanias to Sparta, probably in 478 BC.[15] The Spartans had recently withdrawn their ships from the fleet, and Pausanias their commander had taken them home. A new commander, Dorkis, with a very much smaller fleet had been sent out from Sparta with the aim of resuming the Spartan command over the whole expedition. He had been rejected by the allies, who apparently felt they would gain more under Athenian leadership than Spartan, and the meeting with the island cities, perhaps taking place on board Aristeides' flagship, had been held to decide what was to be done about the fleet now that it was without Spartan participation. The result was a new agreement between the small group at the meeting, which was soon publicised to other interested cities and formalised by the agreement made at a meeting at Delos next year (477 BC).[16]

Exactly which cities attended the meeting, and which actually joined the new alliance at the beginning is not known. The Ionian cities and most of the islands of the Aegean was certainly involved and it is possible that the term 'Ionian' might include some of the colonial cities founded by such Ionian cities as Miletos, though this is probably stretching matters too far. But since the main intention of the alliance was to prosecute the war against the Persians, and since large numbers of cities in Asia were under active Persian threat, close or distant, it is likely that most of them joined the League early on, purely as a measure of defence. The meeting agreed on a military programme, though in vague terms, which emphasised ravaging Persian territory (probably as a means of gathering loot, but also to reduce Persian logistical resources), and to jointly contribute to a fund to finance operations. An oath was taken that the alliance should be permanent.[17]

Specifically in the Straits area it is very likely that the cities of the Troad and the Thracian Chersonese were early members, though Lampsakos stayed out of the League for some decades. Athens and the Ionian cities would, if they were continuing the war, require unusually large quantities of food, and the Black Sea territories were a useful source, so a priority would be to keep the Hellespont open. On the Marmara coasts, both north and south, there were plenty of enemies to propel the Greek cities into the League; along the south coast, the alternative would be to lapse back into Persian domination – especially with an active and able satrap at Daskyleion, such as Artabazos. The Thracians in Europe were similarly, and perhaps more unpredictably, menacing. And yet, the existence of these measures could have contradictory effects, either forcing a city into neutrality, or making its people grasp at the chance of collective defence. Apart from Lampsakos, and perhaps Byzantion, all the Straits cities eventually became members.[18]

The alliance began its war by attacking the posts retained by the Persians in Thrace. In 476 BC Eion was besieged but resisted stubbornly. The Persian commander, Boges, finally despaired and killed himself and his family by self-immolation, after having thrown his wealth into the river.[19] The commander at Doriskos, Maskames, was even tougher and held out successfully until the allies gave up.[20] The place appears to have been still in Persian control ten years later. Easier targets existed elsewhere.

The Thracian coastal cities probably joined the League when Eion's capture made it safe to do so, and when it became clear that the Thracians were hostile – a small Athenian force was beaten up by Thracians when it explored inland from Eion.[21] The continued Persian hold on Doriskos, on the other hand, no doubt also persuaded local cities, particularly Ainos, to join the League. For these relatively small places it was not the prosecution of the Persian War which persuaded them to join, so much as the other aspect of the League's purpose: collective defence. On the other hand, the Athenian detachment destroyed by the Thracians while moving inland was a sign that defence was not the only thought in Athenian minds.

This need for defence applied similarly to the small cities and villages in the Thracian Chersonese. Athens had an old interest in the area as a result of the exploits of Miltiades' family, and the commander of the allied fleet in 476 BC was another scion of that family, for Kimon was the son of the second Miltiades. Here the issue was protection against the Thracians which was the original reason for the summoning of the first Miltiades. Possession of Sestos – or its membership of the League – was clearly a requirement to ensure that the Hellespont remained open. This had become clear in 479 BC when the Persian remnant held the city for some months. This also applied to Abydos across the water. It is reasonable to suppose that with Persians at Doriskos next door, and Thracians menacing still from inland, together with the presence of Athenian settlers from the past sixty or seventy years in several of the Chersonesian cities, the whole peninsula quickly enlisted in the League.

Across the water in the Troad the menace came from Persia, which still controlled the inland areas. The Athenians were no doubt keen to recover control of Sigeion, which had been their expelled tyrant Hippias' base. Lampsakos, at another crucial passage point in the Hellespont, was also important, and manifested a repeated willingness to remain with, or rejoin, Persia for many years. Abydos and a string of small cities along that coast had probably been taken over by the Persian revival under Daurises in 497 BC, and Abydos had been a major base for Xerxes in 480–479 BC, all of which might suggest a lingering attachment to Persia. It also implied a willingness to fall in with the wishes of the most powerful presence in the region, which was now the Delian League's fleet. These cities (not Lampsakos) joined the League, but were clearly quite willing to allow themselves to be captured by its enemy if survival was at stake.

This had been the policy of Kyzikos when faced by Lydian and then Persian power. The city was politically powerful, had a wide land territory and maintained a serious fleet; it was therefore a place useful to any empire. It had joined the Ionian Revolt when the Ionian fleet came into the Sea of Marmara, but had then negotiated its own submission to the satrap at Daskyleion in the 490s before the Phoenician fleet arrived. Its ships probably formed the largest part of the 'Hellespontine' contingent in Xerxes' fleet; no doubt it would have rapidly changed policy when the Greeks under Pausanias and Aristeides came into the Sea of Marmara in 478 BC. As a Milesian colony it may well have been happy to follow its original home city's lead, but not to the extent of fighting if it could be avoided. It was a large and locally powerful city which was fully capable of taking such decisions in its own time; it was also caught between the satrap Artabazos at Daskyleion, only a day's march away inland, and the League fleet in the Sea. Deft diplomacy was clearly required.

The cluster of cities around the Bosporos were all eventually members of the League, but exactly when they joined is unclear. There were half a dozen of these cities. Three of them were of considerable size – Perinthos, Byzantion, Chalkedon – and three were of medium size – Selymbria, Astakos, Kios. Byzantion may be the key. It was liberated from Persian control by the fleet commanded by Pausanias in 478 BC, but it was probably in a very poor condition at the time. Chalkedon no doubt was similarly freed and was similarly in a bad way – both cities' populations had been evacuated in the face of Persian attacks in 496 BC, and it is unclear how many of the people had returned. The return of Pausanias to Byzantion later in 478, and his stay there until (probably) 471 BC or 470 BC may have had some political effects, though it does not seem that he had set himself up as a tyrant. This was a term used in political polemic very freely, but need not always be taken seriously or as a precise classification.

Nevertheless, it is evident that Pausanias wielded considerable influence in the city, in part because of his role in freeing it from Persian control. He returned to it voluntarily after his recall by the Spartans, and was readily admitted to the city; given his reputation his admittance will have been a decision by the city's council. His influence was strong enough for him to be informally regarded as *ktistes*, a founder of the city, even if this was never an honour precisely voted to him; this probably reflects the city's recovery from its depopulation and devastation during the time he was there, and perhaps his organising efforts during that time. Also as a Spartan he was a Dorian, and the Byzantines, founded from Megara, were also Dorians – as opposed to the Ionians and Athenians who comprised most of the Delian fleet. He was able to conduct diplomatic negotiations with Artabazos, and with the Thracians of the European interior, which argues that his influence in the city was strong and that the city and its citizens had confidence in him for a time.[22] In the end, of course, he was expelled by the Athenians in (probably) 471 BC – which must mean by authority of the Delian League.[23]

Pausanias had influence in the city for all of the 470s BC, and Thucydides says that he was only driven out after a siege. From this, assuming Thucydides was correct, several conclusions emerge. First, Pausanias was supported in his resistance to expulsion by the Byzantines. Second, the city was probably not a member of the League at the time, for when the League's misdeeds are listed this is never mentioned, while the attacks on Naxos and Thasos (which 'rebelled') are. And it seems unlikely that he and the city had been blocking the Bosporos. The normal attitude of Byzantion to the Strait was always to profit from it, by taking its fish, and by taxing the passing shipping. To this policy other cities, who would be doing the same when they had the opportunity, did not necessarily object, so long as the charges were not extortionate. We may conclude that whatever position Pausanias held in the city, he was both welcome in the city and moderate in his policies, despite the reputation for extravagance and 'Medizing' he was later accused of. He does appear to have contacted Artabazos at Daskyleion, and to have negotiated with the Thracians, and this was clearly on behalf of the city. It may also be assumed that, if he was acting on behalf of Byzantion in these missions, he had been commissioned by the city government to do so.

Once he was removed, Byzantion was pleased – or compelled – to enlist in the League. It is noticeable that Pausanias was simply expelled, not put on trial, nor murdered, nor assassinated. In fact he went at first to the small town of Kolonai in the Troad, where he was able to stay, unmolested by the League (the city was easily accessible from the sea) for some months or more. Eventually the Spartans extracted him. In all this he does not appear as an enemy of Athens or of the League, but only eventually of Sparta. It did suit the Athenians later, and perhaps the Byzantines, to depict him as a tyrant, but that is not evidence of his tyranny.

The city of Byzantion therefore became a member of the Delian League by the end of the 470s BC. It may be that, by holding out for some years, the city influenced its neighbours against the League, which had not necessarily been popular in the region. If Byzantion remained out, it is probable that Perinthos, its rival and occasional enemy, would join, particularly as it was a Samian colony, and Samos was one of the League's founders. By contrast, Chalkedon frequently acted in conjunction with Byzantion and may therefore have stayed out for a time. It was probably liberated from Persian rule in 478 BC, at the same time as Byzantion, but it would then need time to recover from its own devastation, and the burden of a contribution to the League would be difficult to bear. Of the smaller cities we can say nothing, except that if they looked for protection from the Persians, Astakos and Kios will no doubt have joined the League swiftly; Selymbria, seeking protection from Thracians, will possibly have acted similarly, though the size of the contributions which both Perinthos and Selymbria made to the League funds imply that both cities were actively trading with their Thracian neighbours. This therefore is only an argument from the geopolitical situation, not from the evidence.

There are no events recorded for the cities of the Straits region between the formation of the Delian League in 477 BC (other than those connected with Pausanias) and the record of the regular tribute payments which begins in 454/453 BC, except for the siege of Byzantion in 471 BC or 470 BC. This is a period of two decades, and we may perhaps assume that no records suggest peace. This was not, of course, the case with the Delian League as a whole, which pursued its war with Persia until 449 BC, after which a formal peace agreement may have existed (the 'Peace of Kallias'), but actual conflict continued on a lower level. In that time a series of Athenian actions gradually tightened the city's grip on the League, and it slowly became an Athenian Empire. How far this process was perceived by the non-Athenian members of the League at the time is not obvious, and if they saw what was happening, it is equally unclear how they felt about it. In retrospect, of course, it had clearly been happening from the beginning.

The empire was an unsteady construction. Its power was used as much to dragoon unwilling members as to fight the Persians. To be sure, the members had agreed originally that it was a perpetual alliance, and had solemnly dropped lumps of iron into the sea at Delos, vowing that they would continue in alliance until the iron floated to the surface,[24] but in fact many were clearly less than enthusiastic from the beginning – Byzantion was one such, possibly Kyzikos too – and found that their membership interfered with their own ambitions. Naxos wished to leave the League as early as 467 BC and was forced to disarm and return;[25] Thasos found that Athenian ambitions in Thrace conflicted with its own, and, after a two-year siege, suffered Naxos' fate;[26] the Dolopes of Skyros were conquered and enslaved in 475 BC, and the island was resettled by Athenian colonists;[27] Karystos in Euboia, a city which had made strenuous efforts both in the Persian Wars and in the face of the Delian League to remain neutral, was now compelled into the empire,[28] as were numbers of Karian cities later. The Delian League was being converted into an empire based in Athens from its earliest years.

The tribute which the several cities paid as their membership fees were assessed in the first years by Aristeides, who tended to be described as 'the Just', though he was only a normally adroit Athenian politician. That assessment is not known, except that Thucydides quotes the expected total to be received at 460 talents.[29] This figure has been doubted, but it is largely in line with what was collected when firm evidence for the individual city assessments becomes available. Athens took on, or was allotted, the task of collection, and a set of officials called the *hellenotamiai* were elected for the job. Their task was essentially as accountants, to record (and count) the contributions sent in by the member cities, and to revise the assessments every four years.[30]

The first detailed listing to arrive is for 454/453 BC.[31] The Athenians had moved the alliance treasury from Delos to Athens that year, in fear of a possible Persian naval raid;[32] and next year they had the tribute contributions engraved on a great marble stele in the Acropolis, and then repeated this annually. Between 454 BC and 420 BC the total collected varied between 419 and 498 talents per year. The records before 454 BC may well have been kept on paper, or if engraved, this was done at Delos, where no record of this has been found. However it was that the earliest records were kept, it is the collection of 454/453 BC which provides the first tabulated record. Thereafter many of annual contributions are known, until 420 BC, at least in part.

The cities of the 'Hellespontine' district, as the Athenian accountants termed it, were recorded as a group, ordered into four sections, the cities of the Troad, those in the Thracian Chersonese, and those on the two shores, north and south, of the Propontis. Taken as a sequence they can be ordered by sizes of contribution, which, since they were regularly reassessed, may also be taken as a rough indication of the wealth and economic activity of the cities themselves. Gaps in the sequence (the record is incomplete, since the stone is broken with pieces missing) may at times be linked with political events either in or outside the region.

The history the Delian League/Athenian Empire between its origin at Byzantion in the meeting in 478 BC and its collapse in 405 BC is in fact littered with crises, problems, and wars – Eion, Doriskos, Byzantion, Naxos, Thasos, Cyprus, and Egypt and many others. Later crises are often reflected in the record of the tribute payments. In 449 BC, for example, the war with Persia came to an end (whether or not there really was a 'Peace of Kallias' concluded in 450 BC and ratified in 449 BC) and in that year there was clearly a problem with the collection of the expected payments. The news of the peace had evidently leaked out during the winter of 450/449 BC, and since the purpose of the League had been to fight Persia, the end of the war for many will have implied the end of the League – and more to the point, the end of tribute payments. To concentrate only on the cities of the Hellespontine district, in the Troad section in 449 BC, Tenedos paid less than its assessed contribution of the previous year, as did Kebren, and the Dardanos payment was reduced drastically; in the Chersonese section, the 'Cherronisatai' – apparently the collective term for several small cities who paid as a group – paid a reduced contribution. Of the Marmara cities, Astakos' assessment was permanently reduced, and Perinthos paid in two instalments, though at the full rate, as though it had been expecting a reduction.

The *hellenotamiai* had the task of regularly reviewing the contributions by the members. How this was to be done is never detailed, though the reviewing procedure for the extraordinary assessment of 425 BC seems to have been wholly concentrated in Athens.[33] That is to say the elected assessors worked from the records of previous tribute payments, which had been carried to Athens by citizens of the contributing cities. In 425 BC a new assessment was made, considerably increased from earlier payments, but there was an appeal system set up by which cities could argue for, presumably, a lower assessment. If this was the normal procedure in the regular four-yearly reassessments, we are not told of it, but, either way, it is one more mark of the domination of the League by Athens. It also tends to explain some of the curious anomalies in the record of payments, for these tend to be irregular, and in a number of cases are totally absent.

The new assessment of 450/449 BC is the origin of the sudden reductions of payments by Kebren and Dardanos and Astakos. The spread of the news of the peace is presumably an explanation for the apparent uncertainty of some payments. The contributions for 448 BC are not listed: either no contributions were sent to Athens – highly unlikely – or the money, when it reached Athens, was directed to some other purpose (restoration of temples destroyed by the Persians has been suggested[34]). In 447 BC, the list of contributions is shorter than before or after, but the absentee cities were compelled to pay up twice in 446 BC, in which year there was another new assessment. This was all Athens' doing, employing its determination to enforce and maintain its imperial power. There is evidence of force being employed in several places in these years. Part of Abdera's contribution was directed 'to Eion' where Athenian settlers had been sent, and who were subject to raids by their Thracian neighbours; the redirected contribution is thought to be a direct payment to the Athenian forces which had been sent there to assist in resisting the raids. Another contribution was redirected to Tenedos, no doubt for some other Athenian active force.[35]

This is linked in fact to changes in the Chersonese, carried out by the policy of Perikles, who had emerged as a major political figure in Athens in the previous years. The Chersonese had remained in much the same political condition in which the first Miltiades had put it a century before: there was a coastal ring of minor cities, some of which had been settled by Athenians in the past, while the Thracian Dolonkoi occupied part of the land of the interior. But Thracians from further inland were again mounting a threat to these weak communities. Probably in 447 BC, more Athenian settlers were installed, the Dolonkoi disappear, and were presumably either conquered or expelled, or perhaps incorporated in one or more of the Greek cities;[36] in 446 BC the record of the tribute payments reflects these changes. Where in 453 BC the peninsula had paid as the 'Cherronesitai' (eighteen talents), from 446 BC the cities of Sestos, Madytos, Limnai, and Elaious paid separately, and the rest paid as the Cherronesitai, but the total is only one talent; Athens' colonial settlements did not pay as tributaries, but were taxed as Athenian citizens, so the reduction may be taken to be an indication of the size of the settlement. In the same period a change took place at Lemnos and Imbros as well, where Miltiades' introduction of Athenian settlers in the 490s BC appears to have been reinforced with a new settler contingent.[37]

During 446 BC, Athens faced a major crisis. A defeat in Boiotia led to an Athenian withdrawal from that whole region, which encouraged others to attempt to gain their independence once more: a revolt in Euboia was followed by a massacre of the Athenian garrison in Megara, and the advance of the Spartan army as far as the Isthmus. In the event the Spartans withdrew, Megara succumbed again to Athens, and Euboia was reconquered.[38] But there were further repercussions in the empire – Megara was the home city of numerous colonies, including Byzantion, and while connections between mother city and colony by this time may not have been close, the crisis, preoccupying as it did the bulk of the Athenian forces, was an opportunity for disgruntled cities to shift their political preferences towards independence. There was trouble at Byzantion, a Megarian colony, about this time, when one Athenian and three allied soldiers were killed in fighting – though exactly what was involved is not known, and it may only have been a force sent on shore to support the Byzantines against the obstreperous nearby Thracians.[39] The tribute lists certainly suggest a problem, for the Byzantine contribution for 446 BC is listed in two parts, or possibly three; next door, Selymbria's assessment was reduced between 446 BC and 443 BC by a talent; this could be further confirmation of Thracian trouble in the area. In the Troad and along the eastern (Asian) shore of the Hellespont several of the cities' contributions were paid in sections, either as late payments for the previous year, or possibly as contributions to a fleet in the area.

Certain groups of cities in the northern area are recorded in an unusual way in the lists. In and after 442 BC, several of those in the Troad are not listed at all, and the reason for their absence is difficult to discern. The cities are Kebren, Skepsis, Birytis, Gentinos, and Azeios. All of them were inland and appear to be small and relatively poor. On the other hand, the coastal cities from Sigeion round to Lamponeia are present (in so far as the gaps in the record allow such a conclusion).[40] The *hellenotamiai* operated by receiving payments brought to Athens, either by someone from the city which was providing the payment, or in some cases by a group of cities paying together. The officials did not apparently go out to the delinquents, though in several cases it is clear that a shortage in the payment in one year was made up the next year, and this was probably as a result of a demand sent from Athens where the shortage would be noted. All of these delinquents were small and their total contribution amounted to little more than a single talent in total; possibly the *hellenotamiai* did not feel it worth their while enforcing the collection. But it is also possible that they had banded together to evade payment; less likely is the possibility that Persia had resumed control by advancing from inland, for this would presumably provoke complaints and an Athenian reaction. Apart from Skepsis, which paid up once more in 440 BC, the cities remained absent from the rest of the record right through until 420 BC. Perhaps it simply was not worth the effort for the *hellenotamiai* to dun them for the debt. It looks as though the cities of the interior of the Troad slipped quietly out of the Athenian Empire from 442 BC onwards, and stayed out ever after, in precarious independence.

Many of the cities along the south coast of the Propontis were as reluctant to pay their contributions as were the inland cities of the Troad. In 442 BC, at the same time that the Troadic cities stopped paying, so did several of the smaller cities along that coast, on either side of Kyzikos. Priapos and Kios failed to pay in 442; Zeleia ceased only for that year; Daskyleion (not the Persian satrapal centre, but the small town on the coast), Kallipolis, and Brylleios failed to pay from 442 BC to 434 BC, but paid in 433 BC, Kallipolis paying 3,000 drachmae, perhaps catching up with missed payments; Bysbikos and the Mysoi paid no contributions at all. Again the contributions of these cities and communities were never more than 1,000 drachmae in any one year, and the total missing cash was probably less than a talent. Kyzikos itself continued its payments regularly, but all along the coast from Praisos to Astakos payments from 442 BC to 432 BC were irregular or absent. This is the whole of the coastal cities between the Troad and Chalkedon, with the exception of Kyzikos.

As with the Troadic cities, there is no obvious reason to be assigned for this development – though the settlement of Athenian colonists at

Astakos will have reduced, if not abolished, tribute payments there, and may be a reaction to this gap in Athenian authority. It is, however, noticeable that, once the great war with Sparta began in 433 BC, payments quickly resumed from several of the delinquents, so that most of the cities were paying up regularly from then on. This suggests that there was either laziness on the part of the *hellenotamiai* or there had been a decision that the smallest cities could be forgiven their payments during the earlier period of relative peace. It may well have been more difficult for, for example, Daskyleion to find 500 drachmae than for Kyzikos to pay nine talents, but when the expenditure on the war increased, so did the pressure to pay, or, possibly, the realisation that payment would be a guarantee of protection. All through the period of irregular payments the delinquents continued to be listed on the tables in Athens – they were still therefore regarded as League members.

The empire suffered a serious crisis in 440 BC. Samos was one of the original founders of the League, and one of the few which contributed ships to the League forces rather than simply paying Athens to do the work. It fell into a quarrel with Miletos, which escalated to a war between them. Athens sent a fleet to separate the two, but the quarrel continued until the city of Samos was put under Athenian siege, which was only successful late in 439 BC.[41] This had repercussions elsewhere, particularly in the north. Byzantion, a frequently awkward member of the League/empire, seems to have joined the Samian 'rebellion', though there is no indication that, at least during the Samian War, Athens sent a force to bring the city back to obedience; the assumption that it rebelled is based on gaps and irregularities in the records of its tribute payments.[42]

Probably after the end of the Samian revolt in 439 BC, which had also affected Byzantion in some way, Perikles commanded a major expedition into the Black Sea. This has left no obvious traces in the tribute lists, and indeed is only briefly referred to in a single source, Plutarch's biography of Perikles,[43] but the fleet went as far as Sinope, where the tyrant was driven out, and a group of 600 Athenians was settled in the city, occupying the properties deserted by the tyrant and his expelled followers.[44] In the same region Amisos, next door to Sinope, was also colonised by Athenians at about this time.[45] The accession in 438/437 BC of the new King Spartokos to the kingdom of the Kimmerian Bosporos was possibly not connected with Perikles' expedition, but it brought to power a dynasty which proved to be consistently friendly towards Athens; his kingdom was for a long time a source of grain supplies to the city.[46]

The passage of the fleet through the Straits, past the Thracian Chersonese, recently settled by Athens, and Byzantion, recently a problem, and then into the Black Sea, was a major extension of Athenian power, making the Black Sea region effectively an area of Athenian benevolent influence and alliances for the next generation. Such influence can only have had a strong effect in the Straits' cities, and not just at Byzantion, which would have benefited from the increase in traffic – and yet it had no effect on the payments which were being missed. A further Athenian contingent of settlers was installed at the Marmaran city of Astakos in 435/434 BC. This was a site very exposed to Persian intrigues and power; an Athenian presence there may have reassured the locals.[47]

The Straits cities, from Tenedos to Byzantion, produced a very high proportion of the total payments into the joint League fund. Several of these cities had unusually high assessments. Byzantion paid fifteen talents, Chalkedon nine, reduced later to six, Selymbria six, then five, and eventually nine talents; Perinthos a steady ten. This was a total contribution of about forty talents from these four neighbouring cities. Kyzikos paid a consistent nine talents. At the Hellespont Abydos paid four, then six, talents. Lampsakos paid a constant twelve, and the size of its contribution may explain why the city was so long reluctant to become a League member. While Kyzikos' contribution may be accounted for by its large territory and its profitable coinage, and that of Lampsakos by its gold mines, the other cities were, it must be assumed, all notable trading places, and their high contributions were no doubt, as we know was the case at Byzantion, the product of customs duties of various sorts.

This scale of payment, rough and ready though the assessment undoubtedly was, given the great inaccuracy of any statistics from the ancient world, does suggest also a scale of urban importance among this relatively restricted set of cities. It is noticeable that four of the largest payers are at passing points in the two Straits – Byzantion-Chalkedon and Abydos-Sestos – and their wealth will have come from ships passing, or calling at, their ports; the two Thracian cities, Perinthos and Selymbria, probably profited from a fairly extensive land territory and from trade with the Thracian interior, and Kyzikos from its large land territory and from Asian trade.

The problem, of course, was that such high contributions could breed resentment that local wealth was being drained away for the benefit, as no doubt it was perceived by the 440s, of Athens, where the accumulated treasure was being used from that time to beautify and exalt the city.

These tribute records can suggest a problem, when their fluctuations are analysed, but without further ancient evidence the details cannot explain what that problem was. (In that sense these records, though documentary in the sense that they are written, are more akin to the difficulties of applying archaeological evidence to single political events.) Concentrating on the Straits region, it seems that there was therefore trouble in the area in 446 BC, and in the Troad interior and the southern coast of the Propontis where the small cities were repeatedly failing to pay their contributions from 442 BC onwards, so that they effectively seceded from the Empire, though not in the eyes of Athens.

The Delian League may be assumed to have lasted until 449 BC, when the peace negotiated with Persia by Kallias (if it was so) meant that the League became more obviously an Athenian Empire. This was an evolution which had been in train, of course, ever since the League's formation in the 470s BC, but the peace with Persia, by removing that original reason for the alliance, exposed more nakedly the Athenian aspiration to power and empire. The peace also released and redirected Athenian energies. At first these were directed to enforcing its imperial policies on the members of the League, but by the late 440s BC, Athens was, under the influence of Perikles and the political radicals in the city, deliberately expanding into new territories – the Black Sea, Italy and Sicily (in a tentative way) and, crucially for later events, into the Adriatic.

But the empire was much more restless than the League had been – or perhaps even more restless. The Samian War lasted over a year, and Byzantion, to limit the discussion to the Straits region, was clearly an imperial problem. The collection of minor tribute levies was clearly also a matter which was somewhat haphazard, and when many of the smaller cities failed to pay they found that the Athenian treasurers did not insist. In these matters, that is, imperial diplomacy, and control, and financial administration, the empire was hardly efficient.

Chapter 6

Precarious Independence (405–336 BC)

The final collapse of the Athenian Empire came in irregular stages between 413 BC and 405 BC, and between the defeat at Syracuse and the defeat at Aigospotamoi, though it was interrupted by temporary victories and recoveries. It was perhaps fitting that these two disasters were connected. The personality of Alkibiades dominated both crises, in the first as the bad boy on whom much of the blame for the defeat was fixed, in the second as the man who warned the careless Athenian fleet commanders that their methods were dangerous, but was ignored; the Spartans under Lysander arrived while the Athenian soldiers were resting and eating, and the survivors of the defeat were massacred. Alkibiades had already brought about a late rally of Athenian good fortune, winning victories and capturing cities in the Bosporos and Propontis area between 410 BC and 407 BC, but this could not last, given the suspicion with which he was regarded in Athens. Driven into exile once more, he sensibly made no attempt to return to the city.

Another connection between the two disasters was in their geographical situations. Syracuse and Aigospotamoi symbolised the extreme points of Athenian imperial expansion. They were contrasted in that one was a city, the other no more than a village and a small river, but they were desperate throws by Athens in attempts to secure itself economically as well as strategically. Control of Syracuse would have meant control of Sicily (and possibly much else in the West) and of Sicilian resources, especially of food; Aigospotamoi was close to the Athenian fleet bases which were precisely aimed to keep the Straits open for ships to bring food to Athens from the Black Sea granary, on which the city had come to rely.

It has been argued that the traditional explanation that the Black Sea lands' delivery of food to Athens was a development which actually took place in the fourth century.[1] But Attika in this war was under Spartan occupation, based on Spartan occupation of the fort at Dekeleia. Attika was either a desert or a wilderness during this phase of the Great War. The Athenians could not cultivate their lands – or if the land was cultivated it was for the benefit of the Spartan occupiers. The Black Sea lands were an obvious source of food for Athens between 413 BC and the end of the war (along with Egypt, Cyrenaica, and the West), and traffic through the Straits was heavy enough for the Athenians to collect a duty of ten per cent on every cargo passing through the Bosporos, one of Alkibiades' measures during his campaign there.[2] This collection station was probably at Byzantion while that city was part of Athens' empire; Alkibiades later re-established it at Chrysopolis on the Chalkedonian side, after retaking Byzantion in 410 BC.[3]

The Athenian determination to control the Straits is evident in Alkibiades' expedition, where he began with Byzantion and so established control of the Bosporos exit. Kyzikos, Selymbria, Chalkedon, Byzantion, and possibly others were retaken by the Athenians from the Spartans between 410 BC and 406 BC, while Athens also dominated the Chersonese. But, after Aigospotamoi, the Hellespont was closed to Athenian traffic; the reimposition of Spartan/Persian control in the area contributed strongly to Athens' defeat in the year after Aigospotamoi; as soon as the traffic was stopped the city began to starve. Lysander drove the Athenian garrisons out of their posts but allowed them to go home, so increasing the pressure on resources in the city.[4] The city was thus living on its imports, hand to mouth, and had little or no food stockpiles for such an emergency. People were dying of hunger in the city by 404 BC.[5]

For the various communities in the Straits region the Athenian defeat scarcely altered matters very much, since it was followed immediately by domination by a Spartan fleet and the army of the Persian Pharnabazos, satrap of Hellespontine Phrygia. The basic problems for these communities in a world of Great Powers – their smallness, their independence, their separateness and individuality – remained, and laid the whole region open to external influence – which is to say, to invasion, intrigue, conspiracy, and oppression.

The war had already seriously affected Ilion where the indications of habitation decreased drastically for the late fifth century. Yet the sanctuary received increased recognition. King Xerxes seems to have begun the process, with his visit in 480 BC and extravagant sacrifice of 1,000 cattle.

Athens' domination followed, which was no doubt one reason why the Spartan commander Mindaros sacrificed at the sanctuary in 411 BC, as a symbol of Athenian defeat; from then on it became usual for commanders in the area – Derkyllidas, Agesilaos, Pharnabazos, Chares – to at least gesture their devotion, and the settlement slowly grew.[6]

As a passageway the Sea and the two Straits, ringed by many relatively small states, seemed temptingly easy for the greater states to control, for instance by seizing the strategic points – the Narrows of the Hellespont, between Abydos and Sestos, or the southern exit from the Bosporos between Byzantion and Chalkedon (where Alkibiades established his customs post) – but these outsiders generally failed to exert enough strength to succeed for very long in an attempt at control; if they garrisoned all the cities this would absorb the whole army. The future for the cities of the Straits was therefore much like their past, before Athens gathered them into its empire, which at the beginning was largely done by consent. After Athens' empire vanished, any attempts at independence by the cities alternated with episodes of domination from outside, which was usually soon ended. In the period after Aigospotamoi, a whole series of these outsiders made attempts to emulate Athens in the Straits, but in the event none of them succeeded more than briefly. It was much more difficult than it looked.

The period under consideration in this chapter, therefore, is that between the end of Athenian domination of the Straits and the beginning of the imposition of Macedonian power – which in fact was another of those incomplete episodes of control, only the latest of many such attempts. The cities generally maintained their independence between 405 BC and 340 BC, but this was always easiest the further a city was from the Hellespont, and for all of them independence remained precarious. Control of the Hellespont was the object of several imperially inclined powers – Athens, of course, once it had recovered from its defeat, Sparta the victor, but also Thebes at one point, Persia after the King's Peace, and eventually Macedon. For cities intent on maintaining their independence, it was a fraught time.

Sparta imposed garrisons and governors (*harmosts*) in the cities and installed very limited oligarchies of ten men (*dekarchies*) in place of the democracies Athens had insisted on. This dispensation lasted less than a year.[7] The recall of Lysander, the overall controller of Sparta's system, in 403 BC, was followed or accompanied (or indeed, preceded) by increasingly annoyed complaints from the cities about these oligarchies, whose members, of course, once in power, proceeded to deal out revenge on their enemies among their fellow citizens, and to enrich themselves, often in league with the Spartan *harmost*.

One of the men who handed Byzantion over to Athens in 410 BC in order to overthrow the oligarchy in his city, Anaxilaos, was taken to Sparta and put on trial, possibly accused of treason to Sparta, but he defended himself with the statement that he was a Byzantine, not a Spartan, and that Klearchos the Spartan governor was hoarding all the food for his own men, leaving the 'women and children' to starve; he was acquitted, a sign of Sparta's intended moderation, perhaps, but also of its own feelings of guilt.[8] The original policy of *dekarchies* was changed to ruling through larger oligarchies,[9] but this was a solution which was no solution, since for the cities which under Athens had been democracies, even a wider oligarchy would be oppressive. Above all, the oligarchies were a mark of Sparta's domination; this was a version of Athens' vanished empire, but even more unpleasant.

The method by which Sparta had won its war with Athens – subsidies from Persia, the use of Persian ships, propaganda about the 'liberation' of cities of the Athenian Empire – blew back on it in the succeeding time of comparative peace but oppression. The Persian treaty had included a Spartan promise to return the Asian Greek cities to Persian rule, but this could not be done if 'liberation' was a serious policy. So the Spartans were trapped in the contradictions of their policies, and stalled on performing their obligation to Persia. They became occupiers not liberators, ruling through their oligarchies, collecting taxes, so that the cities could find no difference between Spartan and Athenian methods, other than the even more oppressive Sparta-supported oligarchies. The best-known case is Byzantion, and it appears that Kyzikos, from hints in Xenophon, was under Spartan control. If comparatively major cities such as Kyzikos and Byzantion were in that situation many others, smaller and weaker, may be presumed to be also.[10] In fact Kyzikos may not have been unwilling to be subject to Sparta, at least for a time. Sparta's Persian ally Pharnabazos, based at Daskyleion, struck coins in the city, which was probably done on contract in the city's own mint. It was thus on friendly terms with both Pharnabazos and, later, King Agesilaos of Sparta; a Kyzikene,

Apollophanes, operated as an intermediary between the two; at the time the city probably had a Spartan-controlled oligarchy in charge, though oligarchy may have been its normal governmental system.[11]

The answer to Sparta's policy paradox was to move against Persia, almost inevitably, since the alternative was to hand over a lot of Greek cities to Persian rule. This would have been desperately unpopular in the city, and among its allies, and could well have provoked a wide rebellion. An army was sent to Asia, at first commanded by the Spartan Thibron, who recruited more troops from the cities which were threatened by Persia, and the surviving soldiers of the expedition which had gone deep into Persia intending to place the pretender Kyros on the Persian throne. That army had returned and had been a general problem of the area since because it failed to disperse. It occupied Byzantion for a time, and had recently been employed by King Seuthes of Thrace, but he was unable to pay the soldiers. This made it fairly easy for Thibron to recruit the survivors.[12] No doubt the Greek cities in Thrace were relieved to see them removed into Asia, and the army was more comfortable fighting Persians than Greeks. Thibron, however, was a poor commander, despite his successful diplomacy in gathering an army, and he was replaced by Derkyllidas, an extremely flexible man, especially for a Spartan. He dominated affairs around the Hellespont for nearly a decade. He brought the army to campaign in the Troad. And so active warfare returned to the Straits.

Derkyllidas first captured a string of the small cities along the west coast of the Troad – Larisa, Hamaxitis, Kolonai – which had earlier fallen under the control of the Persian hyparch Mania; then he moved inland, captured Neandreia, and laid siege to Kebren, which fell after the Greek population offered to submit, after which the commander of the city, until then vociferously loyal to Persia, followed them into submission. The siege lasted only four days. Derkyllidas maintained his momentum, taking Skepsis and Gergis and Ilion, again largely thanks to the anti-Persian sentiments of their citizens. It is evident that Spartan rule was preferred to Persian.[13]

Derkyllidas raided into Bithynia, whose people had also been raiding into Persian territory. To reach his target he had to march right across Pharnabazos' satrapy, burning Daskyleion and raiding *paradeisoi*; no doubt some of the pro-Persian landowners in the area also suffered.[14] The

Bithynians were evidently independent but, in Xenophon's account, there is no sign of a central government, or a king. Alkibiades had had dealings with them, when he besieged Chalkedon, with which city they were on friendly terms; Pharnabazos had rescued them from the marauding Greek army, but gratitude did not result.

Derkyllidas was in quest of loot, probably to pay his soldiers, but found the going hard. He recruited a force of Odrysian cavalry and peltasts from Thrace, who mismanaged their raiding, and cost Derkyllidas several hundred soldiers. He did not repeat this experiment, but then he did not need to, but it had been a salutary experience.[15]

He brought his surviving forces back to the Troad at Lampsakos, where he heard that the Thracian Chersonese needed protection from Thracian raids. He was clearly by this time acting largely independently, partly because no specific instructions came from Sparta, and partly because of his constant need for resources to pay his troops. He crossed the Hellespont and built, or repaired, the wall across the isthmus at Kardia, which provided some protection for the 'eleven cities' in the Thracian Chersonese.[16]

Derkyllidas had therefore established control over both sides of the Hellespont. Abydos had also fallen, or remained, under Spartan control about this time and he used the Narrows between Abydos and Sestos as his link between the two parts of his dominion. He remained in control of the Chersonese until at least 391. He had in fact established himself in a little principality which he controlled for almost a decade, in much the same way as Pausanias had a century before at Byzantion. However, the alliance of Athens and Persia from 396 BC brought King Agesilaus to Asia with an army to which he added Dekyllidas' forces. Then in 396–394 BC the Persian fleet, under the joint command of the exiled Athenian Konon and the Persian satrap Pharnabazos, sailed up the Asian coast from Rhodes northwards, removing Spartan authorities, harmosts and garrisons, from a series of cities. The Spartan position in the Straits, however, held firm against the joint naval and land attack; Derkyllidas faced down a large Persian force by bluff, while Agesilaus campaigned through Pharnabazos' satrapy – it was possibly at this point that Daskyleion was burnt. It was, however, possible for the Persian fleet to sail through the Hellespont without Spartan opposition.[17] Derkyllidas apparently made no attempt to prevent its passage, hardly surprising given the discrepancy in power, and his lack of ships. Byzantion, Lampsakos, and Kyzikos took the opportunity to remove any remnants of Spartan authority from their cities, as had those cities further south which the fleet had passed.

Spartan seapower faded after defeats by the Konon/Pharnabazos fleet, and its control of its mainland alliance in Greece also collapsed. Its home territory suffered Persian raids from Konon's fleet and from 393 BC it was involved in the Corinthian War, while Konon supervised the refortification of Athens. Abydos and Sestos remained in Derkyllidas' control for the moment, and so also did the Troad and the Chersonese, but he was recalled to Sparta in 391 BC: presumably his little principality vanished with him; his successor seems to have controlled only Abydos.

The general war continued for several more years, the most important aspect being a modest revival of Athenian naval power, to complement the fading of Spartan strength at sea and its withdrawal from Asia. In 389 BC the Athenian Thrasyboulos cruised in the north Aegean with an Athenian fleet and went through the Hellespont to make alliances with Byzantion and Chalkedon, and probably also with Kyzikos and Lampsakos, thereby securing Athenian access to the Black Sea – and he revived the former Athenian customs post at the exit of the Bosporos.[18] For the cities of the Straits this new naval alliance was, however, less a revival of the Athenian Empire and more a means of joint protection against Persia, though this not necessarily what Athens was thinking of.

The Spartans reinforced Abydos and placed Anaxibios in control in 391 BC. He became active in raiding enemy territory around the city he controlled. In reply Athens sent its own new general Iphikrates to the Chersonese. All this would suggest that this area and the Troad were largely out of Spartan control; no doubt the removal of Derkyllidas was either the cause or the effect of the Spartan position there failing. Iphikrates took his troops, peltasts rather than hoplites, across to the Troad when Anaxibios was out raiding Antarados, which was across Mount Ida to the south.[19] He inflicted a defeat on the returning force, in the process killing Anaxibios and the former governors of a dozen cities who had taken refuge with him at Abydos after their expulsions. But Abydos itself still remained out of Iphikrates' reach.[20]

The war continued until 386 BC, when it ended with what the Greeks called 'the King's Peace'. The Great King was able to dictate a peace which at least stopped some of the fighting, though it allowed Sparta to concentrate on disciplining its empire in Greece. He also succeeded at last in enforcing the terms of the alliance with Sparta of twenty years before, and the Asian Greek cities became Persian once more. Athens had secured control of Imbros and Lemnos close to the Hellespont and this was confirmed in the peace. The fighting in the Straits had continued at Abydos. Iphikrates, reinforced from Athens by a land force under Diotimos, and a force of triremes under a quartet of generals, put Abydos under siege, but the Athenian ships were enticed out by a device of the Spartan commander Antalkidas, who then succeeded in defeating the Athenians in detail.[21] This was the event which at last convinced the Athenians that they should seek peace. Antalkidas was sent to Sardis to collect the king's terms – the Greeks to be autonomous, the cities of Asia to be the king's, Athens to hold Lemnos, Skyros and Imbros. When Athens decided to accept, others who were dissatisfied, notably Argos and Thebes, had to agree; the alternative description of the treaty was the 'peace of Antalkidas'.[22]

The period following the peace is not well recorded, at least if Athens or Sparta are not the focus of attention. For example, in the last three books of Xenophon's *Hellenica* there are no references to the cities of the Straits, the Chersonese, or the Hellespont. The two decades following the peace were occupied by Sparta's continuing attempts to maintain its power over Greece, which involved constant fighting, but mainly within Greece itself, and there was little which affected the Straits region. As ever, it remained on the fringes of affairs, a situation no doubt welcome to the citizens.

The region, however, was still subject to pressure from all sides. Sparta may have displayed little interest, but Athens, now increasingly dependent on food supplies from the Black Sea states, had no choice but to pay attention. The Thracians had long been enemies of the Greek cities ever since the Greek colonists had seized several Thracian towns, and one of the developments in the region while the Greeks and Persians were fighting each other had been the emergence of the Thracians. It was Thracians raiding into the Chersonese which brought Derkyllidas to the cities' defence. He had taken the region in hand, made friends with the Thracian king Seuthes, and repaired the old Isthmian wall at Kardia, a combination of measures which were generally successful. In his earlier campaign in the Troad he was operating against the Persians, these then returned as a result of the King's Peace; the cities had therefore been marked as Persian enemies, or rebels.

Persia was therefore another source of pressure, though the return of its power to the Asian coast as a result of the peace terms was not necessarily violent. It is, however, clear that this return was geographically only partial. Some cities were not subdued in the first years, and these were liable to be attacked by a Persian force at any time, with the aim of finally securing implementation of the full terms. It was a standing temptation to independent minded or ambitious satraps who wished to gain points with the Great King. The northernmost cities – Kyzikos, Chalkedon, and the small settlements between them, were to some extent protected by the continuing independence of the Bithynians along the Black Sea coast, and by Athenian interest. The cities and the Bithynians were apparently friendly much of the time, and would no doubt have understood that the only way to keep out of Persian clutches was to stand together.

Athens, carefully watching Sparta's blundering efforts to hold onto its new power, was the first to project its own power once more into the Straits. In 377 BC a new Athenian League was formed. This had been edging into existence for some time. Athens and Chios, for example, made an alliance in 384 BC,[23] and as Sparta's conduct became increasingly unpleasant, more cities looked to Athens for some sort of protection. By 378 BC Byzantion had joined Athens' alliance, and this seems to have triggered a more general movement among smaller cities to join.[24] Athens converted these alliances into a new league, very carefully defining it as an alliance, since the members feared that it would be reconverted into a new empire. Crucially every city retained its autonomy and every city had just one vote, including Athens.[25]

How wide the alliance had been before 377 BC is not very obvious, but Byzantion's adhesion was described as one with 'the Athenians and other allies'.[26] Envoys went out from Athens to collect new members. The constitution of this 'Second Athenian League', as historians now call it, exists on an inscription from Athens which lists the members, apparently in the order in which they joined, though a break in the stone has caused the loss of some names.[27] Many of the members were small states or islands which were clearly in search of security in a dangerous world. From the Straits, however, there were only four members – Byzantion,

Perinthos, and Selymbria along the Thracian coast, and perhaps Dion ('in Thrace') and the island of Tenedos, which joined along with Imbros and Lemnos as members close to the exit from the Hellespont. Notable absentees were the cities of the Chersonese, and, of course, most of those on the Asian side.

Two implications follow from these members and the absentees. The Chersonese, for example, composed of a dozen small cities which had been targets for invasion several times in recent years, was an obvious candidate for Athenian protection. Athens' growing dependence on shipping from the Black Sea, and the earlier periods of Athenian settlement in and control of the peninsula had shown this. And yet none of these Chersonesean cities became members. It seems from a later event that Sestos at this time was under Persian authority, or perhaps only influence, and it seems probable therefore that the whole Chersonese was in the same situation, probably as a result of the terms of the King's Peace; at least one place, said to be Alopekonessos, was a pirate base, which would suggest a negligent attitude of the Persians to this part of their empire. Athens might thus refrain since the city was on good terms with the Persians at the time.

The second implication derives from the geographical position of the new members and recent events in the region. The Thracians had been threatening the Chersonese in the 390s BC, and the cities there had been rescued by Derkyllidas. The cities further east along the Propontis coast could well be under the same threat, not for the first time. Membership of a league whose leader was very sensitive about the Straits could well seem to be a useful political move by cities which were under such a threat, though strict adherence to the promise of respecting local autonomy was clearly required. The new league was expressly designed not to become an Athenian empire, and so those cities which joined were not coerced, but could consult their own interests in their decision to join. It is doubtful that Athens was seriously interested in wars in Thrace, and the city showed repeatedly that the region was to be the source of diplomatic manipulation, not direct intervention, which was perhaps not quite what the Greek cities required. Combined with the continuing Persian presence in the Chersonese, it is clear that the Second Athenian League had some built-in contradictions from the beginning.

The members of the League did not all join at once. The early members were already, like Byzantion and Chios, allied to Athens before the League was formally constituted. At its formal beginning it had perhaps seventy members. The prospect of the new Athenian alliance alarmed Sparta, which was already at odds with Athens over other imperial issues, including the status of Thebes, and the conduct of Sphodrias, a Sparta commander who had attempted a *coup d'état* in Athens, but was acquitted in his trial at Sparta. A Spartan fleet took up station at Aigina and its patrols blocked the arrival of the food shipped from the Straits and the Black Sea. In reply, Athens brought out its own fleet under its general Chabrias and defeated the Spartan fleet off Naxos.[28]

Sparta then finally gave up any naval ambitions, in effect leaving the sea available for Athenian domination. This persuaded more of the islands in the Aegean to join the League, helped by a cruise under Chabrias along the north Aegean coast, which must have revived memories for non-members. The new Athenian League was, however, only a shadow of its predecessor, and it promised to be fissiparous under pressure. Several mainland members left the League in 371 BC when Thebes took up the banner of the anti-Spartan war.[29] Athens played an intermittent and generally secondary role in this conflict, and eventually took the Spartan side when Thebes looked to becoming too successful.

The brief Spartan threat to Athenian food ships had emphasised Athenian vulnerabilities, and the League was only an uncertain scheme for the defence. At one point the Theban general Epameinondas suddenly built a fleet of a hundred ships and took them into the Propontis, where Byzantion joined the Theban alliance, either under compulsion, or taken by surprise, or even voluntarily. The Theban fleet was large enough to frighten off an Athenian fleet under Laches, but this only withdrew without being damaged – it remained, in effect, a 'fleet-in-being'. It seems that Epameinondas had aimed to detach Chios and Rhodes from Athens' alliance on the same cruise, which was hardly possible, unless the Thebans could maintain their domination of the Aegean Sea by their naval power from then on, which they showed no intention of doing. Without defeating Laches no control of the Aegean would be possible for the Thebans.[30] This brief Theban sea campaign was not followed up, and Athens' domination continued.

The Athenian commander Timotheos made contact with Ariobarzanes, the Persian satrap of Hellespontine Phrygia (who had been given Athenian citizenship sometime before and was now planning rebellion against the Great King). Timotheos was able to get Ariobarzanes to help him to take over Sestos in the Chersonese.[31] The city had been under Persian control until then, probably since the King's Peace, and, with its fellow fortress of Abydos, the two cities had the ability, with a fleet, to control the Narrows of the Hellespont. This the Persians had apparently not attempted to do, so making it clear that they were not interested in the Greek wars, only in keeping out of them.

On the other hand, the Persians, and the satrap of Hellespontine Phrygia in particular, were certainly interested in enforcing the full terms of the King's Peace, even twenty years after the terms were dictated. This must be the reason why the city of Kyzikos was attacked by Ariobarzanes in 364 BC. In fact, it is only an assumption that the besieger was Ariobarzanes; he held the relevant office as satrap, though he had also been busy in Lydia and Ionia. By this time, he was in open rebellion and may have been attempting to burnish his credentials as a patriotic Persian. Ariobarzanes' initial friendly relationship with Timotheos did not last, since it was Timotheos' fleet which arrived to break the siege. Timotheos then enlisted Kyzikos as a member of the Athenian League.[32] This happened in the same year as Epameinondas' naval expedition as far as Byzantion. (It may be that Timotheos recovered Byzantion for the League at this time as well, but this is not certain.) The Straits region, for the moment, was clearly in danger of once more becoming one of the areas of Greek conflict.

The capture of Sestos by Timotheos, at the apparent gift of Ariobarzanes, to which Timotheos added Elaious at the southern tip of the peninsula, and Krithote, a short way along the coast, may have been the trigger for renewed Thracian interest in the Chersonese. By the 360s BC the pre-eminent Thracian king was Kotys of the Odrysai, who was very aware of the new intrusions of Athens onto his doorstep. He marched to attack Sestos, no doubt with the aim of preventing further Athenian incursions. Assisted by Abydos, he captured the city, but it was retaken about 360 BC by Timotheos.[33] That is, Timotheos' adventure at Sestos had developed into a war for the whole Chersonese between Athens and the Thracian king.

There followed a complicated set of operations involving a series of unsuccessful Athenian commanders and some clever diplomacy by Kotys. Iphikrates, Kotys' son-in-law, retired from the field, afflicted by the competing claims of loyalty to his city and his relations. His fellow commander, Charidemos, turned to emulate Derkyllidas; he carved out a little principality for himself in the Troad, possible since the Persians were preoccupied with their imperial crisis. He gained control of Skepsis, Kebren, and Ilion, the same area where Derkyllidas had operated, but he was never safe. A third general had to be sent from Athens, Kephisodotos, since these two had apparently deserted.

Kotys died in 360 BC. His preferred successor was his son Kersebleptes, but he was at once challenged by his brothers. The kingdom was divided. Kersebleptes' portion included the land close to the Chersonese, and he appears to have gained control over much of the peninsula. He was supported by Charidemos, who had returned from the Troad, and who was given the city of Kardia as his principality, and continued to act as Kersebleptes' adviser.[34]

The repeated attempts by Spartan and Athenian generals to build themselves a principality on one or other side of the Hellespont was not emulated elsewhere in the Straits region. It is likely that the Chersonese and the Troad were particularly susceptible to this adventurousness because both consisted of a number of small cities. The other Straits cities tended to be larger, and with considerable territories, and so were more capable of self-defence. Miltiades, Derkyllidas, Charidemos, and later Chares, all made attempts at this – to which can be added the Persian Mania and her husband, while Kersebleptes might be included also. All the cities could be seized with little military effort, but they may also have been willing to become part of a general's fief if it looked as though he would be able to provide protection. So it was generals of the currently most successful Great Power in Greece, men who might be able to call on wider assistance, who would be most acceptable.

By 360 BC or so Athens' League was becoming a burden to its members. Athens had built a large navy, but could neither finance it nor man it, and this led to demands for manpower and financial contributions. It also resorted to several of the practices which had brought obloquy on the first League. It had planted Athenian colonists ('cleruchs') in conquered cities, first Samos, then Potidaia and Methone, a practice Athens had used as an imperialist means of control in its former League (though these three cities were not League members).[35] It had punished two island cities, Naxos and Keos, which had deserted the League in favour of the Thebans,[36] so that it now seemed that resigning from the League was no longer possible – so much for individual cities' autonomy. In other words, Athens had begun to revert to its old imperial behaviour; any recalcitrant member might expect to be punished.

In Thrace, Kersebleptes faced pressure from his co-heirs and offered to hand the Chersonese over to Athens, but the city fumbled the treaty and the handover, and Kersebleptes in effect withdrew the offer. Byzantion had been disenchanted with the league by the 360s, notably after Epameinondas' naval expedition; now the city allied with Chios, Rhodes and Kos as a rival alliance of dissidents, clearly directed against Athens; in effect they defied Athens to punish them as it had Naxos and Keos. They also gained the support of Mausolos, the satrap of Karia, who may have been one of the instigators of the rebellion.[37] An Athenian attempt to force them back into membership by attacking Chios was defeated, and more defections from the league followed.[38]

The war was fought mainly at sea. The allies mustered a fleet of a hundred ships, which Athens countered with 120, they met near Chios, and the Athenians were defeated. The allied fleet was able to raid Samos (with its Athenian cleruchs), Imbros, Lemnos, and many other islands. The Athenian reply was a plan to besiege Byzantion, perhaps because it was isolated from the rest, perhaps because it had been able to block the corn ships from the Black Sea. They sailed for the Hellespont, where the allies met them again. The threatened battle was thwarted by a storm, then two of the Athenian generals, Iphikrates and Timotheos, refused to join Chares in the fight. Chares, by accusing the other two of treason, which necessitated their return to Athens to face trial, succeeded to the sole command, but soon diverted into Asia to assist a rebellious satrap in exchange for which he acquired enough money to pay his men. The Athenian Assembly objected to this conduct when the Great King made explicit threats. The war came to an end in this ignominious way.

Chares had established himself in the Troad as the latest general to hold a little principality there. He held Sigeion and extended his control to Ilion; his rule lasted for thirty years, from about 364 BC to 334 BC, when Alexander paid him a visit. Alexander's action in making Ilion into a regular *polis* probably displaced Chares, but the general may have held onto Sigeion for a while longer. He minted some notable coins which were imitated in local cities such as Kebren and Neandreia, and which thus may well indicate a local alliance under his leadership.[39]

This war was the effective end of the Second Athenian League. Mausolos, rather confirming suspicions that he had an ulterior motive in supporting the allies, seized control of Kos and Rhodes, expelling any democrats, and when some Rhodian exiles asked Athens to help with their return, they were refused.[40] On the other hand, Athens held on to some of the smaller islands, who required its power to aid their defences.[41]

By the mid-350s BC, therefore, for the previous thirty years the Straits region had been buffeted by pressures amounting at times to physical attacks, from Persia and its rebellious satraps, from a series of Thracian kings, and from Athenian naval and military expeditions. Some of the cities had accepted that an Athenian League could be a shelter from such storms. Byzantion, though an early ally of Athens, had been easily persuaded to leave by a single unconvincing Theban expedition, and may or may not have rejoined; Kyzikos joined the League when rescued from Persian attack by Timotheos, but shortly after that one of its ships was seized by an Athenian adventurer, Meidias, who stole five talents from its owner; Meidias was then acquitted (at least at first) on his trial in Athens, which provoked Kyzikos into leaving the League, hardly surprisingly.[42] It was actions of Athenian injustice such as these (strikingly similar to the Spartan injustice in acquitting Sphrodrias), combined with Athenian self-justifying arrogance, as in its punishments of Naxos and Keos, which persuaded many cities that they had had enough when the League broke up over the secession of Byzantion and the other cities. Sending out colonists to Potidaia and Samos had also produced fears of similar treatment being doled out to members.

The War of the Allies (or 'Social' War) which ended in 355 BC, therefore, ended the League. The Athenians' defence of the cities of the Straits had been mainly ineffective, except at Kyzikos, or damaging, as in the case of the Chersonese. Its control of its expeditionary commanders, such as Iphikrates and Charidemos, had also too often failed (usually through lack of financial support for the troops), which led Chares to divert to assist Artabazos in Asia, and Charidemos to take service first with Kotys and then with Kersebleptes, having adventured to seize a principality for himself in the Troad and then at Kardia.

By that time also, attention in Greece was becoming fixed on the growth of Macedonian power, and this became the next threat to the cities of the Straits. King Philip II survived the crisis of his accession triumphantly, and he had then emerged as a major force during the very time that the Athenian League was collapsing. He secured control of Thessaly, but also moved south, threatening Thermopylai in 352 BC, at which a coalition of Greek states sent a joint army to defend the pass. Philip retired. The largest contingent of the coalition force at the pass was provided by Athens, confirming early hostility between Athens and the king.[43] The year before, he had besieged and captured Methone, to which city Athens had earlier sent a party of its cleruchs.[44]

When Philip retired from Thermopylai, he at once moved on eastwards, where Athens' position in the Chersonese might be threatened. He had already penetrated once into Thrace, and had almost clashed with Athens in the process. Chares, the Athenian commander in the Hellespont, had taken the opportunity of an earlier preoccupation by Kersebleptes to seize Sestos, where the citizens were massacred and the rest sold into slavery.[45] This brought Kersebleptes, along with the threat to him from Philip, which emerged soon after, to make a new alliance with Athens, and to hand over the Chersonese to the city. Athens sent cleruchs to the region to secure it, but Kersebleptes had clearly aligned himself against Philip in the process.[46] Philip laid siege to a post on the Propontis, Heraion Teichos, not far from Perinthos. This was part of a wider conflict in which Kersebleptes was at war with his brother Amadokos, who in turn was supported by Byzantion and Perinthos. Philip's activities were steadily multiplying his enemies. Athens mobilized to intervene on Kersebleptes' side, but then hesitated. Athens probably cared little for any of the Thracian kings, but if Philip gained a position on the Propontis he would be much more dangerous. Philip fell ill, and this persuaded Athens that the problem was over. It seems, however, that the king remained in the region, recovered, and probably concluded the siege successfully, but evidently did not keep the place.[47] Kersebleptes cannot have been pleased at the uncertainty and hesitation displayed by his ally, while in Athens the affair was interpreted that Philip posed a threat to its position in the

Chersonese, though this seems unlikely at this point. Philip had, however, marked out his ambition, and he and Athens confirmed their enmity.

Kersebleptes remained quiet for several years, no doubt cowed by Philip's victory, and by the capture of his son whom Philip held hostage. By 347 BC the tension between Philip and his enemies was rising once more. Athens, probably in concert with Kersebleptes, fortified a string of towns and forts in Thrace on either side of the Chersonese, along the Propontis coast and that of the north Aegean, forming a defence line in advance of the Chersonese, but it was Kersebleptes who would have to garrison them.[48] Philip accepted this challenge and attacked the post farthest from Macedon, at Hieron Onos on the Propontis. The Thracians, especially in small garrisons, were no match for the Macedonians. Having taken the first target, Philip returned to Macedon, probably taking the other small forts along the way.[49] In the Chersonese, the message was received and understood, and some of the Athenian cleruchs began returning to Athens; it was evidently too dangerous to go on living in the peninsula. This was a time, it may be recalled, when captured enemies were either killed or enslaved – a practice Athens had indulged in often – so that standing and fighting in a lost cause held no charms.

This was followed by increasing disputes between the Athenians on the spot and the independent city of Kardia, which was suspicious of Athens and its cleruchs. The city's location at the root of the peninsula made it the prime guardian against invasion from the north. If it was hostile to Athens, it could be friendly to Philip, though under Charidemos it had been attached to Kersebleptes. Charidemos, whose principality it had been for a time, had now been reconciled with Athens, therefore separating himself from Kersebleptes; he was certainly back in Athens' employ in 348 BC when he commanded the first Athenian reinforcements going to the aid of Olynthos when Philip attacked it. This presumes that he no longer ruled in Kardia, if he ever did, but who took his place as ruler, if anyone did, is not known; perhaps the city became a democracy; by 347 it had become an ally of Philip, no doubt from a sense of self-preservation. This placed it between the Athenians in the Chersonese and the lands of Kersebleptes to the north. This was certainly an uncomfortable situation, but it was one which may explain why it had become one of Philip's allies. It was evidently seen as enemy territory by the Athenian cleruchs. It was included in the peace 'of Philokrates', agreed between Philip and Athens in 346 BC, as an ally of Philip.[50]

The Athenian war party – the group of politicians who were keen on fighting Philip, seeing him as a threat to Athens and its own power – claimed that Kardia was really an Athenian place which was held by Philip, a deliberately misleading claim, which can only have infuriated the Kardians. The Athenian general Diopeithes, a prominent associate of Demosthenes and Hegesippos as a war party leader, was sent to the Chersonese in 342 BC to install a new set of cleruchs to reinforce those who still remained. He took to raiding Kardian territory, giving the excuse that he was short of funds to pay his soldiers, and went on to do the same to the territories of some of those small forts which Athens had developed along the nearby coasts but which had fallen to Philip during his foray into Thrace in 352 BC. Diplomatic protests by Philip, Kardia's ally, were rejected by Athens, and Demosthenes, one of the war party leaders, asserted that Diopeithes could do as he liked.[51]

This was a clear challenge to Philip. Diopeithes' action was fully in accordance with the war-party's wishes; his methods were, if anyone at the time considered this, those often used by the weaker party in a dispute, and so they inadvertently revealed Athens' poor position. In retrospect, Athens' whole policy towards Philip had shown up the city's weak political and military situation; the war party nevertheless sought war, and seem to have assumed that allies would be forthcoming in the event. In pursuing their chosen aim they had deployed the weapons of the weaker party – lies, fake news, raids, and criminality.

Philip, though he understood what the war party wanted, refused to rise to the challenge, and other hostile incidents took place. Instead, he campaigned in Illyria and then turned to deal finally with Thrace, as he clearly had always intended. In mid 342 BC, his campaign began with a march through southern Thrace to deal with the two Thracian kings who controlled the land south of the Rhodope Mountains, Teres, the son of Kersebleptes' brother Berisades, and Kersebleptes himself. These two were defeated and deposed and their lands annexed to Macedon. This put him in control of all the territory inland of the Chersonese, including the nearby coasts along both the Aegean and Propontis – something Athens had feared since Philip's expedition to Hieron Teichos. He then set about founding a number of Macedonian military colonies in the Hebros valley, a solid indication that his conquests were intended to be permanent, not simply yet another punishment or looting raid. The Macedonian kingdom now stretched right across Thrace as far as the Propontis; Kardia was safe, the Chersonese was clearly under threat, but so were the Greek cities in Thrace, from the Chersonese to Byzantion.[52]

It was this Macedonian success which presumably stimulated an outbreak of violence in the Chersonese between the Athenian cleruchs and the Kardians; no doubt Diopeithes was behind it, presumably hoping to seize control of Kardia to bolster the defences of the Chersonese; as a Macedonian ally, it would be a clear threat in any war. Philip reacted to the subsequent appeal by the Kardians by sending troops to help in the defence.[53] This did perhaps deter Diopeithes, or rather deflected him into a raid into Thrace, into the area which Philip so recently conquered. The aim will have been to provoke a rebellion by the Thracians. It did not work. Philip sent an envoy to see Diopeithes, who seized him, tortured him, and demanded a ransom of nine talents for his release.[54] (This was the second such incident – a Macedonian herald, a species usually left unharmed even by enemies, was kidnapped and taken to Athens at about the same time; he was held for ten months; his letters were read out at the Assembly: Athens, that is, was proud of its bad behaviour.[55]) It was evident that the city, or rather the war party, was intent on provoking Philip to declare war, with the intention of claiming that Athens was the victim of his aggression.

Neither side yet declared war, though Philip's 'Letter' to Athens was later able to provide a considerable list of Athenian hostile actions which had been clearly intended to provoke him. Philip was thus in the stronger position, and, instead of declaring war, he went on yet another campaign in Thrace, aiming to conquer the rest of that land. This took him into the next year (341 BC), and included a winter campaign, during which he secured control, if a little precariously, of Thrace as far as the Danube.[56] The Athenian war party, by carefully exaggerating and distorting what Philip was doing, succeeded in persuading the Assembly to send a deputation of envoys to the former Athenian allies, the group of cities – Byzantion, Perinthos, Selymbria, Chios, and Rhodes – which had broken away a decade and a half before. With Philip campaigning in their back garden, so to say, the Propontid cities were clearly persuadable. Philip took due note of the change in their attitude. They had been his allies until then – the suppression of the Thracians will have seemed a boon to them.[57]

On his return south from the Thracian campaign, Philip attacked Perinthos. This turned out to be one of Philip's failed ventures; Greek warfare, essentially primitive as it was, was hopeless at siege work, and Philip's army was little better, though the Macedonians did use artillery to breach the walls.[58] One of the problems of besieging Perinthos was that, as a city on a peninsula on the coast, it could be supplied and reinforced from the sea, and this task Byzantion and the Persians, among others, undertook.[59] The siege was therefore slowed down drastically, as much by the obdurate and inventive resistance by the Perinthians as by the inherent military difficulty. Philip blamed the Byzantines for this as well as the Athenians, whom he supposed, rightly, had encouraged the anti-Macedonian policies of the two cities in their diplomacy earlier in the year, though the Athenians do not seem to have provided direct assistance to the city.

Philip's attack on the Propontid cities brought together the old Athenian alliance of cities, lining up on the same side. Byzantion, Perinthos, Rhodes, Kos, and Chios, together with Persia, were all involved in supporting Perinthos without actually getting involved in the fighting. Athens' goading had not brought Philip to the point of declaring war, and he had used the city's internal indecision to expand his kingdom and his power greatly. It would soon be too late for Athens to make a good fight of the coming war – in fact, it was already too late though the Athenians did not see it.

Philip now showed that he was as adept at provocation as the Athenians, and did so rather more successfully. He came up with a scheme which would provide him with the necessary seapower in the Propontis to foil Byzantion's tactics, and possibly allow him to capture Perinthos. It might also bring Athens to a clear decision, which Philip probably thought would be against declaring war. He brought forward the Macedonian fleet, which he had to move from the Aegean into the Propontis if it was to be of use. That meant the ships passing through the Hellespont, whose shores were controlled by Athens (the Chersonese) or Persia (the Troad), and where there was an Athenian fleet of forty ships commanded by Chares, one of Athens' more effective generals. It would be dangerous for the weak and inexperienced Macedonian fleet to become involved in a fight with Athens' professional navy, or even with the ships of Byzantion. But Philip also brought up a section of his army, which he could place in a safe base in Kardia.

The two forces, fleet and army, supported each other, the fleet sailing along the west (Aegean) coast of the peninsula, with the army camping at the beaches where the fleet stopped overnight, providing landward defence; then the process was repeated along the east (Hellespont) coast, using the same tactics. The voyage took several days, and the army could not only bring up supplies, but more importantly, by occupying the night camping grounds it prevented any ambushing of the fleet.[60] (It was no doubt in everyone's minds that Aigospotamoi was in the peninsula, and indeed may well have been one of the halting places for the Macedonian fleet; Philip would hardly have passed up such an opportunity to provoke the Athenians.)

Chares and the Athenian fleet did not intervene, probably because Chares was not present, being at a conference, and his fleet was not in the Hellespont but at Heraion Teichos, and it was apparently paralysed by Chares' absence. Diopeithes was apparently dead by now; the cleruchs, in the face of a major Macedonian army marching through their lands, were quite unable to make any challenge by land. So the Macedonian fleet could sail unmolested into the Propontis. Philip brought his full army to attack Selymbria and Byzantion; he probably merely masked the first, but he did make a determined attack on Byzantion.

The purpose of this fleet movement was to facilitate Philip's land attacks on Perinthos and Byzantion, which were frustrated by the intervention at sea by Perinthos' allies; the same would clearly happen at the other cities. Athens' fleet did not challenge the Macedonians'. There were therefore Byzantine, Persian, Rhodian, Koan, and Chian ships in the Sea of Marmara, as well as the Athenians, all of which Philip certainly noted. None of these intervened against the Macedonian fleet's movements.[61]

Philip's sieges all failed, but the military/naval demonstration in the Chersonese made it clear just how vulnerable the cities had become to a Macedonian attack since Philip came to control all Thrace. This was followed not only by an increase in pressure on Byzantion and the other besieged cities, but by another of Philip's exploits. He used his fleet to capture the grain fleet which had been gathering in the Bosporos. It had been waiting to be escorted through the Hellespont and on to Athens and other places by Chares' fleet. How far this had been part of Philip's plan for the fleet from the beginning is unclear, but he clearly knew of the gathering of the fleet, for it was an annual event, and he cannot have avoided looking at it with greedy eyes. It may have been an opportunistic decision to attack it, taking advantage of the fact that Chares' fleet at Heraion Teichos was not yet in place as the escort for the corn ships. But it was a decisive stroke. In Athens, Demosthenes and the war party pronounced that this had been Philip's intention all along, even when he had been campaigning in Thrace.[62]

Philip will have welcomed the wealth which the prize goods provided for him – 700 talents worth, it is said, which became part of Philip's resources and of which Athens had been deprived – and the timber he could use in the sieges, but the capture of the corn fleet, as he must have known, was primarily a blow at Athens' heart. The city depended for its very existence on the cargoes in those ships – out of the 230 ships captured, 180 were Athenian. (Philip let the other fifty, from other cities, go free.) This finally brought the majority in the Athenian Assembly to agree with the war party. It voted for war as soon as the news of the fleet's capture was known.[63]

The war which followed was fought in Greece, not in the Straits region, despite the preliminary crises there which had provoked both sides to fight. Philip had produced a letter saying he was marching away, which he arranged should fall into the hands of the Athenians. This resulted in the withdrawal of the Athenian ships, and then he extracted his fleet, which had been driven as far as the Black Sea and was there blockaded by its various enemies, notably by Athens' fleet.[64] The Athenian ships were now commanded ineffectively by Phokion. Philip withdrew entirely, and attention shifted to Philip's invasion of Greece, and to the final battle at Chaironeia in 338 BC.

Chapter 7

After Alexander (336–301 BC)

Alexander's first serious battle in his campaign of Asian conquest took place at the River Granikos, an eastward march from the site of the city of Troy. He paid little or no attention to the land further east beyond that river, but he did send an army into that area, which had a profound effect on it. His father had sent an army into Asia across the Hellespont before his death, and it had worked its way south along the coast as far as Ephesos.

That expedition had landed at Abydos and turned south, as Alexander eventually did. Meanwhile a Persian mercenary force commanded by Memnon of Rhodes, was instructed by the Persian king to make for Kyzikos.[1] The purpose of this manoeuvre is not clear, though it may have been a venture unconnected with the Macedonian invasion. Memnon arrived by surprise but just failed to capture the city, and then employed his men ravaging the countryside. Parmenion, in command of the main Macedonian force, was engaged in 'liberating' the Greek cities further south by attacking those which refused his summons. His attack on Pitane was interrupted now by Memnon, and at this point it is probable that the main Macedonian force was pulled out after the news arrived of Philip's murder in mid 336 BC. It is a fine point whether it was Philip's murder or Memnon's resistance which stalled the advance, but a year later Alexander recalled it. A force commanded by Kalas remained; it was attacked by the Persians and was driven to the Troad coast near Rhoeteon; from there the troops were presumably evacuated.[2]

To the Persians this probably seemed to be just another Greek invasion of western Asia Minor. There had been several of these in the last two centuries, but none of them had penetrated very far. The Ionian rebels in 499 BC had reached and sacked Sardis, Agesilaos in the 390s BC got no further; and now Philip's army had achieved less than any of them, turning back at Ephesos. Alexander was a new king, still very young, and was not to be taken seriously. There was therefore little reason to expect that his own attack would be any more successful than any of the others. The central Persian government left the task of opposing Alexander's invasion to the local satraps, Arsites of Hellespontine Phrygia, in whose territory the first fighting took place and who therefore took the chief command, Spithridates of Lydia, Mithrobarzanes of Kappadokia, and Alizyes of Phrygia; they were joined by Memnon of Rhodes, fresh from driving out Philip's last force, who would have brought his mercenary force to the battle. That is, the military resources of most of Asia Minor, reinforced by as many Greek mercenaries as could be hired – 20,000 of them – were mustered to oppose Alexander. It should have been enough.[3]

When Alexander crossed the Hellespont, therefore, he found that the local Persian governors had made preparations, warned as they had been by Philip's preliminary campaign. He and his army crossed at the usual place, the Narrows of the Hellespont between Sestos and Abydos. Unlike Xerxes, he used three sailing ships rather than spend enormous resources on a bridge which was vulnerable to the weather (and to his enemies) – though Xerxes had used hundreds of ships to make his bridge. It did allow him to move his huge army across the Hellespont fairly quickly, but it is also a sign perhaps of a Persian fear of the sea. Alexander went on ahead himself, rather than supervising from behind or above, as Xerxes had. But he did do one thing that Xerxes had also done, possibly doing so quite deliberately because Xerxes had done it. He visited Ilion, firmly identified by now as the site of Troy and the Trojan War, and a place where all generals campaigning in the area sacrificed. There he exchanged his own armour for that which the local priests claimed was Achilles', and wore it in his battles. Xerxes is said to have sacrificed a thousand oxen during his visit, supposedly to Zeus, though it was probably mainly to feed his army, not just as a sacrifice to the gods; Alexander sacrificed instead to the sea god on his way across the Hellespont, a good deal less extravagantly, and to Protesilaos at Elaious and to Achilles and Ajax at the Ilion temple, without killing so many animals.[4]

He discovered that the satraps had united their forces into one army to oppose his invasion. They were located somewhere to the east of his landing, the muster point having been near Arsites' governing centre at Daskyleion. Their joint forces probably outnumbered the Macedonian force. Judging by his apparent purpose of freeing the Greek cities,

Alexander seems to have intended to march south in the same way as his father's earlier expedition; by locating their forces to the east of the crossing, the satraps could use the plentiful agricultural reserves of the Hellespontine Phrygian satrapy, and at the same time were a threat to the Macedonian advance. This position would compel Alexander to turn east to face them rather than turn south, or if he did turn south anyway and ignored the satraps' army, they could quickly cut his communications with Macedon and perhaps trap his army between themselves and other Persian forces which were to be gathered to defend the Greek cities along the Aegean coast.

The Persian army approached from the east, having mustered at Zeleia and Daskyleion, and marched along the Propontis coast, where there was a well-used route. As it advanced, it collected more contingents of troops – mercenaries, bodyguards, garrisons – from the Greek cities and from the lordly estates of the Phrygian landowners along the way. The army cannot have been all that well organized, consisting as it did of four different separable armies and a set of other disparate groups. Much of it was cavalry, each unit commanded by its satrap or local lord. A good deal of damage was probably done along the way to the *paradeisoi* and estates which the army passed by or passed through. (The battle appears to have taken place within the confines of a single estate, marked by the tumuli at Dedetepe and Kizoldun, which are only six kilometres apart, and this will give some idea of the size of these estates.) The Greek cities of the coast along the army's route may well have been regarded with suspicion, and collecting the soldiers from each of them would no doubt keep the cities quiet; the men would be hostages, just as the contingents of ships from the Greek cities in Alexander's fleet were hostages for their cities' acquiescence.

Alexander moved his army to meet this enemy, and the two forces met at the Granikos River, in the midst of the estates in that region, an area dotted with manor houses and tumuli concealing the graves of former owners. The tumuli were used by some of the Persian officers to observe the fighting;[5] the present owners were no doubt part of the Persian force. The fight was a fairly desperate one, with Alexander concerned to demonstrate his command abilities to his army, and to impress his mercenaries, who were not permitted to join in the fight. The victory went to the Macedonians, and the Persian force was scattered.

The Persian cavalry had done most of the fighting in the first phase of the battle; the centre of its line had been pierced by the Macedonian attack, and the wings were harassed by archers and Macedonian cavalry; the two cavalry wings then fled; the infantry, mainly Greek mercenaries though no doubt some local conscripts were present, had then been massacred in a deliberate Macedonian attack. The result was that the Persians were deprived of their trained infantry (the mercenaries); their cavalry had largely survived, though damaged in numbers and prestige and presumably in morale.[6]

Arsites, the satrap of Hellespontine Phrygia, fled to central Phrygia, probably to Gordion, and there committed suicide, taking responsibility for the defeat.[7] The other satraps headed for their provinces, and the Persian cavalry was therefore scattered also. Alexander's prime general, Parmenion, was sent to take over Daskyleion, where he installed Kalas, a Macedonian already familiar with the area, as the new satrap.[8] This was the first indication that this new invasion had wider aims than merely local fighting and raiding in the west of Asia Minor; installing a Macedonian satrap implied an invasion to conquer a considerable extent of territory.

Installing Kalas involved a march by part of the victorious army through the satrapy during which Parmenion and Kalas presumably made certain that there were no large organised enemy forces left. (They can have had no concern over Kyzikos, an unusually powerful Greek city, but one recently at odds with the Persians, and which may be assumed to have been friendly to the Macedonians.) Once Kalas was installed, Parmenion withdrew with most of his forces, and Kalas was left to secure the region. This would have included the capture of many manor houses, and the removal of any surviving household troops. The result was a widespread devastation of the Persian estates, much of whose land appears to have been confiscated into royal possession, as suggested by a large royal estate near Zeleia which King Antiochos II gave to his estranged wife about 254 BC.[9] The original owners were compromised by their loyalty to Persia and their participation in the Granikos battle. In the Kios and Myrleia area the local lords were, it appears, descendants of the Ariobarzanes who had been active, and an honorary citizen of Athens, in the 360s BC. Their relationship to the Persian royal house will have made them as obnoxious to the Macedonians as they had become to the Achaimenids; they however, vanish.[10] Certainly the archaeological evidence suggests strongly that the region between the coast and the satrapal capital was partly abandoned after Alexander passed through.[11]

Alexander himself returned to the main army and resumed his original plan. He moved on southwards fairly quickly, leaving the Straits to his subordinates. Kalas' measures in Hellespontine Phrygia included establishing his and his king's authority in the Troad,[12] where Alexander's own visit had not resulted in a permanent settlement. Kalas was successful enough in this early venture to be assigned unconquered Paphlagonia as an extension of his satrapy when that region tendered a formal submission,[13] but a Persian revival from 332 BC compelled the three satraps in Asia Minor, Kalas, Antigonos of Phrygia, and Balakros of Kilikia, to join forces to defeat this counter-attack. (The Persian intention of cutting Alexander's communications with Greece as he campaigned in Syria has a strong resemblance to the Persian strategy at Granikos.) They did block the Persian attack, but Kalas lost control of Paphlagonia in the process.[14] Then he attacked Bithynia and was defeated by the local dynast there, Bas, and was probably killed.[15] When Alexander died in 323, the satrap of his region was a man called Demarchos.

The cities along the Asian Marmara coast therefore got off lightly in Alexander's time, if the rural estates suffered badly. He himself largely ignored them, no doubt assuming they would be at least friendly towards him in his anti-Persian War. In the following period, however, after Alexander's death, when his successors fought amongst themselves for power, they, as fortified cities, became desirable as centres of power. And then they became objects of social and civic engineering by the winners.

In the warfare which began in 321 BC between a constantly changing variety of Macedonian generals, the Greek cities of the Straits suffered along with everyone else, thereby making up for their immunity during Alexander's campaign. By that year the Hellespont, and by extension the Propontis and the Bosporos, formed the dividing area between rivals Lysimachos, the satrap of Thrace, and Eumenes, the commander on behalf of the regent Perdikkas of part of the royal army on the Asian side; Eumenes actually came from Kardia across the water. This division remained a constant feature throughout the wars, though it was often possible for an army to be passed across. As a military frontier the Straits also was a naval passageway, and the cities on the opposing coasts were valued prizes.

Even with the shores garrisoned by a large army and a fleet patrolling the sea, it was relatively easy for the Macedonian regent Antipater and his associate Krateros to cross with their army in 320 BC. Perdikkas' fleet commander, Kleitos, who had controlled the naval passageway, was then persuaded to change sides and join Antipater. Eumenes, commanding the Asian army, was compelled to retire into Asia Minor.[16] And this was the pattern for the next twenty years, a period in which Antigonos emerged to gain control of virtually all Asia Minor. In that time the city of Kyzikos was laid under siege by the satrap of Hellespontine Phrygia, Arrhidaios, who wished to gain control of the Greek cities within his satrapy, but the citizens succeeded in driving him off before Antigonos arrived, coming to the rescue. Antigonos, though, was also intent on gaining control of the city, but pulled back when he found that the citizens had driven Arrhidaios off (as they had earlier the army under Memnon). The city had survived by first drawing out negotiations with Arrhidaios, partly by dressing slaves up as soldiers and putting them on the walls, partly by using its fleet to raid the coast, and to collect citizens who had been cut off by Arrhidaios' sudden arrival. The city also received naval help from Byzantion, which no doubt would see that if Kyzikos fell, other cities in the region would be attacked, possibly including itself. This staunch and inventive defence was a mark of the general situation, for a populous, determined, and fortified city was extremely difficult to capture. Arrhidaios retreated to the much smaller city of Kios which he did capture, but it was a poor consolation. Antigonos' other purpose in coming to rescue Kyzikos had been to begin the process of removing antagonistic satraps from the Asia Minor provinces – he went on to push Kleitos out of Lydia – in pursuit of his new determination to gain full control of the whole country.[17]

Kios was not relieved of Arrhidaios' presence, and that of his defeated forces until 317 BC, when Kleitos arrived with a fleet in the service of Antipater. The soldiers were taken on board to supplement the fleet's soldiers, and Kleitos then defeated a rival fleet commanded by Nikanor in Antigonos' service in a battle near Byzantion. It may be that Kleitos' forces were besieging Byzantion at the time, but they found they were up against Antigonos at his most tactically inventive. He gathered together all his men and the surviving ships and struck at the victors the next morning as they slept the sleep of weariness and victory – shades of

Aigospotamoi. Kleitos' fleet ceased to exist, sunk or captured, and his troops either died or were themselves captured. Byzantion had been an ally of Antigonos, and so ended on the winning side, like Kyzikos.[18]

After a brief pause the wars returned in 314 BC, Antigonos against his rivals, Ptolemy in Egypt, Lysimachos in Thrace, and Kassandros in Macedon; Seleukos, whom Antigonos had expelled from his Babylonian satrapy, was in command – for the present – of Ptolemy's fleet. Antigonos' nephew Polyainos made a march along the Asian Black Sea coast through Paphlagonia and into Bithynia, enforcing Antigonos' authority. In Bithynia he found the local dynast, Bas' successor Zipoetes, attacking the cities of Chalkedon and Astakos; Polyainos' arrival abruptly halted the fighting – two more cities therefore owed their liberty to Antigonos' forces.[19] Meanwhile Antigonos formalised his practice with regard to the cities by announcing his official policy of liberty and autonomy for the Greek cities.[20] It was, of course, popular and gained him support; it was no less obvious that it was particularly advantageous to Antigonos' own power, for it meant that he did not have to garrison the cities to control them, and he could legitimately ask for – demand – contributions in exchange for his protection. Presumably his experience with Kyzikos was partly at the root of this new policy. It was a policy which was followed by his rivals, with varying degrees of sincerity.

A squadron of over forty of Antigonos' ships was apparently stationed in the Hellespont, though we only know this because forty of them were withdrawn to join his main fleet at Tyre in 313 BC. These may, though our source does not specify, have been provided by his 'allies' in the region.[21] He had been compelled to build up his fleet because Ptolemy had controlled the sea in the eastern Mediterranean and the Aegean during the war. Seleukos had sailed past Antigonos' camp at Tyre at one point, shouting insults, and had then campaigned and raided along the Aegean Asian coast. He had a bigger fleet than the squadron in the Hellespont, but had not challenged it, which suggests that much of his activity was designed to lure Antigonos' army away from the siege of Tyre, and perhaps to persuade Asian cities to defect to Ptolemy, though none of them did. Instead, Antigonos ignored Seleukos' pinpricks, and used the time spent in the lengthy siege to build a new navy, which, when the ships from the Hellespont were gathered, was well over twice the size of Ptolemy's fleet. This gave Antigonos' admiral Dioskourides command of the Aegean when he got there, and two of the places he seized were Imbros and Lemnos, the islands, Athenian until then, which in a sense guarded the approach to the Hellespont.[22]

The Hellespont's status as a frontier line was emphasised when Antigonos and Kassandros met there to discuss peace terms, though they could not agree.[23] This was further emphasised in the next year when Antigonos negotiated with Byzantion for an alliance – the earlier association had probably been merely temporary and of the moment – but he was refused. Byzantion was encouraged in this refusal by Lysimachos, who was busy year after year campaigning in Thrace. Byzantion reverted to neutrality, with a leaning towards the dynast who was in control of its hinterland, hardly a surprising condition for the city to take account of.[24] It would have been obvious to the Byzantines that an alliance with Antigonos would bring instant enmity from Lysimachos and Kassandros, and the installation of a garrison – for protection, of course – of Antigonos' soldiers. Antigonos had already sent a fleet of ships through the Bosporos to assist the city of Kallatis on the western Black Sea coast which was under siege by Lysimachos; this was surely warning enough for Byzantion.[25]

A peace of sorts was concluded at last in 311 BC, but the Straits did not cease to separate Antigonos' lands from Lysimachos', even though Antigonos' fleet dominated the Straits. Indeed it was presumably at least part of the reason why both men set-to to establish new cities under their more direct control on both sides of the waters. Possibly a more personal – rather than strategic – reason was that the several rivals all proceeded to establish new cities for themselves, and named for themselves. Kassandros had already done so at Kassandreia and Thessaloniki (named for his wife, Philip's daughter) in Macedon, but neither place was a particularly large city.[26] The real trigger for the acceleration of city founding was the move of Ptolemy's government from Memphis, the old Egyptian imperial centre, well inland, to Alexandria-by-Egypt on the coast. This had been begun by Alexander, though construction had stalled until Ptolemy rebooted the process after taking control of Egypt in 323 BC. By 313 BC enough had been built to house him and his government, and the date had probably been chosen because Ptolemy's negotiations with Antigonos to make peace had failed; the city was therefore in part a gesture of defiance as well as a means of distracting public attention from his failure.

Seleukos, another bitter enemy of Antigonos', followed with Seleukeia-on-the-Tigris in 312/311 BC, a city designed partly as a new regional capital, partly as a defensive bastion against attacks by Antigonos along the Tigris valley, and partly, again, as a gesture of defiance against Antigonos and his pretensions to supremacy. Antigonos had replied by spitefully refusing to include Seleukos in the collective peace made in 311. These two foundations, both new cities on new urban sites, were followed by similar work by Antigonos and Lysimachos. Not one to make a mere gesture, Antigonos established three new urban centres in a strategic line which was clearly designed to confront Lysimachos across the Straits; and Lysimachos replied with his own new city, enclosing Kardia within it. The two men were building four new cities in positions which emphasised the role of the Straits in separating their territories. (Antigonos repeated the plan in Mesopotamia, with a line of cities confronting Seleukos.)

Antigonos had been the most aggressive of the commanders, but now increasingly fortified his share of the Straits in a clearly defensive manner. One of the aspects of the region was the large number of small and militarily weak cities it included. Certainly, there were relatively large and tough cities, such as Kyzikos and Byzantion, both sufficiently well fortified that they could successfully defend themselves, as they both had recently demonstrated, but most of the other cities were little more than small towns. They were vulnerable to easy conquest, as the Troad cities had showed when Derkyllidas and Charidemos and others had campaigned there over the previous century. They were also vulnerable to being seized by a tyrant, as Sigeion by Chares, and the whole Chersonese by Miltiades much longer ago; this was not an aspect which Antigonos is likely to have been very worried about – unless the tyrant involved was rich, powerful, and ambitious (like Antigonos himself).

It is not clear in what order Antigonos worked to found his new cities, though it is obvious that any completely new place would take years to build – Alexandria-by-Egypt had been building, at least in theory, for twenty years before Ptolemy moved in, and another of Antigonos' cities, Antigoneia in Syria, was still conspicuously unfinished in 302 BC, after work on building it for several years.[27] Antigonos, however, was only present for a relatively short time in the Hellespontine region, and it is probable that the essential decisions on number, colonisation, location, and names were made shortly after the peace of 311 BC, possibly as a result of the revolt in the next year by Phoinix, the satrap of Hellespontine Phrygia,[28] and shortly after Antigonos heard of the founding of Seleukeia, and before that, of the occupation of Alexandria.

The various foundations by Antigonos appear to have been tailored to the situation on the ground. Starting from the east, the village (or small town) of Ankore, at the eastern end of Iznik Golu, was taken over and made into the city of Antigoneia, which was planted on it. This will have involved delimiting the site, beginning the construction of walls, temples, and civic buildings such as the theatre, and recruiting a new population. There was a local tradition that it was a Macedonian foundation, which in the context would mean that Antigonos planted some of his time-expired soldiers as part of the initial population, and reinforced this group with Greeks, local Phrygians, and of course the original inhabitants.[29]

About 150 kilometres to the west were the two Daskyleions, founded in the time of the Lydian kingdom. One was the former Persian satrapal centre, on the Kus Golu (Lake Athritis) inland from Kyzikos. The other was on the Marmara coast, east of the mouth of the Rhyndakos River, and about the same distance from the site of the city of Myrleia. One of these places was selected to be neighbour of the new foundation of Antigoneia-near-Daskyleion, but it is not clear which was actually chosen. In a way placing the new city beside the former satrapal capital would help obliterate any local memories of benign Persian rule (if any such memories existed). Yet to found the new city on the coast would be an even more potent power statement, indicating an Antigonid determination to dominate the Propontis. The sources for the foundation of the city are vague and modern students are divided on the city's location. But it may be pointed out that neither site seems to have hosted a city of any size, though there are early Hellenistic remains at Daskyleion, and it is likely that the city failed to flourish.[30] (Antigonos soon fell from power, and it would not have been in the interests of his victorious enemies to commemorate him.)

The city called Myrleia was near the coastal Daskyleion, which certainly continued to exist into the Roman period, and by being renamed Apameia was favoured by the Bithynian dynasty; it may well have attracted to it the Daskyleion population if the coastal site was chosen. The former satrapal capital was the better known of the two Daskyleions, and could provide an already urbanised population to staff it. The precise location must remain unknown for now, but it may be pointed out that Antigonos, whichever place he chose for a new city, was marking out his territory very clearly.

Antigoneia-Kyzikene is defined as a *phrourion*, or fort, by one ancient source. From its name it was within Kyzikos' territory, but once again precision of location is lacking. It is said to have been 'fifty stades' from the 'western sea', which is another unknown. Suggestions have been made for it to be inland of Kyzikos at the village of Debleki, or on the Kyzikan peninsula at the village of Artake. All that can be said with certainty is that it was in Kyzikos' territory and that it was a fort.[31]

This, of course, raises issues concerning Antigonos' policy of autonomy for the Greek cities. An autonomous city would be very unlikely to accept a fort within its territory which it did not itself control, and Kyzikos was sufficiently powerful to insist. It may be therefore that it was built out of Antigonos' own resources and was part of Kyzikos' own defences. It was not unknown for the dynasts and autocrats to give such presents to allied cities. Alternatively, it could have been a Kyzikan foundation which was named in favour of the king who had marched to the city's rescue. Wherever it was, it was close to the coast and, like the two Antigoneias already noted, it faced Lysimachos' lands across the Propontis. The other two were probably planted inland, which might be a clue that this one in Kyzikos' territory was also at some distance from the coast, though that is a notably flimsy argument.

The Troad was the scene of Antigonos' most extensive efforts at social and civic engineering. There were two issues to be addressed here. One was the existence of Ilion, which had slowly become an important semi-religious place during the previous two centuries, though it was still little more than a temple of Athena with a village attached. It had become the custom for invaders to sacrifice there, but they then moved on, no doubt with increased confidence. Athens developed a myth which enabled the city to claim some sort of custody of the temple, which Spartan generals pre-empted when they could during their mutual wars. But there were others interested and involved as well, such as Argos, and Lokris, and now Macedon, so that it had become a minor Panhellenic shrine. Alexander's visit was rather more personal: his favourite reading was the *Iliad*, which he seems to have taken literally. His example was an inspiration to his successors, who tended to cite him as a source for elements in their

The Bosporos seen from the Imperial Palace, looking across to the Asian shore. This was the view of the citizens of the Greek city from their acropolis.

The Bosporos with the Turkish fortress guarding the passage. (*Kerem Barut via Wikimedia*)

The Bosporos, the view upstream from Constantinople.

Constantine – the Wall of Theodosios. (*Carole Raddato via Wikimedia*)

The Bosporos, a satellite view. In this version, the only indication of human activity is the deforestation – Istanbul city is not visible.

The Dardanelles/Hellespont – a satellite view.

After crossing the Hellespont, Alexander the Great lands in Asia in 334 BC to begin his conquest of the Persian Empire. He thrust his spear in to the beach, symbolically claiming it as 'spear-won land'.

Phoenician soldiers construct Xerxes' bridge of boats across the Hellespont in 480 BC. (*Illustration published in* Hutchinson's History of Nations, *1915, artist unknown*)

The Hellespont at Canakkale, the Narrows. (*Adobe Stock*)

Troy, the altar of the later temple, with the more ancient city walls to the right.

Troy, the Bronze Age wall, much tidied up by the excavators; it would have been somewhat higher. (*QuartierLatin1968 via Wikimedia*)

A coin of Byzantion, the design emphasizing the importance of fish to the city – then and now.

The Emperor Theodosios in his box at the Hippodrome, with family and councillors; originally the base for the Egyptian column.

Hagia Sofia. The building was a church from Justinian's rebuilding to 1453, then the minarets were added.

The 'Porte' – the entrance to the Ottoman imperial palace, where diplomats met their interpreters; this became the shorthand name for Ottoman foreign policy.

The shore of the Gallipoli peninsula, where landings were made by Allied forces in 1915, and where similar landings were made 2,500 years earlier by Greek colonists – the former a failure, the latter a success.

policies. When Antigonos came to control the Troad, therefore, from about 318 or so, it was his turn to involve himself in the town's fate.

In 311–310 BC Antigonos organised around the Athena temple and Ilion a new league of local cities. This was something which had existed for centuries amongst the Ionian cities south of the Troad (the Ionian League), and Antigonos had encouraged this league to revive after a period of decline. His admiral in the Aegean, Dioskourides, had already organised a group of island-cities in the middle of the sea into the Kykladic League; now a Troadic League was organised. As with other civic ventures by Antigonos, this was partly a philanthropic gesture to bind a group of cities into a league of friendship and mutual support (which had been conspicuously lacking earlier), but perhaps mainly to provide Antigonos with a useful means of administration.[32]

It was not a cheap matter, however. To make a league organised around the temple, the temple itself had to be made impressive. It was rebuilt and decorated, probably at Antigonos' expense; this had been publicly promised by Alexander, so a pious successor would have a good reason for funding such work. It is known that some buildings were funded by a trust fund set up by Malousios of Gargara, but this implicitly excluded the temple, so the temple works will have been funded by Antigonos or, after his death, by Lysimachos.

The members of the League included a string of cities along the southern Propontis coast as far as Chalkedon. The main membership, however, was the set of mainly small cities in and around the Troad, from Assos to Lampsakos and Parion, and including Antigoneia Troas. Chalkedon and Myrleia were early members, but they dropped out during the next century, and Kyzikos and other cities in that corner of the Propontis were never members, nor, interestingly, were Antigonos' two new cities in that region, the two Antigoneias. It looks as though membership was to some extent voluntary, and perhaps originally restricted to cities near Ilion, but also that old established cities with Greek populations were the only ones eligible – except Antigoneia Troas, of course, which for its size and position could hardly be omitted; it also functioned as the main port of the Troad once it had been developed, so it was the port of entry for many of the festival participants.

The situation of Myrleia is curious. It is recorded later, in connection with the campaign of Ipsos, that Mithridates, the ancestor of the family which ruled in Pontos from 302 BC, held the city for 35 years – that is, he had been in control of the city since the Persian period. He was presumably a descendant of the family of Ariobarzanes, which is known to have held territory in that area after the founder's fall from Persian grace. He had clearly made peace with every Macedonian since Alexander, a notable record, and he enrolled his city as a member of the Troadic League. In the end by his loyalty to Antigonos he fell foul of Lysimachos, not one to accept anyone who may have loyalty to anyone else, and was driven out. He went to Kios, where he died or was killed.[33]

Antigoneia Troas was the one city founded in the region by Antigonos which became a member of his new league. This was a new city, but one founded close to the site of an older one, Kolonai, on the coast facing Tenedos. While it was a new foundation, it was also a synoecism, taking in the territories and populations of several small cities of the Troad, the region which had proved to be so vulnerable to conquest during the previous two centuries, by amongst others, Derkyllidas and Charidemos, Philip and Alexander. The synoecism included three at least of the small coastal towns, the original Mytilenian colonies of Kolonai, Larisa and Hamaxitos, and inland the larger towns of the Neandreia, Kebren, and Skepsis – though Skepsis, a considerable city forty-five kilometres from the site of Antigoneia, in effect resigned from the group later.[34] How voluntary this synoecism was is not known, but these small cities had a tradition of submitting themselves to a greater authority, and becoming part of a principality; the synoecism was in that tradition.

It took some time to begin construction of the new city. It was laid out on a large scale, the walls enclosing an area of 1,000 acres. Building will have begun soon after Antigonos designated the site, but it will have taken, judging by other great contemporary cities, at least ten years before it was much more than a building site, and Antigonos' successor as lord of Asia Minor would claim credit for building the city wall, which meant that it was unfinished in 301 BC. The city did not strike coins until after 300 BC, that is, after Antigonos' death. By that time also it had suffered a change of name, to Alexandria Troas, decreed by Lysimachos, though at least it survived as a city, unlike others of Antigonos' foundations, which were dismantled.

The city continued in existence well into the early Byzantine period as a local centre.[35] (So did Skepsis, the deserter.) The Troadic League was also a modest success, centred above all on the annual festival instituted alongside the League, and held at Ilion, with an especially grand celebration every fourth year. This was in fact largely in imitation of the Panathenaea at Athens, but it made sense to copy a well-known version, and Athens did claim to have an interest in the city.[36] It was one of many festivals of the Hellenistic period, a time when such events proliferated along with the touristic culture of attending them. Such celebrations were popular, partly because they included a strong local element, but also because they brought visitors who spent money in the area.

This colonising, or rather urbanising, activity had resulted in three new relatively large cities being developed. It is sometimes suggested that this was partly undertaken to settle the region down after a minor revolt by Phoinix, the satrap of Hellespontine Phrygia, which had taken place in 310 BC.[37] Antigonos' reaction, in such a case, seems extravagant, and if Phoinix's revolt was involved it was no more than the trigger for the wider reorganization in the area – after all, the revolt probably had little effect in the Troad, which was the main centre of Antigonos' work.

What Antigonos had achieved was a friendly alliance of a string of cities which were included in the Troadic League, backed up by three new fortified cities set some distance back from the frontier, which was the south coast of the Straits, the three cities spread out at intervals of about 150 kilometres. In addition, Antigoneia Bithyniake was placed as a fortified defence against any trouble from Bithynia to the north, Kyzikos was supervised by Antigoneia-near-Daskylion, and perhaps by the fort called Antigoneia-Kyzikene in its own territory, and Antigoneia Troas dominated the western end of the line and the Troad, along with the League, of which it was the largest and presumably the most influential member. The strength of the defensive system would be shown in a few years, though it did not save Antigonos or his kingdom.

This activity, which at times may have seemed frenetic and disturbing, and possibly threatening to Antigonos' neighbours, does seem to have kept Bithynia in line for a time, but it equally stirred up Lysimachos. He, like Antigonos, faced a string of well-established Greek cities along his Straits frontier, from Byzantion and Perinthos to the small cities of the Chersonese. Some of these were, as Philip had found, tough and independent, and while Lysimachos was in no case reluctant to attack such places, as his siege of Kallatis showed, it was not a task which it was worth undertaking so long as the cities remain quiet. Their independence, in a world of competing Great Powers, was often their safeguard; if they attached themselves more than temporarily to one of the powers, they became targets for the others.

On the other hand, the organization of the opposing coast by Antigonos may have been defensive in intention, but it could also become a base for an offensive, and Lysimachos responded. He founded his own new city, called Lysimacheia, of course. He placed it next to Kardia at the root of the Gallipoli Peninsula. The crossing between Europe and Asia in both directions at Abydos–Sestos had been used repeatedly since Philip's preliminary expedition in 336 BC. Planting a large, fortified city at the egress of the Chersonese both blocked any invasion from Asia along that route, and gave Lysimachos an important base for his own purposes if he intended to invade in the other direction. The city was probably the last of the new major cities founded by the successors of Alexander for a decade, all of these men soon calling themselves kings. The city was also a port, considerably larger in capacity, probably, than Sestos.[38]

Since he was building only one city, it is probable that Lysimachos was able to make greater progress than Antigonos, who was building three in Hellespontine Phrygia, and another, even bigger, in Syria. So when the next war between Alexander's successors broke out in 302 BC, Lysimachos was ready, Antigonos was not. And yet it was Antigonos who, in his arrogance, forced the new war. (When asked by Kassandros to name his terms, he suggested that Kassandros retire and hand over his kingdom to Antigonos; Kassandros did not respond, not surprisingly, other than by contacting his equally threatened partners.) Antigonos' son Demetrios had made good progress in acquiring control of southern and central Greece, thereby directly threatening both Kassandros in Macedon and Thessaly and Lysimachos in Thrace. These two allied and pointed out the danger to both Ptolemy and Seleukos, who gladly joined in the war to pull Antigonos down.[39]

It took a considerable effort, in a military campaign lasting over a year.[40] Kassandros had to block Demetrios in Thessaly, which he did by putting his army in a great entrenched camp, but he was also much assisted by Demetrios' own lethargy. Lysimachos, with Kassandros' brother Prepelaos and part of Kassandros' army, took their joint forces across the Hellespont, landing, unusually, at Lampsakos and Parion, avoiding

Antingonos' position and fortifications in the Troad; these had evidently
cemented Antigonos' power in that area so as to deter Lysimachos. The two
landing places did, however, welcome his commanders, as much for self-
preservation in the face of large armies arriving as enthusiasm. Prepelaos
marched south along the coast, while Lysimachos set about conquering
the Troad. Sigeion was stormed, and Abydos besieged, but Demetrios
sent his fleet to assist the city, and Lysimachos turned away to campaign
through Hellespontine Phrygia and further inland.[41] Antigonos came up
from Syria, and the two armies manoeuvred and sparred and eventually
built themselves fortified encampments for the winter. Kassandros and
Demetrios made a truce so that they could both intervene in Asia. This
was much easier for Demetrios than for Kassandros. Demetrios possessed
a major fleet, which carried a large part of his army across the Aegean to
Ephesos. He campaigned through the coastland to retake all the places
lost to Prepelaos and Lysimachos earlier, including capturing part of
Lysimachos' baggage train in a battle at Lampsakos.[42]

Kassandros had much more difficulty in reaching the main
battleground. He sent half his army under another brother, Pleistarchos,
to join Lysimachos, but having reached the Propontis coast he found
that the southern coast was impenetrable thanks to Antigonos' fortified
cities and his established friendly relations with the older cities, and to
Demetrios' quick campaign and dominant fleet. He had to embark his
men at Odessos on the Black Sea coast and sail for Herakleia Pontica,
which Lysimachos had made his winter headquarters. One contingent was
captured by Demetrios' fleet and a second was wrecked in a storm. Only
a third of the reinforcements actually reached Lysimachos.[43] Antigonos'
work along the Propontis southern coast had been very effective.

All these manoeuvres culminated in June 301 BC in a great battle at Ipsos
in central Asia Minor. Seleukos brought his army, including his Indian
elephants, through Armenia, and joined up with Lysimachos, Prepelaos
and the survivors of Pleistarchos' force; Antigonos and Demetrios joined
their forces in reply. The battle was hard but was decided when Seleukos'
elephants blocked Demetrios' cavalry from intervening in the infantry
battle, and Lysimachos' forces ground down Antigonos' infantry, killing
the king in the process.[44]

And, of course, having jointly won the decisive battle, the four victors
almost at once quarrelled over the division of their conquests.

Chapter 8

In the Seleukid Empire (301–223 BC)

The death of Antigonos delivered his entire kingdom into the hands of his enemies, but it did not remain whole, nor did those enemies remain united. Ptolemy seized Palestine and Phoenicia, Lysimachos took Asia Minor, and Seleukos was left with northern Syria and some lands north of there, all of them desolate, mountainous, or desert, and himself angry and feeling cheated. An immediate quarrel between Ptolemy and Seleukos, originally friends and allies, erupted. Kassandros held out for some reward for his brother Pleistarchos, who received Kilikia and other lands in southern Asia Minor. His intrusion there put him between Seleukos and Lysimachos, perhaps in the hope that his neutrality would keep them apart and peaceful. But there was one more warlord at large, Demetrios the son of Antigonos, who held parts of Greece, an army and his father's great fleet, and who was thirsty for revenge for his father's defeat and death. The two men who felt deprived, Demetrios and Seleukos, formed an alliance, Seleukos taking Demetrios' daughter Stratonike as his second wife.[1]

In all this, which surprisingly did not actually result in open warfare, at least in the short term, but was clearly a dangerous condition, the Straits found themselves in a wholly new situation. For the first time ever, both shores of the Straits and the Propontis were largely under the control of one ruler, since Lysimachos held Thrace and now had added Asia Minor to his kingdom. This was a huge territory which brought him great wealth (and an alliance with Ptolemy, both of them feeling threatened by the Seleukos-Demetrios *entente*).[2]

With his new lands, Lysimachos inherited also the new cities founded by Antigonos, while Seleukos acquired Antigoneia-in-Syria. Seleukos dismantled that half-built city and set about building a great array of ten or a dozen new cities to fasten his grip on the part of Syria he had acquired.[3] Lysimachos, however, did not do either of these things. He had no need to develop a new range of cities, since his lands were already well supplied with old cities, to which had been added the foundations of Antigonos and his generals. Indeed, he accepted Antigonos' work on the whole by simply renaming the cities. Antigoneia Troas became Alexandria Troas (and later claimed to have been founded by Alexander). Antigoneia-near-Daskyleion did not suffer the same change, but the name Daskyleion became the part of the name most used, so the 'Antigoneia' section fell away. Antigoneia-Bithyniake was renamed Nikaia, after Lysimachos' wife.[4]

Otherwise Lysimachos followed Antigonos' lead in his state. He always seems the least innovative and lively of any of these kings, which may not have been a bad thing for his subjects. He did not press on the existing cities, leaving them mainly autonomous, as Antigonos' policy had been. So the cities along the coasts of the Straits retained their independent status, and even the Troadic League, a mark of Antigonos' political inventiveness if ever there was one, remained in existence, though no doubt Lysimachos now became the object of any adulation; he paid for a new city wall for Alexandria Troas.[5] His new city across the Hellespont, Lysimacheia, continued, though if he had intended it to be his capital, he soon abandoned the idea in favour of Ephesos.

At Ilion, apart from paying for some work at the temple, he organised the villages and small cities around the village-temple as a new city. This synoecism – in effect, a copy of what Antigonos had done at Alexandria Troas, created Ilion as a city, a *polis*, with territory along the Skamandros River. The exact boundaries are not known, but the new city included the villages in that valley. There is a suggestion that he paid for a city wall, but it looks as though the geographer Strabo, the source of this, mixed up Ilion with Alexandria Troas, because later on the city of Ilion is noted as unwalled. That is, the synoecism of Ilion, unlike that of Alexandria Troas, probably did not involve much disturbance among the candidate villages, which largely continued to exist; so the 'city' was a federation of villages.[6]

Lysimachos' reign was generally quiet in Asia Minor, so far as can be seen, at least until the final disastrous years. He had gained control of Thrace by conquest before the campaign to overthrow Antigonos, though Thrace was a land which was rarely quiet. He attempted without success to subdue Bithynia. This country had resisted earlier attempts to conquer it, the only successful campaign being by Antigonos' nephew Polemaios, who had rescued Astakos and Chalkedon (as Antigonos had rescued Kyzikos), and had concluded alliances with both cities with the king. This balanced situation lasted, of course, only until Antigonos' death, after which Zipoetes rose once more to exhibit his expansionist tendencies, including, after defeating an attack by the generals of Lysimachos, assuming the royal title.[7] The kingdom began a new dating scheme at 297/296 BC, which was probably the date of this self-promotion. Lysimachos is recorded, perhaps somewhat dubiously, as the destroyer of the city of Astakos, an idea possibly connected with his Bithynian war, if the Bithynians had captured the city; on the other hand, the city might not have been destroyed at all, but simply deserted by the population in favour of moving to Nikomedia later.[8]

The interior of Lysimachos' kingdom was thus relatively peaceful, but there was constant trouble on the borders. Bithynia was an example, and he was at enmity with Seleukos, who was to be his downfall, but above all, Demetrios was repeatedly a difficult neighbour. He controlled the main fleet in the eastern Mediterranean and used it. He took over Pleistarchos' kingdom in Kilikia in 299 BC while in Syria to ally with Seleukos, and he also held a series of ports in Phoenicia, Cyprus, and Asia Minor for some years. In 294 BC, he succeeded in making himself king in Macedon after the deaths of Kassandros and his children, and then proceeded to build up his forces, both navy and army – though most of his outlying posts and ports in Asia were taken by his various enemies – Seleukos, Ptolemy, Lysimachos – while he was gaining control of Macedon. The expansion of his power in his new kingdom, as in earlier instances where a single king seems to be becoming too powerful, brought the other kings into a coalition to bring him down, which, along with the disenchantment of the Macedonians at the prospect of yet another massive foreign expedition at their expense, succeeded in 288 BC. One result was increased power for Lysimachos, who secured Macedon to add to Asia Minor and Thrace. It was he who then found he had no friends because of his too-great power, and when his own family dissolved into scandal and murder, he found little support inside the kingdom as well. Seleukos from Syria seized the moment, intrigued against him, and invaded. Lysimachos went down to defeat in the battle at Koroupedion in 281 BC.[9]

Seleukos briefly took over Lysimachos' kingdom but was then distracted into visiting a local altar in the Chersonese and there murdered by a renegade Ptolemy – Keraunos – who made himself king of Macedon, but then he also lasted only a few months. Seleukos had just crossed from Asia into Europe when he was murdered, crossing perhaps by the old route between Sestos and Abydos. He had been on his way to Lysimacheia, an inescapable destination if he was going, as is assumed, to Macedon.[10] Possibly he had avoided that city in crossing because he had been responsible for Lysimachos' death, for, if there was one city where the old king was popular it will have been in the city he founded and which bore his name. Keraunos had immediately fled to that city and there publicly claimed the kingdom, which suggests that he assumed that it was a popular action in the city.

This series of battles, deaths and murders left the region around the Straits in confusion. After Seleukos' death and Keraunos' departure to Macedon, probably no one knew who ruled in Asia Minor and Thrace. The king's body was collected and cremated by one of his subjects, Philetairos, who used his control of a part of Lysimachos' royal treasure, and the obligation he had put the new king under, to manoeuvre himself into independence at his fort-city of Pergamon, though he did not claim the kingdom when he carried through the funerary rites.[11] In the Bosporos region four cities, Byzantion, Kios, Chalkedon, and Herakleia Pontika, all having fleets of various sizes, banded together into an alliance which is usually called the Northern League.[12] They were operating largely in mutual defence against the Bithynian king's ambitions, but also in the face of the general confusion. They could assume that the new king might well try to annex them.

Into the mix came the new kings and a horde of invaders, from several directions. Demetrios finally went down to defeat, in 286–285, and was captured and imprisoned by his son-in-law Seleukos, leaving his fleet and a remnant of his army to his son Antigonus II Gonatas, who was in charge in Athens – though both fleet and army soon broke up, parts annexed by other kings.[13] From the eastern provinces of Baktria came Seleukos' son Antiochos I, who, like Antigonos Gonatas, had been put in command of that difficult area by his father. He now moved west to secure his whole inheritance, which involved claims to Macedon, which had been pre-empted by Ptolemy Keraunos after Seleukos' death, and was also disputed by Antigonos.[14] These kings collided in the Straits, with the Northern League involved as well. Keraunos defeated Antigonos, while the Northern league, mainly seated in Asia Minor, adopted an anti-Seleukid position.[15]

All these attitudes and positions became moot with the invasion of Macedon by the Galatians, who had been infiltrating and conquering in the central Balkans for a couple of generations. The rapid change of kings in Macedon – six in a dozen years – and then the removal of three of the kings of the Great Powers in three years, alerted the Galatians to the possibilities inherent in the confusion. Their aim was primarily loot, at least at first. Invasions of the Macedon in 279 BC and 278 BC killed Keraunos, and for the next two years the kingdom went through six more new kings, none of whom lasted more than a few months. The Galatians reached as far as Delphi in their invasion of Greece, were there defeated, and then recoiled; they finally left Macedon in 277 BC.[16] Antigonos and Antiochos, having briefly clashed at sea in the Straits, cooperated in assisting in the defence of Greece, and both fought the Galatians. Antigonos trapped one band of raiders in the Chersonese and massacred them, which gave him a good claim to Macedon as saviour, and once there, he recruited Galatians to clear the kingdom of other Galatians.

Most of the Galatians removed themselves out of Greece and Macedon northwards to their political centre in the Belgrade area, but others determined to seek new homes in the south. One group decided that Thrace would be their new home, two others knew enough about the region to know that Asia Minor had rich cities which they might be able to loot, and relatively empty lands where they could settle – for those who broke away from the main body were now intending to find a new land to live in.

The Thracian group, led by a man called Kommontorios, established themselves along the Black Sea coast north of Byzantion, constituting themselves into a kingdom called Tylis. They did not, or rather the king and the aristocracy of the kingdom did not, give up their raiding practices, and enslaved Thracians were exported for the next fifty years, which was as long as the kingdom lasted. They also pressed hard on Byzantion, which became accustomed to paying a tribute to the king for immunity from raiding, and he presumably redistributed the proceeds to his supporters. It was an overtly predatory state, and was obviously detested by its neighbours and its subjects.[17]

The other two invading groups, led by Leonnorios and Loutourios, split off from the main raiding force as it retreated northwards out of Greece. They turned east and reached the Straits with the intention of crossing into Asia, virgin territory from the point of view of raiders. In stopping at the Straits, they found they needed ships, but they also quickly discovered and exploited the complex politics of the region. The Northern League seems to have faded away to some extent, but the cities which had been its members were still alert and armed, above all with warships. Their neighbour, Bithynia, was in the midst of a succession crisis, with two brothers, Nikomedes and Ziaelas, disputing their father's throne. And looming over all these was the Seleucid kingdom, where Antiochos I had succeeded in gaining full control. He was pressing on these cities and Bithynia, seeking to extend his kingdom over them. He had already limited his claims by contacting Antigonos Gonatas in Macedon and had given his daughter Phila to him in marriage, signalling friendship, if not an active alliance. But the future of Thrace as well as the Straits and Bithynia were still uncertain.

The Galatians exploited their opportunities like veteran cynical diplomats. They divided, Loutourios' group moving into the Chersonese; Lysimacheia here had suffered a sack recently, and was damaged from an earthquake in 287 BC, and was probably not capable of defence – it would have had to rely on Lysimachos subsidising the repairs, and he may well have been too busy, and no-one else recently had the local authority. The other group, Leonnorios', moved towards Byzantion and camped near the city. Loutourios made diplomatic contact across the Hellespont with the local Seleukid governor of Hellespontine Phrygia, Antipatros. At Byzantion, the city appears to have come to some arrangement with the Galatians, perhaps willing to sell them food, but they also contacted one of the Bithynians, Nikomedes. He was the one man in the region who could be persuaded to accommodate them, because he had been losing in his succession contest, which was also a war of independence against Antiochos, and needed armed support.

Deals were quickly agreed. Nikomedes allied with the Galatians against his brother and Antiochos and arranged to have them shipped across the Bosporos. (It was an alliance, and lasted a long time, not a matter of mercenary arrangements.) It could be that the ships of the Northern League cities, who would have been more than pleased to have them removed elsewhere, did the transporting. The Galatians at the Hellespont meanwhile were refused permission to cross to Asia, which cannot have surprised them, but Antipatros sent a small group of ships across with his envoys, and the Galatians seized them and shipped their people across in stages. Antipatros was apparently unable to interfere with this process. They camped first at Ilion, unwalled and vulnerable, which also implies that they were not under threat, and that they formed a considerable force. Then they set off along the Propontis coast road to join their fellow invaders in Bithynia.

In accordance with their treaty, they helped Nikomedes establish himself as king, but then Bithynia was off-limits to the Galatians, and remained so for the next fifty years. The cities and kingdoms of Asia Minor, on the other hand, were now their prey. An attack on Kyzikos failed, and is commemorated on a stele dedicated to Herakles, who founded that the city. Then they moved south to raid the rich lands of Lydia and Ionia.[18]

This effectively ended the war Antiochos had been waging to recover control of Bithynia and its neighbouring cities. He was fully occupied with the Galatians for the next three years until winning a great victory – the Elephant Victory – in 274 BC, which was then followed by a war against Ptolemy II of Egypt until 271 BC. Most of the Galatians were by then settled, by agreement with Antiochos, in central Asia Minor.[19] By then Nikomedes was also fully established in control of Bithynia, and no doubt had successfully made peace with Antiochos as well; since the Galatians and Nikomedes were allies, it would make sense that a comprehensive peace agreement involving all three had been reached. And so a new configuration of power had emerged at the Straits.

Bithynia was a newly forceful presence at the north-east end of the Straits, and across the Bosporos there was the new Galatian state of Tylis, which, by its blackmail demands, reduced Byzantion to near-vassal status. On the Asian side, Chalkedon was in much the same relationship with the Bithynians, though they were not nearly so predatory. The Bithynian kings were anxious to demonstrate that they were as nearly Greek as their adoption of Greek culture could make them, amongst other things soon marrying into the Great Power families and founding cities in imitation of the work done by Alexander and his successors.[20]

Asia Minor was dominated, though by no means wholly controlled, by the family of Seleukos I. His son Antiochos was king, but there were also scions of the family and various supporters of it installed as lords in various parts. One of his supporters, at least for the present, was Philetairos the lord of Pergamon, whose cautious ambition made a firm foundation for his successors' expansion and independence. He used his patronage methods, of which Antigonos at the Asian side of the Straits was also a master, to extend his political influence. One of the objects of that work was Kyzikos.

The city had evidently suffered badly from the attacks by the Galatians, even if it had not been captured – the Galatians were no better than the Greeks at sieges. Philetairos provided the city with wheat, barley, and other supplies in 276/275 BC, shortly after the Galatian raid; this was at least the fifth year in succession that he had provided gifts for the city. The early gifts had been less emergency aid than minor gifts of assistance. In 280/279 BC the gifts were twenty talents of silver and fifty horses 'for the defence of the country', and next year it was tax exemptions for purchases made in Philetairos' lands. In 278/277 BC he sent a force to help the defence, and money to defray the expenses of the fighting, or perhaps to pay the wages of the soldiers he sent.[21] These defence costs were presumably incurred during the disturbances following the deaths of Lysimachos and Seleukos, but who was threatening the city at that point is not clear, possibly one of the Bithynians. The aid supplied was significant, but in no case would it be much more than a small supplement to the city's own military efforts. If, as suggested, the danger to the city's territory noted in 279/278 BC was the result of the war between Antiochos I and Bithynia, the enemy is still unclear, and the danger may have been the result of a spillover of raids by unregulated forces from either side. No doubt whatever war was involved was the same one for which Philetairos sent a force and expenses next year.

The following year, 277/276 BC, the presents sent by Philetairos consisted of cash to pay for olive oil and for the banquet for the young men graduating that year. There is no mention of warfare or danger, and we may therefore assume that the wars of the previous three years were over, or at least that Kyzikos itself was no longer involved in war. But next year was the time when Philetairos sent food, probably in considerable quantities (wheat and barley, and something more – the inscription breaks off) during the war against the Galatians. The shortage of food which is implied here will be the result of ravaging by the Galatians while they were attempting to capture the city.

Philetairos was therefore using his one political asset, his control of that part of the royal treasure which was stored at Pergamon, to assist a friendly city, and at the same time to extend his own influence. But that treasure was actually part of the Seleukid financial reserve, and Philetairos was a Seleukid official, and a valued friend of Antiochos I. He was obviously doing all this either at Antiochos' behest, or, at the very least, with his permission.

Antiochos was also busy in the region on his own behalf, at least until forced to concentrate on wars in Asia against the Galatians and in Syria against Ptolemy. A cult of Seleukos I was established at the temple at Ilion, which can only have been done after Seleukos had defeated Lysimachos, and perhaps only after he was dead, and by permission, or perhaps at the instigation, of Antiochos, and so probably in the early 270s BC.[22] He also attended to the development of Alexandria Troas, the third king who had to deal with the new city's problematic growth. The wall Lysimachos and Antigonos had been funding was still under construction, and Antiochos probably (the source is unclear) helped in this also, presumably with more money.[23] Meanwhile, Kebren, a small city at some distance from Alexandria, wanted to follow Skepsis in returning to independence; Antiochos I facilitated that move, and refounded the city as Antiocheia.[24] Skepsis, Kebren's neighbour to the east, was even further from Alexandria and had already resigned from the synoecism. It is evident that Antigonos' plan for the synoecism had been too ambitious and had probably been instituted without much consultation. However, so far as we know, this finally solved the problem of the city's extent, though it is possible that Kebren rejoined later. The more cautious synoecism of Ilion and its villages by Lysimachos was not similarly contested.

Antiochos' work in the Straits region was concentrated on the Troad, at Alexandria and its territory, and was, of course, aimed at increasing and cementing his influence and authority in those cities; his agent Philetairos paid some attention also to Kyzikos, of course, but beyond the Troad and as far as the Bithynian king's territories, there was a sort of no-man's-land for the present. The invasion of the Galatians had clearly caused damage, and perhaps a good deal of depopulation, though at no point did they succeed in capturing any fortified city. They were clearly after loot, partly to possess it, partly to use it to buy supplies through the merchants who followed them. The three tribes who had emerged from the crossings divided the rich territories of Asia Minor into three parts and each tribe took one part as its victims. In the north, the Trokmoi held the Mysian and Troad franchise, and it was presumably that tribe which had attacked Kyzikos. There were fewer cities in this region away from the coast, but there was plenty of food available, at least for a short time, by stealing from the peasantry and their landlords. And the peasants themselves could be kidnapped, enslaved, and sold.

It is possible to track many of the activities of the other two tribes, the Tolistobogii and the Tektosages, but not the Trokmoi after Kyzikos. By 274 BC, all three were fighting and settling in central Asia Minor, and the 'Galatian terror' for the cities of the west coast was over. By the treaty by which they were given territory to settle on, they had also agreed to cease raiding.[25] But they had left a wide extent of damage and chaos in their collective wakes, and the region between the Troad, Bithynia, and Kyzikos is one of those disturbed regions – hence my classification of it as a sort of abandoned territory.

The Seleukids favoured Ilion and were commemorated there in some style. Seleukos I was seen in the city as a benefactor who had removed the tyranny of Lysimachos from the city and promoted or permitted the institution of a democratic regime. The city passed a fierce decree, which can be dated to the early third century, and so probably after Lysimachos' demise, condemning in advance any men who advocated, or even were involved in, tyranny or oligarchy.[26] The city clearly felt betrayed: the two most powerful successors of Alexander had failed to carry out Alexander's promises of developing the city, its temple, and its defences. Only three or four years after Lysimachos died, it was occupied briefly by the invading Galatians, thereby making the city's point.[27]

In view of this dislike, even detestation, for Lysimachos, Seleukos' victory was obviously welcome. He was honoured with an altar in the *agora*, with a month renamed for him, and a festival to be held during that month. The dynasty's chosen divine protector and progenitor, Apollo, was given a sacrifice during the festival. The city went one stage further when Seleukos was killed, less than a year after these honours were voted. His son, successor, and restorer of the kingdom, Antiochos I, was voted a gilded bronze equestrian statue, which was placed in the sanctuary of Athena. This is thought to have been the only such image in the city, and the only statue, apart from that of Athena, in the sanctuary. For a relatively poor community, the city was being extremely generous with its honours.[28]

The local powers interested in this disturbed Mysian territory, were Chalkedon, Byzantion, Kyzikos, and Bithynia, with the Seleukid and Ptolemaic kings intervening, if more distantly. Byzantion built up a mini-empire, by a recent theory which is centred on the use of its coinage within the Straits and the Black Sea areas, but also including the possession or acquisition of specific territories. Dating these acquisitions is difficult and unclear, though the city spread its gains along both shores of the Propontis and the Bosporos. The peninsula between the Gulfs of Gimlek and Iznik may have been acquired by the mid-fourth century; one theory puts it back to 416 – though any acquisition while the Athenian Empire was still active is unlikely. The 360s BC or 350s BC may be a more likely time for a city to seize control of territory in this area. It was farmed by Bithynian serfs, likened by some to being in the same condition as the Spartan helots. The Persian Empire was partly paralysed by the 'Great Satraps' Revolt', in the 360s BC, and in 357 BC Byzantion and some other cities broke away from the Second Athenian League, resulting in the 'Social War' of 357–355 BC.[29] It is also not without interest that 360 BC was the year Kyzikos seized control of the island-city of Prokonnesos, so extending its power much deeper into the Propontis than before, and of course, gaining control of the marble quarries of the island, whose product was widely distributed in the Aegean region at this time.[30] One of the principal Persian figures in the satraps' revolt was Ariobarzanes, whose family, even after his fall, controlled the city of Kios, on the Gulf of Gimlek, and sank to the status of a local lordship, after the suppression of the revolt.[31] If Byzantion secured this territory at this time, we have a political context in the troubles of both Persia and Athens.

At some point, also only precariously dated, Byzantion stretched its grip as far as Selymbria on the north Marmara coast; this had been only a small city; now it became one of the villages within Byzantion's *chora*. A further expansion lay to a section of the south Marmara coast into land beside Lake Daskylitis, which it shared with Kyzikos – or to the coastal land of the smaller Daskyleion, or just possibly both. It is reported that control of the land was presented to Byzantion by Ptolemy II, along with a gift of grain. The dating of this depends on the international situation, and in particular on the existence of a war between Ptolemy II and the Seleukid kingdom. The two dates suggested are 275/274 BC and 255 BC, both of them years of warfare between these two kingdoms.[32] The territory would have had to have been Seleukid at the time when Ptolemy's expedition seized the area, though if Daskyleion was independent – an unlikely condition for either place of that name – it might be easier to seize.

Taking a town from Antiochos I and giving it to Byzantion would be the sort of cynical ploy expected of Ptolemy II, since if Byzantion accepted the gift, it would embroil the city with Antiochos. In this war (the First Syrian War) Antiochos may well have been gaining successes, and the more enemies he faced, from Ptolemy's point of view, the better. The gift was certainly received and retained: Byzantion instituted a cult of Ptolemy in a specially built temple later, which may be a response to this.[33] The date 255 BC is much less likely, in part because it was clear by that time that the Seleukid kingdom had established firm control of the interior, and also probably of any part of the coast left to it. In or after 253 BC, Antiochos II gave his estranged wife Laodike a large estate in precisely this region, described in geographic detail in the inscription which recorded the gift, and lying between Zeleia and the coast, precisely next door to the Lake Daskylitis which the two cities shared. Thus, by the 250s BC, the area which had been a no-man's-land in the 270s BC had been claimed by the various neighbours.[34]

The final acquisition by Byzantion – that we know about – was at the northern mouth of the Bosporos, and was bought from 'King Seleukos', who was probably Seleukos II, a king who was under severe pressure, who would no doubt have preferred to reduce his responsibilities and increase his cash receipts. The place was Hieron, at the north-east entrance of the Bosporos from the Black Sea. This was a somewhat holy place, hence the name, but also a major control point for the traffic through the Bosporos, a place where ships stopped to prepare for the run through the Strait. The reasons for acquiring it, according to Polybios, included the Byzantine wish to prevent anyone else from controlling it. But it seems probable that the Byzantines also aimed to establish control over the traffic, and placed a customs house there to collect duties. By securing this point, they were also aiming to establish their full control over the whole Strait.[35] This went with their acquisition of the promontory between the Gulfs of Iznik and Gemlik, and also Selymbria, since collectively these gave them more or less full control over the eastern half of the Propontis, and therefore of all the shipping and trade between the Black Sea and Kyzikos on the south and Perinthos on the north – a minor empire based on taxing trade and shipping.

Kyzikos, of course, also had its small empire, not only its own island, now connected by a bridge with the mainland. This bridge and the post on the mainland were probably fortified since the Galatians could not get across. They were also defended by the city's fleet. The city held the island of Prokonnesos, and probably the smaller islands next to it. Prokonnesos, of course, was the source of the much-prized marble, which at times was exported all over the Mediterranean, and might be considered as important to Kyzikos' revenues as tunny fish to Byzantion's. The extent of the city's territory on the mainland is not known, but it is likely that it reached to the Rhyndakos River to the east, and beyond to take in Daskyleion, and along the Marmara coast to the west to the boundary with the next city in that direction, Priapos; inland it stretched to Lake Daskylitis, and as far as Zeleia and beyond, where a boundary stone has been found.[36] Given the disparity in strength between Kyzikos and Priapos, the boundary between them is most likely to have been at the Granikos River. Inland the city had connections with Miletopolis and Apollonia, both of which appear to have been independent cities at this time. But even only possessing the territory along the coast between the coastal Daskyleion and the Granikos River, as far inland as the Lakes, would have provided the city with a reasonably extensive resource base for its food supplies – unless people such as the Galatians camped on it. But its island territories were perhaps just as productive.

In the 270s BC, therefore, both the Seleukids and the Ptolemies intruded their power actively into the Straits region, and both Byzantion and Kyzikos expanded or firmed up their control over parts of the territory, no doubt in response. Further, the king of Bithynia and the lord of Pergamon were also active in seeking to expand their influence and territory in the area, and the city of Alexandria Troas controlled much of the Troad. The days of the many small independent cities appeared to be over.

The date of Nikomedes of Bithynia's intrusion is not clear, but his action is. He moved south to the head of the Gulf of Iznik and built a new city, Nikomedia, close to the site to the ruined Astakos. This blocked the land route from Seleukid Mysia across the Sangarios River and exploited a site which had already been spotted by the colonising Greeks as both economically and strategically useful. There was, it seems, no obvious reaction by anyone to this Bithynian move, but it perhaps stimulated Antiochos II, who had become king in 261 BC, to pay more attention to the region.[37]

Another new ruler in the region was Eumenes I, the nephew and successor of Philetairos at Pergamon. Eumenes quickly dissociated himself from Seleukid suzerainty, apparently fighting a successful battle and so establishing his freedom. He seems to have taken advantage of the death of Antiochos I and the fact that his successor almost at once found himself at war with Ptolemy II (the 'Second Syrian War'). For the Seleukid king, Eumenes' presumption was a minor matter, and the dynasty would continue for the next seventy years to attempt, with some success in the end, to fasten their control on the Attalid state once more. Eumenes expanded his territory towards the sea by gaining control over the small port town of Elaia at the mouth of the Kaikos River, and this he developed into a naval base. He planted a group of mercenaries, probably men recruited by Philetairos who were now too old to serve in arms or who did not wish to serve Eumenes – some of them had mutinied soon after his accession – at a site on the slopes of Mount Ida in the Troad. Named Philetaireia for Philetairos and distinguished as 'by Ida', the site was probably somewhere on the eastern slopes of the mountain.[38] Like Elaia this was a deliberate move to extend Eumenes' lordship into an area with no clear master. Once established for a time, both places were taken by others to be permanent Attalid possessions.

The Second Syrian War, between Antiochos II and Ptolemy II (260–253 BC), was fought only in part in Syria, though both sides were firmly planted in their respective sections of that country so that dislodging either would take a very great effort. The secondary area of fighting was in the Straits, where there were vulnerable territories and allies to be attacked. Antiochos II seems to have taken the initiative here and campaigned across the Hellespont into Thrace, at one point in 255 BC besieging Byzantion. He took control of Lysimacheia and the

Chersonese, if he did not already have them, and minted coins there, no doubt in part to pay his soldiers. Ptolemy subsidised Byzantion with the aim of keeping Antiochos preoccupied. The city received his contribution and restamped the coins with the city's own mark. The siege was unsuccessful, but certainly did not generate permanent ill feelings. The relationship of Antiochos with the rest of Thrace, and in particular with the Galatian Tylis kingdom, is not known,[39] but the Tylis king cannot have been too pleased to see his milch cow of Byzantion being attacked by anyone else. The blackmailer would wish to protect his victim from any other intruder. Unfortunately, there is no record of what any of the three involved did about it. But it is worth noting that Antiochos had no difficulty in reaching deep into Thrace, even though he was at war with Ptolemy everywhere else, and that his siege of Byzantion failed.

The result of the war, concluded with a peace treaty in 253 BC, was therefore a qualified Seleukid victory. Antiochos had fastened his grip more securely in parts of Thrace, notably the Chersonese, and, combined with his domination of the Troad, this gave him control over the Hellespont and its traffic. The other major item in the peace treaty was Ptolemy's surrender of his daughter Berenike to become Antiochos' second wife. This was a major concession, since in Ptolemaic political theory a royal daughter carried to her husband a claim to the throne. Antiochos had put aside his first wife, Laodike, to whom he gave the large estate near Zeleia in Mysia mentioned earlier, precisely in the area which had been encroached on by Byzantion and Nikomedes in the recent past. Choosing that estate implied that Antiochos or his father, as might be expected when such advances were made by their enemies, had asserted his control in the area.[40]

In this connection there was another geopolitical move in this region, which is again undated, but which would fit very neatly into these events in the Straits area. Part at least of the population of Miletopolis was moved to reinforce and refound the town of Gargara. Miletopolis was an old foundation in Mysia, inland of Kyzikos, which claimed to be a foundation of Miletos, but may better be seen as a renamed native Phrygian town, and was in the Seleukid sphere. Since the advance of the Bithynians to Nikomedia, the place was in the borderland between the Seleukid and Bithynian kingdoms. Gargara was a town on a hilltop on the southern slopes of Mount Ida. Moving part of the Miletopolis population to

Gargara and re-founding the city on the coast asserted Seleukid authority in the Troad, and confronted the newly founded Philetaireia-by-Ida with a new and stronger Seleukid guard post. The vulnerability of Miletopolis was removed by presumably some other means, a new garrison perhaps. The date of these developments is not known, but the encroachments of Nikomedes from the north and Eumenes from the south, both Seleukid enemies, is a most appropriate moment; Antiochos II's authority in the area is attested at Zeleia and in Thrace at this time. The Miletopolis/Gargara move seems most likely to have taken place in this context.[41]

Antiochos II died in 246 BC; and so did Ptolemy II. Their successors, Seleukos II and Ptolemy III, fell into war at once. One of the earliest victims was Berenike and her infant son, murdered at Antioch in Syria, it is said at Laodike's instructions. Ptolemy invaded Syria during the subsequent confusion, but the Seleukid kingdom compounded its difficulties by Antiochos' two sons each claiming the succession. Seleukos II concentrated on recovering Syria; Antiochos Hierax, the younger of the two, was supported by his mother and laid claim to ruling the Asia Minor lands. Civil war followed throughout the 230s BC. The Ptolemaic War (the 'Third Syrian', or 'Laodikeian' War) ended in a new peace in 241 BC, but by then Ptolemy had seized large parts of the outlying Seleukid lands, including the Chersonese.[42]

Antiochos Hierax, regarded in modern accounts as a Seleukid rebel and usurper, was in fact a ruling king in Asia Minor for well over a decade. He made himself king in defiance of his brother Seleukid II, probably in 241 BC, but he had been the ruler, or others had ruled in his name, since 246 BC or 245 BC. He defended his kingdom until 228 BC, when he was driven out by Attalos I of Pergamon. In that period of nearly two decades, Hierax concentrated a good deal of his attention and considerable resources in the Troad.

Development in the area had been slowly growing since Seleukos I's conquests. Alexandria Troas and Ilion had become royal mints.[43] The Troadic League, though a fairly loose system which shed its more distant members Chalkedon and Apameia Myrleia, had benefited from a long generation of peace, as evidenced to some extent by the appearance of gold wreaths deposited in local tombs, suggesting local wealth.[44] The two delinquent members were named on an inscription to indicate that they had failed to pay their annual contributions and were to be fined for this dereliction, though there is no sign of their having paid up, nor did they continue as members; by the mid-century both had become engulfed in the Bithynian kingdom and this may have been the reason for, in effect, resigning their membership.[45] The royal mints had been started under Antiochos II, who had campaigned in Thrace, an expedition which probably brought more royal expenditure into the Troad, but the mint production continued after his death, at first in the name of Seleukos II, but then in that of his usurping brother Hierax. By then the coins of other states which were members of the Troadic League were a strong indication of the slow integration of the League itself.[46]

Ilion also showed an unusual moment of aggressiveness. At some point in the third century, it mustered enough strength to attack and destroy the small city of Sigeion. This had been Athenian for a couple of centuries though whether it still was under Athenian control when Ilion attacked is not known. And 'destroy' may be taken in the sense of depriving the victim of its independence rather than physical destruction, since excavations suggest it was still occupied a century later. What brought on this outburst is unknown, but Sigeion occupied a position where it could block some access to Ilion from its post on the coast, so this may have been the reason.[47]

The apparent prosperity of the Troad in the third century was new for the area. Alexander's unfulfilled promise of favours was in part due to his dismay at the smallness and poverty of the temple-plus-village he saw on his visit, though he organized it as a *polis*. His two successors, Antigonos and Lysimachos, were less than generous to the city, but, judging at least by the continuing honours offered to the Seleukid kings, this was mended after 281.

The new prosperity was something fairly general for the Hellenistic world, thanks to the release into circulation of the accumulated treasure of the Akhaimenids, and to the spending of the new kings on their armies, their new cities, and so on. Ilion was also in the fashion in its new festivals, which proliferated in the third century. There were three of these at Ilion – that of the Panathenaia, copied from the Athenian celebration, that of the Seleukeia, instituted from 281 BC and celebrated during Seleukos' name-month, and that of the Ilieia, whose beginning is not clear, but which is recorded in a local inscription of the early third century which laid out the festival's regulations. Since the city had been generally poor until about 300 BC, it seems probable that this festival involved minimal expenditure at first, and was regulated and continued when it was seen that the Panathenaian festival brought in visitors spending money in the city.[48] The growth of the neighbour Alexandria Troas, which was growing wealthy from trade, and from the passage through the city of visitors heading for Ilion's festivals, was a spur to Ilion's growth. Alexandria was favoured by Antigonos and Lysimachos with buildings, including the city wall, one of the promises of Alexander implemented by others.

Antiochos Hierax went some degrees further than many of his predecessors, from Alexander onwards, in his favours to the Troad region. He appears to have made Alexandria Troas his main residence – though he was as mobile as any other king during his time – and so it was the nearest thing to a capital of the Asia Minor kingdom there was during his reign.[49] And because he favoured Alexandria with new building and a very busy royal mint, he also favoured Ilion, which could be regarded as the prime religious seat of his kingdom. No doubt fully conversant with the relative neglect of earlier kings and the unfulfilled promise of Alexander – and if he did not know of them before he came to the Troad, no doubt the Ilians would enlighten him swiftly and forcibly – Hierax was able to make political capital by at last providing the city with what it needed.

In what looks like a planned development programme, the city at last was given a surrounding wall, the temple was rebuilt, enlarged, and given a wider precinct, an operation which involved flattening and enlarging the platform on which it was built, and a much larger *bouleuterion* was laid out. The planning of all this also involved the laying out of the grid of streets within which the city would grow.[50] The large *bouleuterion* may have been intended for meetings of the city council and for the regular gathering of the meetings of the *koinon*, the assembly of the League; the enlarged temple and its precinct clearly were intended as the theatre for more expansive religious displays and festival celebrations. The city wall was laid out to enclose not only these buildings and the existing settlement, but an area on lower ground which had not been inhabited since the Late Bronze Age – indeed the city wall followed in part the ditch dug to defend that Bronze Age city a thousand years earlier.

The wall was about 3.6 kilometres long, which was about half that of Alexandria Troas. It enclosed an area of seventy-two hectares (178 acres), which made it a fairly minor city in size.[51] The new grid was on mainly level ground, and expansion was clearly possible if it became necessary. Until the wall was laid out and construction began, this 'lower city' had seen little recent occupation; now it became the main residential area. The extent of the settlement has been investigated by excavation and by electronic survey, though neither of these is specific as to dating or the extent and density of occupation.[52] Nevertheless, the money which went into the new developments clearly stimulated the growth of the city, and especially since the building programme continued for several decades, and, at the temple at least, continued with new temples and replacements for a century and a half. The foundation of wealth in the city was royal generosity and tourist spending.

Seleukid control of the Hellespont, established by Antiochos II, (and perhaps secured earlier by Antiochos I) was replaced in the Third Syrian War by Ptolemaic control of the waterway. An inscription honouring the Ptolemaic governor of the region, Hippomedon, a Spartan, defined his authority as over 'the Hellespont and the Thracian provinces'.[53] The latter is somewhat vague, even exaggerated, because Ptolemaic power did not extend much beyond the coastal cities of Ainos and the Maroneia and a little way inland. But the 'Hellespont' is a precise and correct description of his authority. It included, of course, the Chersonese, taken from the Seleukids by the Ptolemaic fleet during the war, and to this was added the town of Larisa on the Troad coast facing west.

The evidence for this is that the town was renamed Ptolemais, and the only time when Ptolemaic power was exerted on land in the area was between c.240 BC and c.220 BC, the reign of Ptolemy III. Larisa had in fact been one of the towns synoecized into Alexandria Troas in 309 BC by Antigonos and, by renaming it Ptolemais, Ptolemy III was partly destroying that union – but then it had been fragile from the start, losing first Skepsis and then Kebren. This excising from the body of Alexandria (the towns to north and south of Larisa, Kolonai and Hamaxitis, remained with Alexandria) was also a display of power which humiliated the Seleukids. Further, Ptolemaic possession of a post on that coast, together with the Chersonese opposite, enforced control over the Hellespont route, already implied by the inscription honouring Hippomedon.[54]

Ptolemy III's ship the *Isis* is recorded in a painting on a tomb at Nymphaion in the Crimea. There is some doubt about the size of the ship, but it was either a trireme or, more likely, a quinquereme – the more likely because it clearly made a major impression in the city, which would not have been the case with the more common type of warship, a trireme.[55] This was hardly the first time Ptolemaic ships had sailed through the Straits and into the Black Sea, but the *Isis* may be taken as a symbol of these earlier events and of the new Ptolemaic victory. *Isis'* voyage in fact may well have been one of those events which were widely publicised by the Ptolemies as a symbol of their triumph in the Third Syrian War, in which the Seleukid kings were defeated and their kingdom collapsed. And, along with the alliance of the Ptolemies with Byzantion, the Ptolemaic control over the Hellespont amounted to the allies' control of the whole passage from the Black Sea to the Mediterranean.

This was, however, only due to the temporary breakdown of Seleukid control over Asia Minor, in which the Seleukid Antiochos Hierax remained as king for a decade, after which Attalos I briefly took his kingdom from him, and then lost it to an expeditionary force commanded by Akhaios, a Seleukid kinsman, who in turn was eventually suppressed by Antiochos III in 212 BC. Given the obvious instability in the region, it was perfectly possible for the Ptolemies to control the Hellespont; as soon as Antiochos III resumed full Seleukid control of Asia Minor, the Ptolemaic position became in its turn untenable – the existence of a Ptolemaic post at Larisa in the Troad may be assumed to be one of the first to go.

Chapter 9

Seleukids, Romans, Attalids (228–133 BC)

The civil war in the Seleukid kingdom went through a series of bewildering changes. Antiochos Hierax survived in Asia Minor for a time but was attacked by King Attalos I of Pergamon, with such success that he was driven out of the country, despite having an alliance with the Galatians and being married to the daughter of King Ziaelas of Bithynia. He escaped from his final defeat by fleeing to Thrace, where he fell in with a group of Ptolemaic mercenaries; possibly he was killed on instructions from Ptolemy III.[1] This left Attalos as king in much of Asia Minor. He survived an attack by Seleukos III, who was murdered by two of his officers, but in 223 BC was attacked by a more skilful commander, Akhaios, who had inherited estates in Asia Minor which Attalos had probably confiscated, if Hierax had not already done so. Akhaios was also a cousin of the latest Seleukid king, Antiochos III, and had the backing of the Seleukid army. Attalos was defeated and driven back to his ancestral kingdom at Pergamon, but then Akhaios decided that his victory was good enough to make himself king. He began to march his army towards Syria to overthrow Antiochos, only to find that his army, mainly men from Asia Minor, who had no wish to go to Syria, refused to go with him, though he continued as king in Asia Minor alone. Then in 216 BC he was attacked by Antiochos himself, and by 212 BC he had been defeated and killed.

In the midst of all this, the long-simmering crisis between Byzantion and the Tylis kingdom of Galatians in Thrace finally blew up into a much wider crisis. The king of the Tylis kingdom, Kavaros, made a new and very much greater demand on the city. It was Tylian practice to accompany such demands with a raid in the Byzantine *chora*, which, as noted in the previous chapter, was of a considerable size. But Byzantion's wealth came from taxing the passing traffic along the Bosporos in various ways, and Kavaros clearly understood this; the demand made in 220 BC was for eighty talents, a huge sum even for a wealthy city like Byzantion.[2] The city appealed widely for help, but only Herakleia Pontike responded. No doubt all cities whose ships had run the Byzantine taxation gauntlet were quite content to let the city suffer.

So Byzantion was compelled to find the blackmail money itself, though it had no intention of beggaring itself in the process. A tax was revived which had been collected by Athens in its imperial heyday, the *dekate* – ten per cent of the value of the goods carried in a ship. That had been collected in order to fund the escorts of Athenian ships on the voyage through the Bosporos and these ships had protected the merchantmen against piracy. The Byzantine revival of the tax, even though the amount was the same, was in order to collect enough to pay Kavaros' blackmail demand: that is, the Byzantines were shifting the burden of paying the Tylian king's blackmail from themselves onto the general trading community.

Complaints by those cities injured by the *dekate* went, not primarily to Byzantion, though no doubt the city was not omitted as a target for these complaints, but to Rhodes, which had a powerful fleet and had a reputation for guaranteeing free trade on the seas, as well as an interest as a major trading city. (It is interesting that the appeals did not go to Ptolemy, whose fleet was the greatest in the Mediterranean, and was an old friend of Byzantion; but the Ptolemaic fleet was in decay by this time, and there was a new king in Alexandria from 222 BC or 221 BC, amid much murderous intrigue in the court there, together with a developing war in Syria, against the new Seleukid king.) Rhodes gathered up some of the complainants' representatives and sent an envoy to Byzantion; it refused to rescind the tax. Both sides cast about for allies. Rhodes sent its fleet to the Hellespont, including several ships from its maritime allies, and made an alliance with Prusias I, the Bithynian king; Byzantion allied with Attalos of Pergamon and Akhaios in Asia Minor.[3]

Of the four states which thus became involved, Rhodes' fleet went no further than the Hellespont, which it blockaded for a time. (Here again the Ptolemaic authority in the area is seen to be in disarray, since it had controlled the waterway for the past two decades, but apparently did nothing to either keep it open against Rhodes or block it in support of Rhodes.) On Byzantion's side, to ally with Attalos and Akhaios at the same time was to ally with two princes at enmity with each other, and neither was interested in intervening; in fact, neither was able to intervene without exposing himself to attack by the other. The only one of the four who took serious measures was Prusias of Bithynia, who was particularly eager to attack Byzantion for his own purposes. He was Byzantion's neighbour in Asia Minor and he sent his forces to occupy Hieron at the Black Sea entrance to the Bosporos (the place where Byzantion collected the fees), and to attack the city's territory south of his kingdom, no doubt using Nikomedia to seize the peninsula belonging to Byzantion between the Gulfs of Iznik and Gimlek.

From Rhodes' squadron in the Hellespont another envoy went to Byzantion, but that city had been equally busy in its diplomacy, and this included contacting an exiled member of the Bithynian royal family, Tiboetes, who was in Macedon, and who nursed a frustrated claim to the kingship. But then, when all this seemed to be in place, Byzantion's whole diplomatic construct fell apart. Attalos could not move because Akhaios threatened him. Akhaios failed to move when Rhodes successfully persuaded Ptolemy to release his imprisoned father, which is probably why Akhaios was pleased to be involved in the first place. Tiboetes died on his way to Byzantion. No ally was available. Rhodes tried again to negotiate peace.

Into the situation at last came Kavaros, who by this time could see that Byzantion's plan to pay his blackmail out of the *dekate* revenues was not going to work. Either the blockade would stop the shipping in which case no one would be paying the tax, or Byzantion would give up the tax; in neither case would it be able to pay his blackmail. He produced a set of proposals, whereby Byzantion would cancel the *dekate*, and Prusias would withdraw from the lands he had seized, restoring all goods and slaves which he had taken. General agreement followed, though Kavaros still presumably maintained his claim to a large ransom. It seems unlikely he got much of it, and a few years later his kingdom collapsed after a rebellion by its Thracian subjects. This was presumably a result of Kavaros' failure to pay out subsidies to his followers.[4] Byzantion and Prusias returned to their own guarded enmity. Since many of the slaves or serfs captured by Prusias were Bithynians, it seems unlikely that they were returned, but then compliance with agreed peace terms was always unlikely in this period.

One of the reasons for the collapse of the Tylis kingdom may well have been the defection of some of its Galatian population. In 217 BC, the year after the end of the Rhodian-Bithynian-Byzantine War, a Galatian tribe, the Aigosages, appeared at the Hellespont and was hired by Attalos as mercenaries, and these may have been former subjects of Kavaros; this is only speculation, but it is difficult to see where else they had come from. After they had campaigned for him along the Aiolian coast, Attalos decided that they were too unruly to be employed any longer. He settled them in the Troad somewhere, probably not far from Ilion, but their unruliness provoked the Alexandrians, whose militia drove them away. If they could be defeated and driven off by the amateur soldiers of a single city, they were not a serious problem for anyone else, but they were certainly a nuisance. Prusias intercepted them, defeated and massacred their soldiers, and sold off any survivors into slavery.[5]

The collapse of the Tylis kingdom is attributed to the revolt of its Thracian subjects, and if the Aigosages had defected, this would certainly have encouraged the revolt, and would have reduced the Galatians' authority over their unwilling subjects. But this did mean that the Thracian region was even more disturbed. Meanwhile in Asia Minor, Antiochos III, the Seleukid king, had decided to remove his cousin Akhaios, and in a campaign out of Syria he drove him into Sardis by 214 BC, besieging him there; the city and Akhaios were captured in 212 BC, and Akhaios was executed.[6] Antiochos then left Zeuxis in charge in Asia Minor and embarked on a long campaign into the eastern territories. In his absence, little changed in the Straits region which was a clear indication that power now lay squarely with the Seleukid king.

The abstention of the Great Powers – the Seleukids, the Ptolemies, and Macedon – from the Rhodian-Byzantine War in the Straits is unusual. The Straits region was an area in which all the powers would normally be interested, thanks to its important role in international trade. Antiochos III had perhaps a good excuse for abstaining, since he was beset by his own crises at the time, and his kingdom no longer stretched further west of the Taurus Mountains until after 216 BC, but both Ptolemy IV and Philip V of Macedon were, in effect, close by and could be involved had they chosen. But both were, like Antiochos, hard pressed in crises nearer home.

Ptolemy IV was engulfed in a court crisis, which involved the murders of several of his siblings, and of his mother. In such circumstances he could not take much interest in distant Aegean affairs; in addition, he faced an attack by Antiochos III on his possessions in Syria from 219 BC onwards (which also helps explain Antiochos' lack of concern in the Aegean). Philip V was concerned to extend his power into Greece, and was also watching the developing crisis in Italy (which became the Second Punic War); in 219 BC a Roman army had campaigned close to his western border in Illyria, an area Macedonian kings had long been interested in.

The Byzantine War therefore involved local powers only – Bithynia, Byzantion, Rhodes, with several other cities equally concerned. Attalos failed to get involved, pinned down by the threat of Akhaios; Akhaios himself was only concerned to extract his father from Ptolemaic imprisonment, and clearly he used Rhodes' involvement to achieve that, then went no further; other Aegean states simply followed Rhodes' lead.

This political isolation of the region was not merely a temporary phenomenon, but remained a condition in the area for over a decade after the end of the war. All the Great Powers remained fixated on their own problems until 204 BC or 203 BC, leaving the cities and kingdoms in the Straits to themselves.

When the Rhodian-Byzantine War ended, Akhaios suddenly turned to campaign in Pisidia and Pamphylia. This released Attalos from his confinement in Pergamon and allowed him to reclaim some of the lands he had been deprived of by Akhaios in the previous years. This was when he hired the Aigosages as reinforcements and campaigned to recall the cities of the Ionian coast to his allegiance. The second part of his expedition was to have been into Mysia, but he could not control the Aigosages. He had got as far as the valley of the Granikos, where he captured two posts, Didymoteiche and Karseai, held by Akhaios' men.[7] It seems then that he got rid of the Aigosages by planting them in a settlement in the Troad, and moved along the Troadic coast renewing friendly relations, broken by the intrusion of Akhaios, with Lampsakos, Ilion, and Alexandria Troas. By this time Akhaios was emerging from his own campaign, and Attalos, weakened by the loss of the Aigosages, but strengthened by the new and renewed allegiances of the cities he had visited or taken, returned to – or scuttled back to – Pergamon.

The true extent of his authority in the Troad and in that part of Mysia where he had campaigned is not clear, but it was not permanent. He was assailed once more by Akhaios, but the war was inconclusive and so fairly long. This did mean, however, that the cities were left to their own devices, which explains why it was a citizen militia of Alexandria Troas which drove away the Aigosages. They evidently retreated eastwards into the Mysian no-man's-land, where they were intercepted by Prusias.[8] In doing so Prusias was, of course, equally demonstrating his intent on expanding into Mysia when he had the chance. His brief control of the Byzantine territory in Asia in 219–218 BC had been a similar signal, but he was only able to venture south of his border, but still near to Nikomedia, because the stronger powers, Attalos and Akhaios, were mutually engaged – that is, absent. And if Alexandria Troas was able, or compelled, to act on its own against the Aigosages, so could other cities in the Straits region act against their own enemies. It seems likely, for example, that the failing strength of the Ptolemaic navy in the Aegean would have enabled Alexandria to recover Larisa from Ptolemaic control in the confusion of the Aigosages' presence, Attalos' wanderings, and Ptolemaic preoccupation. (That city's period under such control can only be dated to the reign of Ptolemy III (243–222 BC); it is also quite possible that the town was taken by Antiochos III later, when he in turn campaigned in the area.)

One connection of the Attalid family with the Straits region was strengthened by Attalos I. He married a lady, Apollonis, from Kyzikos.[9] His predecessor Philetairos had begun the friendly relationship with the city in the 270s BC, and this was a strong reinforcement for it. Apollonis was one of the more notable royal women of the period and was widely admired for her beauty and her character. She married Attalos in about 220 BC or a little before. For once a royal marriage also meant a political friendship, though one might suspect that the physical separation of king and city helped this political relationship to continue and flourish.

The one intrusion of the Great Powers into the Straits area between 212 BC and 204 BC was a brief conflict between Prusias and Attalos; neither of these, of course, could be counted as a Great Power, but both were allied to states which were, and they had no compunction about dragging them into their greater wars. Attalos involved himself in the war in Greece between Philip of Macedon and the Roman Republic (the Second Romano-Macedonian War), taking the Roman side. Philip activated his friendly relationship with Prusias – the Bithynian king had married Philip's daughter, Apama – and Prusias was happy enough to attack Attalid territory. Attalos had moved across to Greece, and had taken part in the capture of Oreus in Euboeia, but while he was gloating over his victory and shaking down the defeated citizens of Oreus, Philip arrived by surprise with an army and drove him and his forces out in disorder. At about the same time Attalos heard that Prusias was invading Mysia, and he took this as the best excuse yet to return to Pergamon, leaving Philip and Rome fight it out.[10] The war between the two kings is otherwise unknown, and even the peace which was made in the end is only assumed to have been part of the settlement arrived at in Greece in 205 BC.[11] But it was one more item in the growing animosity between the two kings and their kingdoms, an animosity which, given their similar ambitions for expansion, was as inevitable as anything in international politics at the time. Another war between them was only waiting for an opportunity to begin.

The temporary oblivion of the Straits area from greater affairs ended with an invasion in 202 BC in which several cities were captured and destroyed. The trigger for the business was the death in 204 BC of Ptolemy IV. This was the start of another internal court *coup* at Alexandria by those who had conducted the earlier one in 221 BC; the dead king's widow was murdered, and their child-successor fell into the hands of Agathokles, as regent, and his disreputable family. A nationalist Egyptian rebellion in the south of Egypt which had begun in 207 BC, developed new strength, and the war lasted twenty years.[12]

Ptolemy IV's death cancelled any previous international agreements made in his name. In particular, this referred to the peace made with Antiochos III at the end of the previous Syrian war, the Fourth, in 217 BC. Since then, Ptolemy IV had sunk into a lethargy of self-indulgence, leaving affairs to his ministers, while Antiochos first campaigned into Asia Minor to eliminate Akhaios, then made a spectacular campaign as far as the borders of India to enforce his authority throughout Iran and Baktria. When Ptolemy IV died, Antiochos was again in Asia Minor attending to numerous details, and steadily expanding his authority over the borderlands, pressing on his neighbours and enemies, including Ptolemy, whose authority in the borderlands had faded in the latter part of his reign.[13]

Most of Antiochos' attention was directed at Karia, where a regular campaign of conquest was undertaken. He did not, at this time, reach into the Straits area. He was friendly with Attalos, for they had been allies against Akhaios, and he carefully kept clear of Attalid territory on his visits to Asia Minor. It is noticeable that at Ilion he was not honoured as his dynastic predecessors had been – Seleukos I, Antiochos I and II, and Antiochos Hierax – and had he visited the city some sort of commemoration could be expected. (The memory of Hierax' extensive work in the Troad may have left Antiochos III jealous and unhappy.) He was busy enough in the two years or less he spent in the country, on this occasion, and then he was called away to the Egyptian crisis.

An envoy arrived from the regency government of the infant Ptolemy V. The envoy, Pelops, had been sent by the regent Agathokles, to protest at Antiochos' encroachments in Asia Minor, and to request that Antiochos continue to observe the conditions laid out in the peace treaty of 217 BC. These were, essentially, that peace should obtain between the two kingdoms – the complaint about his Asia Minor encroachments was all part of that overall request. It had been the security afforded by this agreement which had allowed Antiochos to go off on the long campaign in the east and to busy himself in Asia Minor during the previous ten and more years, but the death of one of the parties to such an agreement (Ptolemy IV in 204 BC) rendered the continuation of these terms problematic, and it is evident that Antiochos was in two minds about it: he had not attacked the Ptolemaic lands in Egypt or Syria during 204–202 BC, but he was certainly moving against them in Asia Minor. Before long, Antiochos knew that a further envoy, Ptolemaios son of Sosibios, had gone to Philip V of Macedon asking for help in case Antiochos did attack the Ptolemaic lands – and another man was supposed to go to Rome, but did not get beyond Greece.[14]

Then during 203 BC there was a further *coup* in Alexandria, Agathokles was driven from power, and he and his family were murdered in a brutal episode of mob rule. The new regent was a soldier called Tlepolemos, who soon began to exercise dictatorial powers, but also to wallow in the sort of luxurious debauchery which had given the regime of Ptolemy IV a bad name.[15] It was obvious to all who watched that the central government of the Ptolemaic Empire was unstable and was weakening fast.

There is no evidence that Antiochos had decided anything in this matter in the year since Ptolemy IV died, though it may be taken as certain that he had considered it and discussed it with his council. It may have been information reaching Alexandria that these discussions had been taking place which prompted Pelops' mission, which was not sent for some time after the king's death. The envoy sent to Philip V was clearly an attempt to keep the two potential enemies divided, for their dynasties had managed to stay at peace with each other, whereas both had frequently fought Ptolemaic Egypt. In fact, the reminder of Egypt's vulnerability was heightened with the overthrow of Agathokles, and this made it clear that the Ptolemaic state, particularly in its more distant possessions, had become very vulnerable. The possibilities for conquests now clearly rose for both kings. Which of them first suggested joint action to partition the Ptolemaic empire is not known, but it seems that an envoy to Philip went from Antiochos; the agreement, listing the parts of the empire each would seek to acquire, was quickly reached.

Philip would operate against the Ptolemaic lands in Europe, and Antiochos would therefore be able to concentrate on the real prize for him, which was Ptolemaic Syria. The planned division therefore gave Syria to Antiochos and the European and Aegean cities and islands, and Cyrenaica, to Philip. All of these had long been of interest to the previous kings or their families, and none of them are at all surprising.[16]

It took Antiochos almost three years to conquer Syria, and in that time Philip operated in the Aegean and the Straits. He found it as difficult as Antiochos to reach a victorious conclusion, in part because of the absence of any authority in Egypt which could make peace, while his task was far more complicated and his resources less. His earlier aggressions had ringed his kingdom with enemies, in particular Rome and the Aitolian League; Rhodes was involved in a war in Crete which Philip had engineered, and an agent of his had attempted to burn Rhodes' main shipbuilding dockyard. Whatever actions Philip took, therefore, would almost inevitably anger someone almost at once. He could rely on Prusias of Bithynia, but Attalos of Pergamon, though a subordinate ally of Antiochos, was also Philip's enemy, and since Antiochos was busy in Syria, Attalos would be free to act on his own account. To Philip, despite these likely antagonists, the opportunity and the prize were too enticing to forego.

At some point in the recent past the Aitolian League – another of Philip's enemies – had allied with three cities in the Straits area, Lysimacheia, Chalkedon, and Kios. This was presumably part of their reaction to the earlier war in which Prusias and Attalos had been involved. Chalkedon had been threatened earlier by Prusias, and Lysimacheia had been part of Ptolemy's territories since the 240s. Aitolia had long been friendly with Ptolemy, and it may be that its association with Lysimacheia in particular – it installed an Aitolian *strategos* in the city – had come about as a result of Philip's all too open ambitions. Whatever the origin of this Aitolian connection, it meant that he regarded all three cities as enemies. The Aitolian League was itself in no condition to defend the cities and had no wish to become involved in this distant war, while Philip had a useful fleet which allowed him to campaign in the Propontis. For him they were easily collected prizes which had some distant Ptolemaic connection but, more immediately, in taking them he would damage Aitolia.

Using his fleet, Philip compelled Lysimacheia to accept his alliance in place of that of Aitolia and installed a Macedonian commander and garrison in the city in place of the Aitolian *strategos*. He sailed on to Chalkedon and imposed the same conditions, apparently without any fighting. But Chalkedon had been an old ambition of the Bithynians, and Prusias would hardly take kindly to seeing his father-in-law seizing it. So together Philip and Prusias attacked Kios, another Aitolian ally, captured, sacked, and pillaged it, and sold the population into slavery. Across the Propontis Philip imposed his alliance on Perinthos, which had an alliance agreement with Byzantion. The desolate site of Kios was annexed by Prusias, but the other captures, with their Macedonian commanders and garrisons, were in effect annexed to the Macedonian kingdom.[17]

During the siege of Kios a delegation arrived from Rhodes and other Aegean cities, with a request that the city be spared. Philip put them off, and sent an envoy back to Rhodes with them, but then went ahead and destroyed Kios anyway (a result not at all pleasing to Prusias, as it happened, who would have much preferred to acquire a functioning city, though he did not refuse to accept the empty site). Philip went on to attack Myrleia in the same way, and Prusias acquired that site also. Rhodes, hearing the news of the fate of Kios, declared war.[18]

All this activity by Philip in the Straits area was not really a part of the partition agreement with Antiochos, and the only Ptolemaic connection was the tenuous link with Lysimacheia. Philip was in fact being very careful to avoid a clear break with the Ptolemaic government. His next move included seizing Samos, a Ptolemaic naval base, but all he did was to beat down local resistance, and then use the resources of the naval base to repair and maintain his fleet. He may therefore have been attempting to avoid open war with the Ptolemaic regime, but he had successfully angered enough states in the region to conjure up a serious war and many enemies. Perhaps the lack of reaction at Samos convinced him of Ptolemaic weakness and supineness – though the Ptolemaic government was fighting hard in Syria – but he then went on to take the city of Miletos, which had been Ptolemy's, and which he treated as an annexed place, just like Lysimacheia and the rest. By this time, an anti-Macedonian coalition had formed, and Philip's fleet found it had to fight a battle against the Rhodian and allied fleet nearby. Philip's fleet won the fight, though a draw might be a more accurate description of the result, but this was then followed by a declaration of war by Attalos of Pergamon, to Philip's surprise. Rhodes' allies now also included Byzantion and Kyzikos, and Kos joined as well. But to have the two strongest cities in the Propontis at war with him did not bode well for his new possessions in that region.[19]

Attalos' declaration of war provoked Philip into a raid through parts of Ionia and against Pergamon itself, where his campaigning reputation convinced the inhabitants to gather in their harvest and hide behind their city walls.[20] He began to run short of supplies, and the loot was fairly thin also. He was able to get some assistance from Antiochos' viceroy in Asia Minor, Zeuxis, but not enough to keep him going for long.[21] He tried to attack Chios, and had to fight another naval battle, which he lost with heavy casualties.[22] He went on to campaign in Karia and ended up trapped for the winter of 201/200 BC in the small town of Bargylia.[23]

All this was not gaining him much, and nothing he could count on as permanent. It would clearly have been better had he confined his aggressions to Ptolemy's territories alone. Any conquered community had to be held down by the threat of force, and the number of his enemies steadily grew. He escaped from Bargylia in the spring and returned to Macedon. But then he picked a quarrel with Athens, which declared war, and suffered the consequent ravaging of Attika in reply. This was witnessed by a Roman commission of enquiry, which came to understand the wide revulsion he had evoked, and the wide ambitions his activities implied. Rome had not forgotten the unsuccessful early war against Philip, and its resumed interest was followed by a series of appeals to that city from Rhodes, Attalos, Athens, Egypt, and others, all seeking help against him.[24]

As it happened this suited Rome well enough, where the failure to win the previous war against Philip continued to rankle, and the prospect of Philip expanding his kingdom and his military resources provoked fear and trembling. A series of demands was dispatched to him from Rome, which Philip ignored, because they seemed irrelevant and made no sense in the context.[25] He set out on a campaign in Thrace and captured the city of Ainos (betrayed to him by the Ptolemaic governor) and Maroneia (taken by storm). He campaigned through southern Thrace and captured several towns, and on to the Chersonese to seize more, to add to Lysimacheia. Then he crossed the Hellespont and laid siege to Abydos.[26]

Like Kios and Perinthos, Abydos was an independent city, but in this case, its geographical position was crucial. Philip had already taken Sestos, its twin across the Hellespont, and control of Abydos as well would gain him, with his fleet, control over the waterway. Holding Chalkedon and Perinthos, and allied with Prusias of Bithynia, he already dominated the Propontis, and held part of the Bosporos exit. All this was clearly too much for the Aegean cities, who would be subject to his blackmail if he won. Abydos was sent help from Kyzikos and Rhodes, having set the example itself by a determined resistance to Philip's attacks.[27] The people twice attempted to surrender, however, but Philip imposed such harsh terms that they felt they had to fight on and, when conquest was inevitable, they committed mass suicide rather than accept any part of his authority and Philip cynically allowed them to get on with it, since it would mean he gained the city. But it was all ashes in Philip's mouth, for, even as he was victorious, he was visited by a Roman envoy who delivered a new declaration of war. This time, Philip paid full attention.[28]

Pausing only to install a commander and garrison in the ruins of Abydos, which amounted to annexation, Philip returned to Macedon.[29] All through the war which followed he left the cities he had conquered under occupation, with the exception of Lysimacheia, from which his garrison was withdrawn at the end of 199 BC.[30] When peace terms were discussed late in 198 BC in Lokris, the demands of the allies included that Philip leave Perinthos, Sestos, Abydos and 'all commercial depots and harbours in Asia', showing that these were still under his control. Some of the other demands were purposefully vague, but the Aitolians wanted their former league members to be returned, and in discussion this appears to have included Lysimacheia, which Philip insisted he no longer controlled.[31] Next year, after his final defeat, Philip's agreement to the peace included his abandoning the four places mentioned, so he had held onto them all through the war. His withdrawal from Lysimacheia had left that city defenceless, while his campaign through Thrace had roused the Thracians; the Chersonese was invaded in 198 BC by a Thracian group, the year after his withdrawal, and the city was sacked and depopulated, as he pointed out at the Lokris conference.[32] When Philip's forces withdrew, his record in the Straits therefore was four destroyed cities, three by his own forces, and one by his enemies (as well as others which had suffered in various ways in his campaigns).

The war ended in 197 BC, effectively in June with Philip's defeat at the battle of Kynoskephalai. In Syria, Antiochos had completed his conquest of Ptolemaic Syria the year before, and spent the next year preparing for the next stage of his annexation of the Ptolemaic Empire. For this he needed a fleet, which was not something the Seleukids had much bothered with before, but which he built in the next year, or recruited from the Phoenician cities he had acquired. He moved westwards, beginning shortly after Philip's defeat, the timing probably not by coincidence. The fleet moved along the coast of southern Asia Minor, and his army marched by the old Royal Road through central Asia Minor, heading for Sardis. There was no serious opposition, except by a Rhodian fleet, which was easily bluffed into allowing passage, and a few places which resisted, principally Korakesion in Pamphylia, but by using the fleet and leapfrogging the cities of the coast, Antiochos was able to avoid other fighting. By early 196 BC, he had reoccupied all the south Asian coastal cities, except those subject to Rhodes, had bypassed Rhodes island and city and was settled at Ephesos.[33]

He did not stop there but moved on at once to the Hellespont. He landed in and occupied the Chersonese, decreed the restoration of Lysimacheia and sent out for the scattered citizens (including those who had been enslaved) to return, and then moved on to campaign in Thrace.[34] In September, he returned to Lysimacheia to meet a squad of Roman senators who were to negotiate a settlement in the wake of the peace made with Philip. The Romans claimed a supervision and protectorate over Greece and had already warned Antiochos to leave free cities free, specifying in particular Alexandria Troas, Lampsakos, and Smyrna.[35] But all three were former Seleukid cities, and the whole rationale of Antiochos' expedition was to restore to the Seleukid empire all those territories it had once ruled or claimed. These included the cities mentioned, the Chersonese, Mysia, the Troad, and Thrace, as well as the former Ptolemaic Syria and the cities of the south Asian coast. All these, except the cities specified by Rome, had been reacquired or conquered in the last four years. (He might also claim Macedon, from Seleukos I's defeat of Lysimachos, but did not actually do so; he might have done so later if matters had turned out differently.)

The restoration of Lysimacheia, where the conference was being held, was a clear sign to the Romans that they were dealing with a very different political figure than Philip and his destructiveness. Another traditional aspect of Seleukid dynastic policy was to encourage the founding and development of cities everywhere in their empire. The conference, from the Roman point of view, was a failure but for Antiochos it was a success. The problem was that, to the Romans, this was only the first round of a conflict; to Antiochos, the issue had been settled. But he did leave alone the three cities which were in dispute, though he pressed Lampsakos briefly to submit, offering the city retention of the usual status of autonomy; but he did not insist.[36]

Antiochos campaigned three times in Thrace between 192 BC and 196 BC, finding the accomplishment of control in the country just as difficult to achieve as every other invader. Exactly where he reached to is not recorded, but in 196 BC one of the Roman commissioners tried to reach him by landing at Selymbria, which implies that he was well inland and to the north.[37] But by 192 BC it seems he had reduced the area mainly to obedience; he had not intruded on the Macedonian lands, but both Philip and the Romans were made nervous by his activities in 'Europe' as the Romans defined it. Philip had been forced to disband most of his forces by the peace treaty with Rome, and so his kingdom was clearly vulnerable, and Antiochos could put forward a claim to Macedon almost as strong as to Thrace. The cities of the Propontis coast were left alone, though he took Byzantion into some sort of protection, but again without exerting any serious pressure on the city. Byzantion, seeing the Thracians subdued for the most part, and the ruler of Asia from the Hellespont to India looming over it, no doubt felt it had little or no choice.[38]

When he had been campaigning in Thrace, he had also been conducting a long-range negotiation with Rome, in effect to decide on the division of the Hellenistic world between them. It is a catalogue of misunderstandings, of which the worst was Antiochos' belief that the Roman military withdrawal from Greece in 194 BC was also a political withdrawal – which is what it would have been in the east. (Philip's withdrawal of his garrison from Lysimacheia had been both a military retreat and a freeing of the city from his political control; he did not object when Antiochos took over the city.) The Romans were also guilty of misunderstanding Antiochos' overall restoration purpose, though his policy was made clear to them in the negotiations. They had this odd belief that once they had a relationship with a community, that community was part of their empire. This got them involved in many wars, often to their advantage, but it was a concept alien to Hellenistic political practices. So when Antiochos moved into Greece in 192 BC, believing he could establish his protection there as well as elsewhere, the Romans were outraged, or at least claimed to be, and declared war.[39]

The subsequent fighting scarcely affected the Straits region. The Roman army approached along the Thracian coast, taking control of Ainos and Maroneia and the Chersonese and crossing to Abydos.[40]

The commanders visited Ilion to sacrifice; the Roman myth of a Trojan origin could only be burnished by its armies camping in the Troad.[41]

There seems to have been enough of Abydos left after Philip's attentions to accommodate at least some of the Romans, but the army partly camped at Ilion, and then soon moved south to fight the Seleukid forces. The war went on in various ways until 189 BC, when the consul, Cn. Manlius Vulso, having campaigned into Galatia, extracted plenty of loot from the Seleukid cities, and presided at the conference at Apameia Kelainai which settled affairs, at least for the moment, then returned westwards with his army, only to be ambushed by Thracians on the march along the Thracian coast.[42] In all this none of the cities were seriously involved. The Romans passed through the Troad and the Chersonese, Scipio Africanus made an offering at the temple at Ilion, but the rest of the Straits were untouched.

The result of this warfare was the expulsion of Macedonian power from Thrace and the Propontis, and the expulsion of Seleukid power from all Asia Minor. The treaty negotiated at Apameia assigned to King Eumenes II of Pergamon the Troad, the Chersonese, Hellespontine

Phrygia, and 'that part of Mysia Prusias has taken from Eumenes'.[43] When that happened is not known, but it was not referred to in the settlement of Greece in 196 BC, when Prusias' possession of Kios was called into question. So presumably Prusias had helped himself to the land in question during the war of Rome and Antiochos. There is no suggestion that he gave up Kios, and his other encroachments in Mysia were equally not something he would willingly surrender. It seems probable he kept them. The area, of course, was that part of the borderland which had been in dispute between the Bithynians, the Attalids, the Seleukids, and the cities since the emergence of the Bithynian kingdom and the death of Lysimachos. Whether Prusias had really encroached on Attalid territory is not known. But it seems unlikely that any of the Attalid kings had ever established any more control in the area than any other potentate. One might suppose that this was an attempt by Eumenes II to get control of the land by the use of the treaty rather than making any serious effort himself.

The cities were declared free, and Alexandria Troas and Lampsakos celebrated with issues of coins. Perinthos and Byzantion were freed of Macedonian and Seleukid attentions, but Thrace was abandoned by all the powers. On the Asian side of the Straits, Kyzikos had not been involved since involving itself in the siege of Abydos; Prusias probably retained his section of Mysia; the condition of Chalkedon is unknown. (The city had not been mentioned in any of the peace negotiations involving Philip, where Abydos and Perinthos were demanded to be freed; the city may have been evacuated by Philip at the same time as he brought his garrison out of Lysimacheia, and like Lysimacheia it was technically an ally of Philip, not a conquest.) West of Kyzikos, at some point Parion seized some territory from Priapos, apparently by licence from Attalos or Eumenes. It was not compelled to give it back and, in a fit of exuberance, built the largest altar in Asia and advertised it on the city's coins.[44] Dardanos was declared free, probably from Seleukid control, but in doing this the treaty also blocked any Attalid takeover. The synoecism of Ilion was extended to include Rhoeteon and Gergitha. So the Troad now was largely partitioned between Alexandria and Ilion, though the cities of the south coast, the interior (that is Kebren and Skepsis), and along the coast eastwards, including Abydos and Lampsakos, were independent. By declaring the cities free and in several cases naming them so specifically, the kings were deliberately being excluded, not something they wholly appreciated.[45]

The expansion of the Attalid kingdom into Hellespontine Phrygia, the Troad, and across the Hellespont into the Chersonese and nearby parts of Thrace seemed to establish that kingdom in much the same dominating position as earlier powers, from Antigonos to Antiochos III. But this was soon seen not to be the case. By claiming part of Mysia from Prusias of Bithynia, Eumenes II had converted his enmity to the Attalids into a confirmed enemy, and in less than a year a war had broken out between the two kings.

The war was initiated by Prusias, the aggrieved party, and continued for four years (187–183 BC).[46] He had given refuge to Hannibal, whom the Romans had forced to leave Carthage, but this does not seem to have given the king any serious military advantage. Eumenes was hampered by a simultaneous war with some of the Galatians in central Asia Minor, while Prusias had the opportunity to expand eastwards, annexing the city of Kieros in 184/183 BC, which he refounded as Prusias-ad-Hypnios.[47] This guarded his eastern border against the unorganised Paphlagonians and Herakleia Pontike.

In the same time he refounded Kios, naming it Prusias-by-the-Sea, and Myrleia, which was renamed Apameia (after his wife).[48] The Bithynian kings, one after another, were all enthusiastic hellenisers, and re-founding these two destroyed Greek cities was a very public way of demonstrating that. It is said that Hannibal Barka of Carthage was involved in the re-founding of Prousa, which might explain why he was not involved in the fighting, and this would therefore date the founding to the 180s BC, the time of the Attalid War.[49] The cities, of course, like Kieros/Prusias, were also planted with strategic care. They acted as guards along with Nikomedia (formerly Astakos) along his southern border, and their *chorai* extended into Hellespontine Phrygia. No serious attempt was ever made to dispossess Prusias of these city-sites, if this was the territory referred to in the Apameia judgment, and the failure to do so was an effective recognition of the legitimacy of his possession.

This series of city foundings expanded the Bithynian territory eastwards (Prusias-ad-Hypios) and to the south. The three cities planted in the Mysian borderland were quite clearly intended to expand the kingdom into this disputed territory. One advance had already secured

Nikaia (though the date of its annexation is not known; a suggestion of c.280 BC is based on a very flimsy piece of evidence) which would bring the Bithynian boundary as far as the Iznik Golu and the river connecting that lake to the sea. The city's territory stretched east to the Sangarios River, so the land between the two gulfs was now shared between Bithynia and Byzantion. The three cities south of the Gulf and the lake pushed the Bithynian boundary to the northern slopes of Mount Olympos, a well-chosen defensive line. By annexing the territory from Nikomedia to Prousa and Mount Olympos, the Bithynian kings had doubled their territory; by securing Kieros (Prusias-ad-Hypios), it was extended still further.

The war was brought to an end by the (somewhat tardy) intervention of Rome in the person of T. Quinctius Flamininus, in 183. This is presented, in Livy, as actually a mission to persuade Prusias to surrender Hannibal (though he committed suicide), but this was no more than Livy's Rome fixation. No doubt in Asia, it was the bringing of peace between the kings which was the crucial event that was recalled.[50]

There followed almost at once a new Asian war, in which a coalition including Prusias and Eumenes (who thus switched from war to alliance in a moment – very Orwellian) sought to contain Pharnakes of Pontos. In the peace treaty which ended this war in 179 BC, a long series of other kingdoms and cities were included, some of which were actually neutral, including Kyzikos. One region from which Pharnakes was expelled was Paphlagonia, and Prusias was awarded the city of Teion, beyond Herakleia Pontike on the Black Sea coast. The date of the founding of Kieros as Prusias-ad-Hypios was 184/183 BC, which is about the beginning of the Pontic war, and may best be seen as another defensive measure taken by Prusias.[51]

One of the Attalid kings, probably Eumenes II, planted a new but small city on the north Propontis coast. The name was Panion, and the exact reason for founding it is not known, but fairly early in the Attalid expansion seems most probable. Attalos II fought and defeated the king of the Caeni, a Thracian tribe, though the date is not known. The new colony was placed towards the boundary of Perinthos, which was still closely linked with Byzantion in an alliance, and so the new city may have been intended to block any further expansion of the territory of this civic alliance westwards, as well and keeping a watch on the Thracians; it was in a good position from which to attack if a Thracian raid was projected on the Chersonese.[52] It means that the north coast of the Propontis was divided between the Attalids, in control from the Chersonese as far as Panion, with the Byzantine alliance from there to the Bosporos.

The Romans, for the third time, made war on Macedon, beginning in 172 BC, having deliberately prepared and intrigued to bring the war about for several years beforehand. As usual, the war spilled over to involve those who had no real interest in the conflict. The arrogance of the Republic was now such that all neutrals were regarded with suspicion, and any state which offered to intervene, or attempted to broker a peace, was taken to be hostile. The most obvious victim of this attitude was Rhodes, but others took note, and deliberately involved themselves on the Roman side, though often unenthusiastically.

Byzantion had made the inadvertent mistake of accepting assistance from King Perseus of Macedon in fighting against Thracian raids (well before the outbreak of this Romano-Macedonian War), in this supposedly acting, according to Rome, against a treaty agreed twenty years before with the Romans.[53] It did not help that Perseus clearly regarded Byzantion as a friend during his fruitless negotiations aiming to avoid a war – fruitless because Rome was impervious to any argument which might prevent war; what was required was immediate and unquestioning support. Kyzikos, Ilion, Chalkedon and Byzantion were all in receipt of gifts from the Seleukid king Antiochos IV, a ruler regarded with some suspicion at Rome, as by this time were all kings.[54]

The Straits area managed to keep clear of the Macedonian War almost entirely, and Eumenes proved to be so necessary for the Roman war effort that he was able to exert some influence over the Roman commanders, most of whom were either incompetent or greedy for booty, or both, as well as lacking in honour. But the end result, after the final conquest of the Macedonian kingdom, was another display of Roman mistrust directed at the Attalid kingdom. Sensing Roman antagonism, Prusias II of Bithynia, who had taken a small part in support of Eumenes during the war, joined with some like-minded local enemies of Eumenes to levy accusations against him. But these were either so vague, or so inaccurate, that even the Senate refused to believe them; yet the hostility remained.

This helped to incite Prusias to launch a new attack on the Attalid kingdom. This was the Second Bithynian-Attalid war, beginning in

156 BC. Until then, Rome had frequently demonstrated its support for the Attalid kings, sometimes to the extent of ensuring their victory in a war. By the 150s BC that policy had changed, probably because the Attalids seemed to have expanded their power more than Rome wished. Prusias II attempted to take advantage of what seemed to be Attalid political isolation. His attack took Attalos II by surprise, and Prusias' army had a splendid time ravaging and looting the countryside between Bithynia and the Attalid homeland, including besieging Pergamon for a time. That is, he overran the old borderland in Hellespontine Phrygia and Mysia. Rome was dilatory at intervening, and not inclined to take any effective measures. But Prusias went too far when he attempted to kidnap Attalos and attacked him while he was with a group of Roman commissioners. This turned them, and Rome, against the Bithynians. By this time, 154 BC, Attalos had gathered together a serious army, with which he invaded Bithynia, while his navy took control of the Propontis. He had also gathered a group of allies who assisted him with troops and ships, and these included Kyzikos. The Roman commissioners visited those who had joined Prusias and insisted (or persuaded) them to abandon him. Byzantion is named as one of these, possibly because it felt threatened by the Attalid presence in Thrace. 'The country near the Hellespont' is also listed as a Bithynian ally; this must mean cities on the Asian side, presumably Ilion and Alexandria Troas at least, since the European side was Attalid territory. How much the cities helped is not clear. They were raided by Attalos' allied fleet, listed by Polybios as five Rhodian, twenty Kyzikene, and twenty-seven Attalid ships, with other ships from minor allies making up the fleet of eighty. A Roman intervention, more forceful and therefore effective than before, finally persuaded Prusias to withdraw and agree to terms.[55]

Another Macedonian crisis emerged in 149–148 BC, when a man, a soldier, Andriskos, claiming to be a son of King Perseus, invaded the republics in Macedon which the Romans had set up in place of the united kingdom. Their governments collapsed, and he made himself king as 'Philip VI'. This happened at a time when Rome had begun a new war with the aim of destroying Carthage, and it became mixed in with another crisis in Greece. Andriskos had received help from a variety of people and cities who disliked the Roman control of Macedon – exiled Macedonians in the Attalid kingdom, including a few members of Perseus' court and army, and one lady who had been the mistress of Perseus and who had married into the Attalid family. She kitted Andriskos out in royal robes and a diadem. More practical support came from the Thracian king Teres, who had married a daughter of Philip V, and who provided Andriskos with an armed force. He failed in his first attack, but once inside the kingdom, he was able to defeat a Roman force – Macedon was full of trained soldiers no doubt more than pleased to defeat a Roman army. A second and larger Roman army came to defeat him, and he died in the pursuit. He had received support from at least two Thracian kings; these were always interested in raiding richer territory. Teres' relationship to Philip V (his wife was therefore Andriskos' 'sister') was clearly important to him. Andriskos was also welcomed at Byzantion, which had been assisted years earlier by Teres at Philip's behest. Andriskos had clearly struck an international network which was anti-Roman, and which extended into the royal palace of the Attalid kingdom.[56]

It is noticeable that of all those who assisted Andriskos, only Byzantion, the most vulnerable, is said to have been the recipient of Roman displeasure,[57] but that was not the first time – it had happened earlier when Teres had helped the city against other Thracians. What form this displeasure took is not recorded, but soon afterwards Rome and Byzantion came to an agreement and alliance – unless the Roman alliance was the punishment, for such an alliance involved a considerable loss of autonomy by the city. The exact date is not known, nor the terms, though alliance is the term used. Without Philip at its centre, the anti-Roman network was clearly of little use.

Given this network, a poisonous inheritance of Philip V lying in wait for the Romans, one might expect Prusias II, the son of Apama, Philip's sister, to be roped in to join. Prusias, however, had raised up his own internal enemies. He was unpopular with his people, and his conduct of external affairs, as Attalos could attest, was erratic; he had alienated both his son and his senior minister. These two went to Rome on a diplomatic mission, discovered their mutual discontent, and conspired to murder the king. This happened in 149 BC, Andriskos' year of achievement, and the conspirators were supported by an expedition led by Attalos II; the heir, Nikomedes II, became king, and he and Attalos remained at peace – but he was not in a position (neither was Attalos) to involve himself in the Macedonian crisis.[58]

Chapter 10

Into the Roman Empire (146–30 BC)

The end of the Attalid dynasty, with the untimely death of Attalos III in 133, brought Rome finally into Asia as a physical presence rather than as an interfering busybody. It was only thirteen years since the Roman eastern frontier had moved from the Adriatic Sea into the eastern Balkans with the annexation of Macedon and Greece. Now it advanced into the middle of Asia Minor. The agency was the will of the last Attalid king, who left his kingdom to 'the Roman people'. This was not to the liking of the anti-Roman element in the population, who supported the ambition of Aristonikos, an illegitimate son of Eumenes II, to make himself king. After a delay, the bequest was accepted in Rome, but for Roman reasons. War resulted and lasted until 129 BC, and it spilled over, as wars tended to, into the territory of Pergamon's neighbours. At one point, for example, Aristonikos laid siege to Kyzikos. The city, as it usually did, had quickly identified the most powerful element in crisis, Rome, and had cleaved to it for protection. The city was rescued by Nikomedes of Bithynia with an army, at Rome's request.[1]

The Attalid kingdom, once conquered, was divided up. This may well have been in conflict with the terms of the will, but Attalos had already separated out the Greek cities in confirming their independence, and, after all, this was a Roman decision, and Rome always interpreted matters in foreign affairs to its own advantage, legal elements notwithstanding. The richest area became the Roman province of Asia; other peripheral areas went to neighbours, including Nikomedes II, who, however, found that Mithradates V of Pontos had been allocated the same territory – a repetition, in a way, of the decision to award Eumenes II territory supposedly occupied already by Prusias II at the time of the Treaty of Apameia. Both kings appealed to Rome, of course, but it was decided that both claims would be denied and Rome kept the territory for itself.[2]

Attalos III's will specifically set up the cities of his kingdom to be 'free', and Rome confirmed this. This hardly affected the cities of the Straits, most of which were not Attalos' to dispose of. No doubt some, like Kyzikos, suffered from the general warfare, but none seems to have been directly affected, though a contraction of the settlement of the 'Lower City' at Ilion has been dated to c.130 BC, and consequently Aristonikos' War, if not Aristonikos himself, has been blamed.[3]

Having acquired these two distant provinces, Macedonia and Asia, Rome made a serious attempt to apply to them a measure which they (and every other empire before and after them) no doubt hoped would bind their conquests into one empire. In Macedonia, once the country had been converted into a province in 146 BC, the Via Egnatia was 'constructed'; then in Asia the Via Aquillia was organised, both roads named for their supervising magistrates, C. Egnatius, probably the governor of Macedonia in 136–133 BC, and M'. Aquillius, the consul of 129 BC and the man who finished off the war with Aristonikos, and then stayed in office in his provincial command until 126 BC, sorting out the conquests, and supervising the 'construction' of the road which bears his name.

These two roads clearly were organised in close succession, with the aim of providing a clear and marked route from the usual landing place of Roman forces at Epidauros (Dyrrhachium), on the Adriatic coast of Epeiros to the easternmost point of Roman authority, or rather the final area of Rome's conquests in Asia Minor, at Side on the Mediterranean coast in Pamphylia. But the fact that must be noted about the source we have for these roads is that, although it is credited to Polybios (who actually died c.130 BC, and so could only have discussed the Via Egnatia in his book) the actual source for both roads is in the *Geography* of Strabo, who produced his account a century after Polybios' death. (There are also a few inscribed milestones, but details of routes and reasons are only in the written sources.)[4]

The Via Egnatia has been traced, in accordance with Strabo's description, from Epidauros on the Adriatic to Byzantion on the Bosporos.[5] But the Via Aquillia, built in the 120s BC, within a few years of the Egnatia, runs from Abydos on the Hellespont to Side at the eastern end of the Pamphylian Sea, which is a pretentious name for the wide bay on the south coast of Asia Minor.[6] The latter road traversed Asia Minor from north-west to south-east, but according to the later description of the Egnatia by Strabo, this road did not connect with the crossing used by the Egnatia, which was described as terminating at Byzantion. This is where the fact that Strabo's account is a century later than Polybios' is crucial.

Polybios' account takes the Via Egnatia as far as Kypsela in Thrace, no doubt because that was more or less the boundary of the Macedonian province as set up in 146 BC, and because, not far beyond Kypsela, the land became Attalid territory. Once the Chersonese and the nearby land in Thrace had been annexed by Rome in 133 BC, the Egnatia could be extended to connect with Aquillius' new road through Asia. It is evident that Aquillius' road, by commencing at Abydos, was intended to be a continuation of the Egnatia, and so together they formed a clear route from the Adriatic to the Syrian border; the Egnatia will have been extended, once the Aquillia was organized, to fill the gap between Kypsela and the Hellespont, no doubt by Aquillius as governor of the former Attalid territory; this extension turned south from Kypsela to reach the usual Hellespont crossing point at Sestos-Abydos. Later, when the Roman Empire included all Thrace (which was not until after 30 BC or later), the road was provided with a new terminus at Byzantion. From there the crossing into Asia gave access to a much more important, but later, road along northern Asia Minor.

For it must be recalled that the purpose of these roads was to enable Roman forces, marching, to reach trouble spots in record time. Crossing at Byzantion would allow a force from Italy or the Danube frontier to reach the Parthian frontier in Armenia much more quickly than using the crossing at Sestos-Abydos. When the Egnatia was organised, the most likely potential enemy lay in Thrace, and the Roman governors of Macedonia in the first century of its provincial existence had to repeatedly fight to hold on to their province – just as had the Macedonian kings for half a dozen centuries before them. From the point of view of the Roman governor of Asia, however, the potential enemies would be rebels in and around the province, or attacks from one or other of the kingdoms of Asia Minor, or perhaps by the Seleukid king in Syria. That kingdom was going through one its periodical succession crises in the 120s BC, but this would not necessarily last for very long; until 129 BC the king was Antiochos VII, a vigorous and powerful king. He was followed by the usurper Alexander II Zabinas, a weak ruler, but then Antiochos VIII secured full control by 121 BC, though later, in 113 BC, Antiochos IX reactivated the dynastic war. But the kingdom still consisted of all Syria and Cilicia, from the Taurus Mountains to Gaza, and united it would pose a serious threat. The last of these kings had been educated in Kyzikos, and so was fully aware of the situation in Asia Minor.[7] Kyzikos had been a longtime ally of the defunct Attalid kingdom and had successfully maintained its independence against all conquerors since the sixth century BC.

It is relevant to explain why the term 'constructed' was put in quotation marks. These roads were not 'built' in the sense of a modern road, or like one which had been carefully laid out in Italy by Roman magistrates over a period of decades or centuries. The 'new' roads, of course, already existed. This was a region which had been inhabited, travelled over and traded over, for millennia, and roads, whether paved or not, seamed the whole of the several regions. What the Roman magistrates had to do was to select the routes most favourable and most direct for their forces to use, bearing in mind their likely destinations. In Macedonia this was relatively straightforward, in that the obvious route lay almost directly west to east, with the termini at Epidauros and Kypsela equally obvious, and the intervening stops mainly the cities along the route. In Asia, the route chosen for the initial road led from Pergamon to Side. The starting point at Pergamon is a clear sign that Aquillius was using an existing road, one which had been in existence in the Attalid kingdom, and was directed through its former territories; his work therefore consisted in recognising an existing road, and in designating the connection between Kypsela and Pergamon.

What the Romans actually did was to decide the route and then to mark it with milestones, giving the distances from the last town, and on to the next. The discovery of the 331st milestone of the Via Aquillia at Side both illustrates the method and confirms the destination. The use of existing routes was sensible; the signing of them with milestones, inscribed in Latin and Greek, with Latin first, made it clear that Rome was stamping its authority on the whole region; one wonders how many in Asia Minor could understand Latin in the second century BC, but the commanders of the Roman forces marching along the road could understand it.

The expansion of Roman control into Asia Minor was accompanied, preceded, and followed by the arrival of Roman merchants who came to take advantage of the commercial possibilities of the region. Some of them settled in the cities, some were merchants and traders, some were slavers, and some were tax collectors. Romans had been in the area since the third century BC,[8] but it was only after the conquest of Asia and the imposition of Roman control that they became numerous, and from then on ubiquitous. Records of their presence, however, are mainly from the first century BC.[9]

The dividing event of Roman presence, and indeed of the second transition of the region into Roman control, was the conquest of western Asia Minor and Greece by Mithradates VI, king of Pontos, in 88–86 BC. The notorious massacre of Romans in Asia in 88 BC at Mithradates' behest, may be taken as that dividing point, since it was clear that before then the Roman presence was unpopular and resented but was accepted; after Mithradates' War the Romans' control was fastened firmly on the whole region.

It is difficult to date many of the individual items of evidence for the Italian presence, especially in the Straits area, where they seem, in the pre-massacre period, to have been fairly few. In Bithynia, when King Nikomedes III was asked to send soldiers to assist Rome in the wars against the Cimbri and the Teutoni, he replied that he could not since his kingdom was largely depopulated, and many of his people had been taken as slaves to Italy. The Senate reacted by ordering those from 'Allied' states to be freed. But what Nikomedes did not say, perhaps because he did not need to say, was that he himself had gathered up his free subjects and sold them to the slave traders. This is, of course, not evidence for the presence of Italians in Bithynia, other perhaps than a small number who arrived occasionally to collect their living merchandise.[10]

On the other hand, the activities of the *publicani* were clearly apparent. These Roman/Italian oppressions were due to the taxation system, whereby the collection of taxes in a province, or a region, or a city, was sold to a company of Italian *publicani*, who then proceeded to levy more than the tax in order to pay their expenses and make a profit, and to loan sums to those who could not immediately pay, at high rates of interest. Nikomedes had clearly got himself entangled in this by 104 BC, when he explained the lack of recruitable men in his kingdom. In 89 BC, however L. Julius Caesar placed himself as a patron of Ilion and prevented the *publicani* from levying their charges against the estates of the temple,[11] though this, of course, would not protect the city. We may conclude therefore that Italians, in the form of the *publicani*, were hardly unknown in Ilion, and probably other cities of Asia as well, though they were not necessarily very familiar in Bithynia. The Ilion temple was lucky in its patron, but elsewhere appeals heard in the governor's courts resulted usually in judgments in favour of the *publicani*, without regard to the justice of the case, and no doubt the *publicani* were well equipped with the necessary paperwork.

By the 90s BC much of the region was in distress, relieved only by the occasional governor who dispensed justice rather than punishment. In Bithynia, still under its kings, the tribute due to Rome was exploited in the same way. Slave traders therefore did not always need the excuse of tax collection, but simply bought the enslaved, and this seems to have been the practice also in Galatia.

This exploitation was the social background to the expression of hatred released by Mithradates' War. Until then he had gradually emerged as the leading potentate in Asia who took up a policy of opposing the Roman Empire. He was clever, rich, cunning, and long-lived, all qualities necessary for his task, but he was unable to prevail against the legions, or, eventually, against a couple of unusually capable Roman commanders.

The presence of Rome as controller of the province of Asia from 129 BC was a situation which the cities and kingdoms of the Straits area might have thought was relatively familiar. They had largely survived the Akhaimenid, Antigonid, Lysimachid, Seleukid and Attalid empires and kingdoms; optimists no doubt saw Rome as just another empire.

In a sense these people were right. Rome, as it encroached on the east, adopted eastern ways. Eventually, after much trial and tribulation, it adopted a monarchic system, in which the external show was largely a copy of the Hellenistic monarchies; the Greeks in the east were fully familiar with this. In some cases, such as Asia and Egypt, the transition was instant, and Rome took over the legal and constitutional places of Attalos III and Kleopatra VII whole and entire. But there was something more about Rome. First, it was a much more militarised state than the Hellenistic kingdoms; second, and more than the Hellenistic kingdoms, it financed itself by the loot acquired in its conquests,[12] and its public figures, elected or appointed, were, when faced by the riches of the east, avid to acquire some of that wealth for themselves, and thus, at the very time when the Senate chose to accept the bequest of Attalos III, the city became engulfed in the political crisis which was the first stage in what became a succession of ever deeper and more violent crises. In this case the wealth of the new Asian province was allotted to finance a party political programme of colonisations within the empire.[13] The crises followed for a century and only came to an end, more or less, at the moment Kleopatra committed suicide, leaving, though she had no intention of doing so, her kingdom to her enemy. And these repeated civil wars and internal crises caused major casualties amongst Roman subjects and citizens, but even, or especially, more so among those who had no interest in the reasons for the fighting. The Greek East, in particular Asia and its cities, were left looted, widely damaged, and impoverished by the conflict, and it took them perhaps a century to recover.

The wealth of the region attracted a variety of Romans. There were the merchants and the slave traders, already noted – these were often the same – and the tax collectors, who were part of the political decision to exploit Asia. The bequest of the Attalid kingdom to Rome was seized on by those who discerned in the bequest a possible solution to the developing social crisis of Italy; the wealth in tax opportunities of Asia Minor could be used for colonising schemes to benefit the Italian poor; and to avoid employing bureaucrats to collect those taxes, the task was farmed out to Italian companies of *publicani*.[14]

The result was a deepening immiserisation of the new province as the tax farmers collected what they wanted rather than what they were entitled to. The population became increasingly anti-Roman, until the eruption of Mithradates VI king of Pontos, revealed to Rome just how disliked it had become. The agony spilled over into other lands. Bithynia is the prime example, even though the Bithynians were not paying Roman taxes.

Mithradates VI had for some years been attempting to expand his kingdom in the time-honoured Hellenistic (and Roman) way but was repeatedly blocked by Roman opposition. He had some success in securing the Cholchian lands under the Caucasus, and in seizing the Bosporos kingdom in the Crimea, but attempts to expand his inherited kingdom into Paphlagonia and Cappadocia had been foiled. These frustrations, unsurprisingly, made him unwaveringly hostile to Rome.[15] In 88 BC, the Romans organised a trap for him, attempting to provoke the king into war, though it was so obvious and incompetent that he did not move. Instead the trap was sprung on the Romans, who impatiently moved first themselves, and sent their ally, Nikomedes IV of Bithynia to invade Pontos; three Roman armies had been assembled to attack Mithradates but they, and Nikomedes, suffered comprehensive defeats.[16] Mithradates' army and navy then overran most of Asia Minor, and at his signal, his partisans turned on the Romans in the region, murdering all they could reach, supposedly up to 80,000 people: men, women, children and freedmen.[17] Mithradates – and this may have been his main purpose – confiscated the wealth of those who were killed, said to amount to 700 talents; this had been extracted, of course, from the people and cities of Asia Minor, but it was not returned to them, though he did grant the province three years' tax relief; it all provided the king with a large war chest.[18]

Mithradates attacked Rome while it was in the midst of another major internal crisis, and he went on to overrun a large part of Greece. He was then attacked by an army commanded by L. Cornelius Sulla, but soon after he began his campaign a *coup d'état* in Rome removed his legal authority, but not his army, which was loyal to him before it was loyal to Rome. A new army, commanded by L. Valerius Flaccus, came into Macedonia. The two rival Roman armies avoided each other, though some of Flaccus' men deserted to Sulla.[19] The two men concentrated on fighting separate enemies. Sulla besieged Athens and defeated two large Mithradatic armies which came to its relief, while Flaccus' army marched east to invade Asia; on the way he was murdered by his subordinate L. Flavius Fimbria.

Flaccus had got most of his army, those who remained, across into Bithynia by the ferry to Chalkedon, staging through Byzantion, where the quarrel between Flaccus and his second-in-command Flavius Fimbria, heated up. Flaccus' murder took place soon afterwards near Nikomedia, which city had closed its gates to the army, presumably because it was, or was held by a force, loyal to Mithradates.[20] Fimbria claimed the command – it was in effect a *coup d'état*, of course – and campaigned through Asia with considerable success. He had an army of two legions, less those who had deserted to Sulla, and the relatively small size of his force rather suggests that the Asian opposition was fairly feeble. Mithradates had certainly been resorting to massacres and deportations to enforce his rule and had been faced by revolts as a result. L. Licinius Lucullus had collected a fleet from Egypt and other places in the eastern Mediterranean (which Mithradates had hoped would be on his side), and he now arrived to defeat Mithradates' own fleet. The Asian cities had to face the same choice as everyone else in a Civil War such as this – who to support – and that choice had to be made whenever Fimbria's army arrived at the gates of any city, with dire results if they submitted too late. He was successful in hunting Mithradates into a series of retreats and flights, until the king took to his ships to escape.[21]

The Straits area was the scene of three of Fimbria's more notorious actions in his campaign – Flaccus' murder (at Nikomedia) being the first. He laid siege to Ilion, which proclaimed its loyalty to Sulla. The city's walls enabled the citizens to hold off the assault for eleven days, but Fimbria's forces then broke through, and in the fighting the temple area was burned, though not the Athena temple itself; the rest of the city was looted, much of the population murdered, and large parts left in ruins.[22] Then, as Fimbria and his army approached Kyzikos, defeating a Mithradatic force near Miletopolis on the way, the city opened its gates. Fimbria's force entered, but he treated the city as if it had been conquered, executed some citizens and plundered others.[23] This was no longer a fight against Mithradates, but a further episode in the Roman Civil War.

Sulla, faced with two enemies, first made peace with Mithradates and then dealt with Fimbria. In a meeting at Dardanos on the Hellespont, a member of the Troadic League, Mithradates agreed to a set of terms (which he had in fact rejected sometime earlier) – withdrawal to his ancestral kingdom, payment of an indemnity of 2,000 talents, and the surrender of many of his ships.[24] It may have been widely recognized that these terms only guaranteed a further conflict, as some historians assert – and they certainly gave ammunition to his Roman enemies – but Sulla's intelligent peacemaking might have worked, and it certainly allowed him to proceed to polish off Fimbria. Having thus removed Mithradates from the war by his lenient terms, Sulla was able to remove Fimbria, whose forces gradually deserted to Sulla until Fimbria himself committed suicide.[25] And yet, Fimbria had accomplished a great deal of the work Sulla would have had to do, in recovering control over both Bithynia and Asia.

Needless to say, none of the indemnity provided by Mithradates went to any of the victims, Greek or Roman. Sulla did promise Ilion freedom from taxation, though whether it was because the city had resisted Mithradates or Fimbria is not clear – the conclusion must be that resistance to Fimbria was the more important consideration.[26] This exemption proved useful when Sulla announced his terms of peace to the rebels of Asia for having supported Mithradates and having murdered the Romans – a fine of 20,000 talents.[27] To pay this most cities had to borrow at exorbitant rates from Roman *publicani*. The impoverishment which had led to the cities to support Mithradates in the first place, and which was in effect confirmed by Mithradates' confiscations, was deepened by Sulla's and the *publicani's* extractions. No doubt the *publicani's* first priority would be to recover their losses.[28]

Lampsakos, however, did stand up to the rapacious C. Verres, who was saved from a rioting mob by the interventions of the local Romans when he became even more obnoxious than usual, but the affair no doubt left a good deal of bitterness; Verres got off scot-free; his unwilling host was prosecuted for the death of Verres' lictor, and he and his son were condemned and executed. Typical imperialist justice, of course.[29]

As was to be expected, the lenient peace terms agreed with Mithridates did not hold for long. Romans felt the king should be punished, understandably; Mithradates, on the other hand, felt he might win in a second attempt. The second war, however, was in fact his defence against a blatant and unauthorised Roman attack; this was called off by Sulla, now in power in Rome, before it became too serious.[30] But Mithradates was encouraged by the victories he had gained in defence, and he spent the next decade building up his strength.

The third war originated once again with Bithynia. Nikomedes IV died in 75/74 BC, and bequeathed his kingdom to Rome;[31] it was at once declared a province, and so Rome's boundary was advanced that much closer to Mithradates' kingdom, with only uncontrolled Paphlagonia separating them. Mithradates had built up his fleet to 400 ships, and his army to well over a hundred thousand men in the previous decade.[32] The consuls for 74 BC were assigned to Bithynia (M. Aurelius Cotta) and Asia and Cilicia (L. Licinius Lucullus), which was in effect a clear invitation for them to invade Mithradates' territory. He had already developed relations with a variety of Roman enemies – Egypt, Cyprus, the anti-senatorial rebel Sertorius in Spain, pirates operating in the Mediterranean – before the crisis over the annexation of Bithynia. He clearly hoped that these friends would assist him; it was probably news of his agreement with Sertorius which brought the Senate to decide on war.[33]

The annexation of Bithynia would give Rome control over the Bosporos, the entrance to the Black Sea which Mithradates dominated with his new fleet; this was probably another nudge towards war. For Rome, a Mithradatid war was unfinished business; for Mithradates it was a chance to reverse the result of the first war. The extent of his territorial ambitions is not known, and probably varied with opportunity, but it can be assumed that he aimed for at least Asia Minor – Bithynia, the Asian province, Galatia, and Cappadocia – and was probably thinking of a restoration in some way of the Seleukid Empire – he had Seleukid ancestors – which was currently on its last legs in Syria.

Both sides, therefore, knew the war was coming and both prepared for it, so that it only took a move by one or other of them to ignite it. Cotta in Bithynia had the usual consular army of two legions; in Asia Lucullus had recruited vigorously, and had a force amounting to five legions, and both armies including forces recruited locally.[34] Cotta also had a fleet commanded by Rutilius Nudus, but this was quickly defeated, leaving Cotta with 64 ships, partly recruited from local cities such as Kyzikos and Byzantion.[35] Lucullus in Asia moved his army eastwards and so threatened an invasion of the Pontic kingdom from the south; this was countered by a Mithradatic force sent into Cappadocia, while Mithradates himself took his own army into Bithynia. He was clearly aiming to eliminate Cotta's army and fleet while Lucullus was held in Galatia, and so gain access to Asia from the north. Mithradates was exploiting his control of the central position, which in this war was Pontos itself.

Mithradates was accompanied in his march along the north coast into Bithynia by his huge fleet, which had no difficulty in passing into the Propontis when Cotta withdrew into Chalkedon. Part of the Pontic fleet was sent to contact Sertorius in Spain in the hope of receiving assistance of some sort, or perhaps of provoking a distraction. Mithradates sent forty ships, a substantial section of his fleet, on this errand which suggests that he hoped either for a considerable reinforcement of Roman trained soldiers, or to attract a major Roman force to the west. The remainder of his fleet – several hundred ships – dominated the Propontis by sheer numbers.

The conquest of Bithynia was straightforward, and Cotta sensibly, outnumbered as he was, withdrew into Chalkedon, which was a well-fortified city. The Roman land forces, however, became trapped between Mithradates' army, which advanced very quickly, and the city wall, whose gates were shut. Some of the Roman officers were rescued by ropes sent down from the wall, but the troops they had commanded were killed or captured. The Mithradatic fleet sailed into Chalkedon's harbour, breaking the bronze chain across the entrance; four ships were burnt, and the rest, sixty vessels, were captured and taken out of the harbour. This eliminated the Roman naval forces for a time.[36]

Ten of the captured ships and a considerable number of soldiers had been sent by Kyzikos to assist Cotta. This was probably not the only Greek contingent to go to Chalkedon but the main source for this fighting, Appian's *Mithradatic Wars*, does not specify any city other than Kyzikos because of what happened next. Indeed, he only says that 'Romans' went to join Cotta from other cities, but that Romans exclusively did so seems unlikely.[37]

This victory by the Pontic forces brought Lucullus back to the west. Mithradates, lacking control of Chalkedon, and perhaps Byzantion, which would have been as difficult to capture as Chalkedon, decided he needed the naval facilities of Kyzikos, but the city's losses in the fighting had hardened the city's resolve to oppose him. Capturing Kyzikos would compensate for not capturing Chalkedon, and would be a much more valuable prize; it would count as a major victory to be proclaimed throughout Asia and Greece; no king had yet taken the city by attack, and Mithradates had ignored it back in his first Roman war. He may have been dazzled also by the rapid conquest of Bithynia, and possibly he believed his own propaganda, that Rome was divided and therefore much weakened. He was correct that it was divided, but it was not so much weakened and the friends he had cultivated, from Sertorius to Egypt, turned out to be of little use. Sertorius did indeed send him some technical help, and the pirates were pleased to have the excuse of raiding throughout the Aegean. But Sertorius was dead by the time Mithradates' ships arrived, and the use of pirates would turn many cities against him. No-one else stirred.

Kyzikos' resistance attracted Mithradates' forces, and Mithradates' huge stationary besieging forces in turn attracted Lucullus' army. The very size of the two contending forces became the real problem, since they required enormous amounts of food. This was less a problem for the city, oddly enough, because it had a considerable hinterland in its islands. Lucullus, who swiftly appreciated the opportunity, carefully organised his own supplies by recruiting – conscripting – large numbers of non-military people to transport the food for his own army from all over Asia.[38] He was also able to take up a fortified position close to Kyzikos from which he could deny supplies to the enemy.[39]

The siege is described in some detail by Appian, possibly even largely accurately, but the essential point is that the citizens were clearly well acquainted with the methods of besiegers, so that whatever ploy or device Mithradates attempted the citizens were able to block it. This included ships displaying captured Kyzikenes threatened with death, battering the walls, constructing a huge mound designed to overtop the walls, setting fires to crumble the walls, and building enormous siege machines. In each case the Kyzikenes seem to have had an answer. A history of failed sieges of the city no doubt provided abundant examples of how to resist such an attack; at the same time the suspicion must exist that Appian's account simply repeats typical siege warfare incidents gathered from elsewhere. It is the fact, however, that Mithradates' efforts were unsuccessful.[40]

The logistical problem and the resistance of the Kyzikenes defeated Mithradates. Other parts of his army were similarly unsuccessful in Mysia, in Karia, in Phrygia and Pisidia, in part because the major part of his forces were engaged with Kyzikos.[41] There was discontent enough in the cities of the Asian provinces, but with his army's failure to win anywhere, Mithradates' appeal was dimmed. In the winter, when his ships could not sail, and local food supplies had been consumed, he broke away from the siege. The horses and pack animals were sent away, presumably for them to recover, but Lucullus ambushed the convoy – or herd – at the Rhyndakos crossing and destroyed it.[42] Soon afterwards Mithradates sent his ships to Parion, westwards towards the Hellespont, and his infantry army (the cavalry having been destroyed at the Rhyndakos) marched to seize Lampsakos; presumably this was the first stage in a new invasion of Asia. But the army was defeated on the way, though the survivors did get into Lampsakos, to be blockaded there by Lucullus.[43]

The move of the ships towards the Hellespont, like the army's march, was presumably aimed at moving out of the Propontis to carry the war into the Aegean and Asia. His subsidiary armies in Asia had not succeeded, but he knew well enough that the cities did not like Roman rule, and the appearance of his great army could well set off a wider revolt. The army's defeats at Kyzikos and Lampsakos, however, scuppered that idea. The fleet he had sent to Spain found that Sertorius was dead and suffered damage from a storm during its return; off Tenedos it was met and defeated by Lucullus' fleet, which had been gathered from the seaports of the Aegean, and was commanded by L. Valerius Triarius. It had not been necessary to hunt through the Mediterranean for Mithradates' ships, for wherever the king was, that was its destination, and while he was blocked up in the Propontis the fleet had to attempt to pass the Hellespont. All Lucullus' fleet need do was wait off Tenedos or Alexandria Troas and let the enemy come to it.

In the Propontis, Mithradates took his ships across to the north shore to attack Perinthos. Again, this could have been an attempt to link up with the Thracians, who were as anti-Roman as anyone. In the previous generation they had been regularly battered by Roman armies stationed in Macedonia, including Sulla's, who had attacked them just to give his soldiers exercise and practice. Perinthos was untakeable,[44] just like Kyzikos – all the Greek cities which had survived on the Thracian coast were tough and well-fortified; those which were captured suffered that fate repeatedly, as did Lysimacheia. Attacking Perinthos was a final desperate throw. Blocked in every direction, Mithradates collected his remaining army at Lampsakos, and took the whole force to Nikomedia. On that fairly short voyage he lost many ships (and no doubt many of his men) when a storm struck them.[45]

The war returned to being one for control of Bithynia. The Roman aim now was that Mithradates and his ships were to be bottled up in Nikomedia and its gulf by a Roman squadron, while other Roman squadrons seized the cities on the coast. Apameia Myrleia had apparently taken Mithradates' side, possibly involuntarily, and suffered a massacre in consequence. Prusias-on-the-Sea was taken and from there the captors moved inland to capture Nikaia. The attempt to blockade Nikomedia, however, failed, and Mithradates got his fleet (about a hundred ships still remaining) out and on its way to Pontos; almost inevitably in this difficult year, however, it was struck by another storm which sank some ships and scattered the rest; Mithradates himself had to be rescued by one of his pirate allies.[46] Lucullus scoured the Propontis coast for any remaining Pontic ships, finding thirteen at the Harbour of the Achaeans in the Troad (Bezika Bay) and drove them and the other ships to take refuge on a 'barren island'. There the troops held out but were bombarded from the Roman ships until they broke and fled, to be killed or captured. Mithradates, having been rescued, went back to his kingdom. Lucullus and Cotta were able to reoccupy Nikomedia and hold a conference there.[47] The war moved eastwards.

This was the first time since the last decade of the Athenian-Peloponnesian war that the Straits area had been the scene of major warfare, and it had been a most unpleasant experience. Several cities had suffered damage, including Lampsakos, Kyzikos, Chalkedon, Nikomedia, Apameia-Myrleia, Prusias-by-the-Sea, and Nikaia, either by capture and sack or ravaging in their *chorai*, if an army camped there, or even if one passed by. Probably the worst to suffer, ironically, was Ilion, the city most revered in the region by Romans. Sulla had declared it free and immune after Fimbria's capture and sack, as had every warlord who passed by since Alexander. It did little good for the city; it may have not paid taxes, but since the city was evidently impoverished, and the festivals suspended for a time, immunity from tax was scarcely relevant – the Roman state could hardly collect tax when there was nothing to be taxed. The city did continue the festivals, whereas the general impoverishment caused by the Roman-Mithradatid Wars meant that other cities decided that spending on such frivolities was at the bottom of everyone's priorities. No doubt being one of the few cities to continue with its festivals would have been profitable, but the festivals were Ilion's economic purpose.[48] Ilion's experience was no doubt extreme – few cities were taken by assault – but not necessarily atypical in suffering damage, loss and depopulation. It and many others had depended on royal grants and handouts ever since Alexander, and even before. It was somewhat protected by its Roman connections, but Rome was much too preoccupied to continue such largesse, at least until Caesar's and then Augustus' time.

Another threat which the Romans eventually faced up to was the problem of piracy. This had long been endemic in the Aegean, with its many islands and numerous sailors and ships, but the menace tended to increase in the wake of civil warfare, in whatever land the fighting took place. It had grown in the 140s BC, for example with a war of Seleukid succession, but it was the Roman wars which gave it a major boost – in both cases because one of the contenders, Tryphon and Mithradates, deliberately enlisted the pirates; this encouraged their activities, but they were not reined in again afterwards. Mithradates had allied with the pirates more than once, and this gave them a licence to raid almost anywhere. Ilion appealed to Rome for protection from them, for example.[49] One cannot help feeling that for a man with a fleet of 400 ships, an alliance with the pirates was hardly necessary, and in reality it was counter-productive in public relations terms.

It was not, however, just the threat of a sudden pirate raid which was so disturbing, but the Roman demands for manpower and ships when they finally nerved themselves to make the attempt to suppress the pirate pest. This may be a reminder that much of the fighting in these eastern wars was done by Greeks recruited or conscripted into the Roman armies (and those of Rome's enemies). Lucullus, for example, began with his one consular legion, added the survivors of Fimbria's two, and quickly recruited two more locally in Asia. Some of their men no doubt were Italians domiciled in the east, but most would be local inhabitants, probably men reduced to poverty by the exactions of the Roman *publicani*; he also conscripted many thousands, particularly from Galatia, to carry his supplies to feed his army at the siege at Kyzikos. And anyone who was not conscripted, or any city not otherwise affected, was taxed to pay for the campaign, to pay for supplies, and to pay the soldiers.

For the piracy wars, for example, Byzantion supplied a ship to M. Antonius for his Cretan campaign in 69 BC, and if so distant a city was called on, one must assume every settlement around the Aegean and the Propontis had to contribute. The same will have happened with Lucullus – Kyzikos lost ten ships at Chalkedon – and Pompey's later campaigns against both the pirates and Mithradates will have been similarly costly, in men and ships and money. With the Roman civil wars, almost continuous between 49 BC and 30 BC, the impoverishment would have been crushing. The cities were always caught between two sides, and whether their cooperation with one warlord was coerced or voluntary, punishment by his enemy was imposed without hearing any contrary argument. The warlords were in constant need of resources and had few scruples about acquiring them.

During this period, and earlier, the whole area became host to increased numbers of Italians. The number massacred at Mithradates' instigation in 88 BC is put at 80,000 (the lowest ancient figure suggested – obviously a guess and probably an exaggeration) though not all Italians present in the east died, and the prospects for personal or corporate enrichment, especially in the 80s in financing the demands of Sulla, were such that the Roman losses were soon replaced by new migrants. For example, in Mithradates' third war (74–73 BC) a group of Italian tax farmers living in Herakleia Pontike were murdered; they had clearly moved in since the previous massacre.[50] In Bithynia the tax farmers' company set up its headquarters in Nikaia, as a result of which this became the Roman officials' chief city when the tax farming system was eliminated, and was regarded as the chief city of the province by Augustus.[51]

The numbers of Italians in this post-Mithridates period was much greater than before 88 BC. In Bithynia, where a careful survey of the evidence has been made, there had been one or two Italians before Mithridates' massacre, say in the thirty years before 88 BC – some were clearly active before 104 BC, according to Nikomedes III – but in the half-century after 88 BC, and particularly between 66 BC and 30 BC, there were seven recorded in Cicero's letters, and fifteen Italian families recorded in inscriptions. These were clearly only a part of the total, and this applied only to the Bithynian province.[52]

It is impossible to provide much detail about the fate of individual cities in this period, though Ilion's fate is well documented because of its fame, the extant written sources, and the recent excavations.[53] One of the more ironic consequences of the serial defeats of armies recruited in the east by those coming from the west (Caesar against Pompey at Pharsalos, Anthony and Octavian against Brutus and Cassius at Philippi, Octavian and Agrippa against Anthony and Kleopatra at Aktion) is that each victor tended to find himself honoured in some way in the eastern cities after the victory, presumably on the news of the defeat of the most recent warlord arriving – so Pompey, Caesar, Brutus, Anthony and others were all serially honoured before their defeats and deaths – Miletopolis, a minor city if ever there was one, honoured Pompey in extravagant words,[54] while Ilion probably honoured Caesar – he certainly visited the place and was its patron;[55] and in the end everyone honoured Octavian/ Augustus, perhaps in self defence.[56] These evanescent honours illustrate as well as the results of battles and campaigns the central uncertainty and frantic fear of the cities during these bloodthirsty wars. And every warlord wanted money and took the most drastic measures to acquire it.

Chapter 11

In the Roman Empire (30 BC–AD 180)

Induction into the Roman Empire on a permanent basis was never a pleasant experience, since only very rarely was it in any way voluntary. Kings, such as Attalos III and Nikomedes IV might will their kingdoms to Rome, but their people, perhaps justifiably resentful of the cavalier treatment of their homelands, usually resisted their new 'owner'. In the Roman Republic, these takeovers invariably involved violence, usually violence perpetrated on the new subjects by Rome, and this was followed by their exploitation. Even the best-intentioned Roman governor was expected to enrich himself by his period in provincial office, in the guise of having the provincials pay his expenses, and, if he had one, his salary. In 30 BC when Octavian – C. Julius Caesar (Octavianus) – after fifteen years of striving, finally removed the last of his opponents, much of the eastern part of the empire was damaged and impoverished and scattered with communities of Italian emigrants.

All this applied with probably greater force in Asia Minor than anywhere else. This region saw repeated bouts of warfare and, with its reputation for wealth, it was a region which was squeezed more systematically than any other, both by the frequency of the occasions it had to pay and by the tax farmers' demands and profits over and above these taxes, on top of which were the interest-bearing loans the Roman warlords imposed. It still comes as a shock to find that M. Iunius Brutus, styled 'Liberator' for his participation in the assassination of Julius Caesar, was collecting interest from a loan he had made to Cyprus (illegally) at the rate of forty-eight per cent; he was presumably not the only such exploiter.[1]

After this sort of treatment, it took decades for the region to recover. Nothing could be done during the period of civil war, since money was short, and any work of recovery was liable to be interrupted. The poet Lucan essayed a description of the condition of Ilion on a visit by Julius Caesar in 48 BC, forty years after Fimbria's sack. It depicted the whole city as burnt and in ruins.[2] It was a grossly exaggerated description (though it has been taken as accurate in both ancient and modern accounts) and the recent excavations have shown that the burning was restricted to the temple area – the actual Athena Temple survived – and the city itself, if not undamaged, was not ruined completely, though damaged houses in the Lower City remained as ruins for decades. These excavations also show that nothing was done for many decades to revive the city or to repair the damages, despite promises by Sulla, Caesar, and Augustus (shades of Alexander's promises). The temples remained in ruins, the burnt debris was still in place all that time – there are signs that the only clearance of the burnt area was done by small groups of men, probably workmen, who cleared areas where they could camp and light their fires.[3]

Julius Caesar, on a brief visit to the region, ordered the plantation of two colonies of soldier veterans at Apameia Myrleia and Lampsakos. These were precarious at first – a colony at Herakleia Pontike failed.[4] The Roman world's collapse into war after 44 BC not only prevented building in old cities but damaged the prospects of the new colonies.

From 41 BC, however, the east generally was under the rule of Mark Antony, and he paid much attention to Asia Minor. It is likely that Alexandria Troas was reinforced with a group of veterans, and so converted into a colony at his behest.[5] His work is not always easy to detect, since it was ignored or blanked out after his death, but he had been active in colony founding in Italy, and establishing colonies was a good way to plant his authority in any particular region.

Augustus, as Octavian had become, visited the East in 21–19 BC, in part to negotiate a peace with the Parthians, but he dealt also with a series of local and imperial problems. He visited Ilion in the process, and made promises about the future, and seems to have provided some of the materials from imperial sources for the rebuilding, though most of the materials came from cannibalising the ruins of earlier buildings.[6] Other matters were dealt with and initiatives taken. Close to Ilion was the port city of Alexandria Troas, one of Antony's colonies; it was now, after 30 BC, reinforced by more veterans sent by Octavian, possibly to dilute the Antonians already present.[7] A second colony was established at Parion, east along the coast. Parion had been expanded at Priapos' expense by a grant of Attalos I or II, and its reception of Roman veterans made it a powerful local Roman presence, diluting the local power of the Greek inhabitants; it evidently absorbed Priapos, marking its victory in the long struggle between the two cities.[8] Between them, these cities along the Hellespont Asian coast – Alexandria Troas, Ilion, Lampsakos, and Parion, all Roman in sentiment and loyalty – were in control of the Asian side of the Hellespont, as far as the lands of Kyzikos.

A curious episode in the history of Prusias-by-the-Sea saw the city being the refuge of two of Mithradates' relatives: his daughter Musa Orosabios, and Orodaltis, daughter of Lykomedes. They appear to have been given the city by Mark Antony, in a gesture not altogether to the liking of the citizens. The city suffered a demotion when the two women were expelled; it ceased to be a free city – but this was not necessarily anything connected with the women, but more part of Augustus' policy of reducing free cities to dependent status.[9]

Across the water in Thrace, there had been major changes. After decades of intermittent warfare, the Roman Empire finally reached the Danube during Augustus' reign, having conquered the several Thracian tribes. Thrace itself was organised as a kingdom for half a century or so, under kings of the ancient Odrysian tribe. This was a tribute, in a sense, to the resistance put up by the Thracians. Beyond the kingdom, the territory along the Danube became the Moesian province, and for the present this marked the limit of Roman ambitions.

In the south of Thrace, the old Greek cities of Ainos and Maroneia still continued, but Lysimacheia at the root of the Chersonesos Peninsula had apparently finally been allowed to die, and the elder Pliny notes that the city was deserted by the time he was writing (before AD 79); it had suffered yet another Thracian destruction in the time of Attalos II.[10] These were the fates also of several of the old and small Greek cities along the coasts of the peninsula. Two changes took place, probably imperceptibly for a time: first, the peninsula as a whole had become an imperial estate, which in Augustus's early years was granted out to M. Vipsanius Agrippa, Augustus' imperial partner and general – the latest example of the peninsula as a principality. It was left to Augustus in Agrippa's will.[11] It had no doubt been a royal estate under the Attalids. It remained an imperial estate from Augustus' time on.

The second change was the growth of two new cities. Coela, a little to the south of Sestos, appears to have grown as the administrative centre, from which the area was controlled by the Roman officials; this presumably meant, from Augustus' time, the procurator who ran the imperial estate. The founder may thus have been Agrippa, though the place did not become recognised as urban until Hadrian's reign, and had probably been growing since the estate came to the Romans; it would probably have attracted a local population of traders and merchants, as well as slaves.[12] There is also a reference to the 'Chersonites of the Hellespont', who came together for an imperial dedication; one must assume these were the inhabitants of the imperial estates, an indication that there was a lingering sense of community in the peninsula.[13]

A second new town developed not far from the defunct site of Lysimacheia; it was named Flaviopolis, which suggests an origin, or perhaps only an official recognition, in the Flavian period, though it is described as a colony by Pliny, and so by the mid-first century AD at the latest.[14] Inland from the Propontis coast, a veteran settlement was developed at Apri (or Aprus), which was the royal city of the Caeni, the Thracian tribe occupying the land just north of Lysimacheia (and so probably the tribe which had so repeatedly sacked the city). The royal family had been suppressed during the Roman conquest, and the tribe was probably still seen as dangerous; the veteran settlement was founded by Claudius, but probably it had been going for some time before then; the fact that it was at the tribal centre was a means of Roman control.[15] This area of the Chersonese and its neighbourhood had always been a place of villages and small towns, and this did not change in the Roman period; it would seem to be its normal condition of human settlement.

The cities along the European Propontis coast appear largely to have survived and prospered in a small way. Some of the smaller sites, as on the Asian side and in the Chersonese, faded away, but this had been happening for centuries. Bisanthe, for example, is never heard of again after about 400 AD; Selymbria, engulfed in Byzantion's grip, lost its population, probably to the larger city; it was still in existence in 196 BC when some Roman envoys landed there on their way to visit Antiochos III during his Thracian campaign, but there is no further record after that, though it was refounded in the fifth century.[16] Panion, the Attalid new foundation after 188 AD, west of Perinthos, is still recorded in the fifth century, and presumably continued to exist all through.[17] Perinthos, which survived the threat of Mithradates' fleet in 73 AD, became the capital of one of the *strategeia* in the Roman administration of Thrace, and being a government centre was able therefore to survive with some prosperity.[18] Byzantion, of course, went on, having largely kept its head down in the civil wars, and so it had survived well; it was included in the Roman province of Bithynia-and-Pontus. The extension of the Via Egnatia to the city was partly a consequence of the conquest of Thrace and the stationing of the legions on the Danube frontier and made the city for the first time a major crossing point to rival that at the Hellespont. The stabilisation of the Parthian–Armenian frontier by Augustus' treaty in 20 BC, and the repeated threat of its destabilisation as a result of the intermittent threats of Parthian wars over the next two centuries, only enhanced Byzantion's importance as a transport point. For the first time in its history Byzantion had become more important than as a mere guard on the Bosporos and a source of pickled fish. Its status as a free city was abolished by Vespasian, presumably because its role in providing cross-Bosporos transport made its independence an obstacle.[19]

It is high time that it is more generally recognised that Byzantion was of only minor importance throughout its history until its refoundation as Constantinople. Its absence from any role in the Roman civil wars is a clear mark of its essential unimportance. It was certainly a city of note in the Straits area, but so were Kyzikos, Chalkedon, Alexandria Troas, Ilion, and others. Its geographical position did not give it any special importance until it was built up as a great city; it had no 'natural' geographical advantages until then.

As an illustration of all this, under Augustus, just as its importance as a transport point grew, it was reduced in political importance. It lost its lands across the water in the peninsula between the Gulfs of Astakene and Kios (Iznik and Gemlik), which was transferred to the new city of Caesarea (or Caesarea Germanike), founded by Augustus on the Asian Propontis coast between Apameia-Myrleia and Prusias-by-the-Sea, and later refounded by Germanicus. The new city also took over land belonging until then to Kyzikos. The boundary between the Bithynian and Asian provinces was deemed to be the Rhyndakos River, and the lands of Kyzikos east of that river were then handed over to the new city.[20] All this was clearly the Roman way of tidying up the map, while at the same time weakening the two strongest cities of the area. Veterans had been planted at Alexandria and Parion for much the same purpose: now Byzantion and Kyzikos, both cities which had displayed a degree of independence all during their history – especially Kyzikos – were being cut down.

Kyzikos was in fact treated to a long process of alternating imperial favour and punishment. Augustus in the east in 21–19 BC, visited Ilion and promised help to the city, but then he went on to Kyzikos where the city had been demonstrating its status as a free city by arresting, punishing, and imprisoning some Roman citizens who had done something of which the city disapproved. But Roman citizens were sacred. Augustus reacted by depriving the city of its free status.[21] In fact, the city had also played a curious and devious path in the preceding civil war. In 48 BC it sent help to Julius Caesar when he was entangled in his Egyptian war, but had then served as the naval headquarters for Brutus and Cassius after Philippi.[22] Following this it was in Antony's part of the empire, in the course of which he helped to defend the city against a raid by the sea-king Sextus Pompeius by lending the city a force of gladiators for its defence – though it was probably as much due to the local sea militia that Pompeius was driven off.[23]

This record hardly looked good from Augustus' viewpoint – the city, after assisting his adoptive father, had then helped several of his enemies, whether or not voluntarily. And now Roman citizens had transgressed in some way in a city which had no doubt suffered from the greedy attentions of tax farmers and uncontrolled Roman officials. As a free city Kyzikos was exercising its legal powers, and Augustus took exception as much to the city's free status as to its treatment of Roman citizens, while its free choices of whom to support in the civil wars cannot have pleased him. Freedom for cities was not a status welcomed by the new dictatorship.

On the other hand, sycophantic honours for members of the imperial family were always welcome. Ilion honoured every Emperor and several family members with statues and cults;[24] Kyzikos did the same, perhaps after a pause. Its free status was returned later in Augustus' reign, but then again removed by Tiberius, to be finally returned by Caligula.[25] By this time no doubt the city was quite clear about how far it could go. Alexandria Troas and Parion, the veteran colonies, did similar homage, as would Caesarea.[26]

However, the vindictiveness of Augustus at Kyzikos and the apparent punishment of Byzantion by Vespasian also occurred at the royally favoured Ilion. Agrippa in his tour along the Asian Propontis coast in

17–16 BC,[27] was accompanied by his wife Julia (Augustus' daughter). She was caught in a flood of the Skamandros River, not having notified the city of her approach, and so nobody was there to help. Agrippa instantly punished the city with a fine of 100,000 drachmae. (The crime was presumably not having the foresight to guess that Julia was on the way.) Ilion had to get Herod of Judaea to intervene (presumably by way of some Jews living in the city) to have this rescinded. All of the Romans with authority were capable of such impulsive injustices.[28]

Apameia-Myrleia was elevated to the status of a colony by Julius Caesar and no doubt it put up the usual statues; its official name was Iulia Concordia.[29] Nikaia became the chief city of the province, and as such would have grown and flourished. And so on. The gradual recovery from the damages done in the Civil War went on fairly steadily throughout the first century A.D.

The results of this prosperity, which was general in the empire, of course, was that there is little information about any events in the region. Some cities were honoured – Prusias-by-the-Sea was raised to colonial status and reverted to its old Greek name of Kios[30] – and the festivals of the Hellenistic period revived; honours for emperors were widely voted. But the cities themselves were increasingly subjected to provincial and central authorities' control. The model, or threat, had perhaps been the treatment of Kyzikos, singled out no doubt because it was the most prominent and powerful and independent city in the Straits area. With its clear and repeated subjection by both Augustus and Tiberius, no other city would be inclined to assert itself in any way other than by obsequious honour-voting. And, of course, the great peace gave them less opportunity to either act independently or defy governors or emperors.

For the next century and more after Augustus and Tiberius, tensions in the Straits region relaxed, as in most of the rest of the empire. It was a sort of digestive torpor, as the empire absorbed the new provinces gained in the violence of the Civil Wars, and the provinces and cities which were now part of the empire gradually worked out how to exist and flourish in the new conditions, which in Kyzikos' case took five decades. As ever when within an imperial grasp, events in the region remained obscure – it had been the same under the Akhaimenids and the Seleukids – and the changes which took place worked often invisibly so that only a crisis, of which there were few, brought out what had been happening. As in any state in which the central government interfered and meddled in the local affairs of provinces and cities and individuals, local initiative withered and became distracted. If a city like Ilion, for example, felt that it was favoured for its connections back to ancient Troy and by the Roman elite because of that, it would emphasise that aspect, and become all too used to the subventions when they arrived, and would seek them when they did not; several buildings were constructed in the century after Augustus' visit, and the city must have received the finance for that work. It was visited by Agrippa, C. Caesar, and Germanicus and Agrippina, after which the emperors stayed in and about Rome – until Nero.[31] Other cities felt that they were in some sort of competition with their neighbour, and then their energies went into that affair, to the detriment of more useful and helpful activities; Augustus granted Nikaia the right to put up a temple of Rome and Julius Caesar, but Nikomedia one to himself – possibly an attempt the sow division between the two cities.[32] That is, one of the causes of the civic extravagance was imperial policy.[33]

This emerges from the investigations carried out – by an imperial order – into the affairs of the cities of Bithynia by the younger Pliny in 111–113 AD. He was chosen because he had a certain familiarity with the province even while he lived at Rome. He had defended two earlier governors of the province who had been prosecuted for malfeasances at the instigation of the provincials, which suggested that something was wrong in the province; he was also a leading expert in Rome on finance, and it was apparently in this the Bithynian problem lay.[34] He wrote back to Rome frequently, reporting to the Emperor (Trajan) on his progress and asking advice on various matters. The letters were collected and published after his death, as a final volume to complement the nine books of correspondence he had already published. Given that all the letters in book ten are concerned with Bithynia it is evident that they are only a selection of his correspondence in the two years he was in the province. It is not believable that an assiduous letter writer like Pliny will have restricted himself to Bithynian affairs in all that time; similarly it has been pointed out that, since the letters all deal only with Bithynia, it seems likely that other topics he discussed were filleted out, either by discarding whole letters or by removing non-Bithynian references from the existing letters. And yet the correspondence was mainly with the

Emperor, who may well have insisted that each letter dealt with a single topic for his own ease of dealing with matters.

Pliny did not complete his investigation, still less did he produce a considered final report, dying in the midst of his work early in 113 AD. Two further investigations into the province followed in the next years, so it does look as though the problems in Bithynia were particularly deep-seated and intractable. He visited Prusa, Nikomedia, Nikaia, Claudiopolis, Byzantion, Apameia, and was working his way through the cities of Pontos, visiting Sinope, Amastris, and Amisos when his correspondence ends with his death.

The inability of the cities to take even minor spending decisions for themselves – Amastris had to get imperial permission to cover a noxious sewer and Nikomedia was forbidden to form a local fire brigade[35] – combined with earlier incompetent extravagance in contracting for public buildings which they could not pay for, left them at the mercy of governors and emperors. (This incompetence was hardly new – Athens had been attempting to complete one particular temple for the last five centuries, and even with imperial help did not succeed.) The corruption of a number of governors did not help, of course. Pliny's investigations revealed the problem, but did not reveal the answer, and it is doubtful if any report he made would have done so either. The real answer was to remove the interfering imperial oversight, which was never going to happen. So the Roman imperial system would continue to gradually remove any real authority from the local councils, which in turn reacted by becoming irresponsible.[36] The reduction of free cities, like Byzantion and Kyzikos, to dependent status, was another part of the problem. That is, the Roman Empire was unlikely to last for very long as the quasi-federation of cities it liked to think it was; it was all set to devolve into the penetrating autocracy which emerged with the revolution of the 190s AD.

The *amour propre* of the imperial house was always a priority. The disciplining of Kyzikos by Tiberius was ascribed to the city's failure to complete the building of a temple of Augustus.[37] Thus, as early as this reign, failure of the cities to complete public buildings was a problem – though given Kyzikos' treatment by Augustus it is quite possible that not finishing the construction of his temple was a deliberate local insult, and that Tiberius interpreted it as such.

The emergence in this same period of Bithynian men who were wealthy enough to enter the Roman political system and stand for election at Rome was a further social development. Most of the cities produced a number of Roman magistrates, sometimes a succession of men from a single family, but the effect was hardly to enhance the well-being of the cities. One of the requirements of a senator was to possess estates of a certain value in Italy, which could only be acquired by purchase, using the wealth the family had acquired in their home town and local province. And then the elected man had to attend in Rome for election or nomination, and was then employed in various provinces – very rarely in his own province of origin – as an administrator. He might pose as the patron of his home city, but this hardly redounded to the city's prosperity. The net effect was always to drain wealth from the local area and to take away capable men for the benefit of the empire (and Italy), to local detriment.

The spread of Roman citizenship in the Bithynian cities was slow, perhaps in part because it was a senatorial rather than imperial province, and so had its governor selected by the Senate, but it is a fact that the Greek part of the empire was notably less enthusiastic about adopting Roman citizenship than the west. No doubt civic pride was part of the explanation for this reluctance, but the extensive damage of the Civil War period and the slow recovery afterwards were also elements, as no doubt was general resentment at the assumption that Roman citizenship was more valuable than their own local citizenships. One result was that the east was slow in providing men in the public offices, but Bithynia seems to have been especially so. The veteran colonies of Alexandria Troas and Parion had a better route to elective or appointive offices, but Apameia, also a colony, was as slow as the other Bithynian cities. The earliest example is a Catilius Longus of Apameia, who began as a military tribune in Claudius' reign, and was adlected to praetorian (that is, senatorial) rank by Vespasian in the Emperor's great adlection of AD 73/74.[38] That is, Longus would probably not have risen so high but for the gaps in the senatorial ranks caused by the casualties of the civil war of AD 69, and the fact that this new emperor had emerged from the army in the east, where Longus was serving as a soldier.

The Catilius family was in fact one of the more notable imperial families of the next century and more, probably originating by immigration in the Republican period, but producing a line of three senators in the four generations after Longus.[39] Nikomedia produced two families with successive senators, the Flavii Arriani and the Cassii, both families producing notable historians.[40] But once these three families are counted there are only four more men who reached the Senate from the cities over a period of two and a half centuries. Those who took posts of equestrian rank, usually as procurators, were a little more numerous, but even so there were only eight of them.[41] There was evidently little enthusiasm for serving the empire – or perhaps the spread of wealth was sufficiently wide to preclude its concentration in more than one or two families in any city, and even the lack of wealth.

These men are spread throughout two centuries, from the reign of Claudius to their latest appearance; it is a very thin spread, but they are virtually the only indications of any events in the region before the revolution and imperial affairs that brought a new Civil War in 192–197 AD.

In the rest of the empire there was intermittent warfare on the frontiers and over the century, from Tiberius onwards, the new strategic situation was revealed. Augustus had directed the final conquest of the Balkans as far as the Danube, and a series of legions were posted along the river in fortified camps, which soon attracted civilian settlements alongside them. This northern frontier was rarely quiet for very long, but the legions stationed there could usually cope. In the east there was the constant worry about the possibility of a Parthian war. There were six legions available in the east for deterrence, but this was not enough when a war actually came in Nero's reign. This was followed by the Jewish uprising in AD 66–73, during which the commander in Palestine, Vespasian, successfully made his bid for the empire.

All these wars required much movement of the legions. Corbulo, in command against Parthia from AD 55, took two legions from Syria, and was given a further one, IV Scythica, from Moesia, where it was replaced by VII Claudia from Dalmatia. In AD 62, V Macedonica was shifted from Moesia to Cappadocia and suffered with others in the Armenian campaign. Neither IV Scythica nor V Macedonica were returned westwards when the Parthian war ended, since the Jewish War followed almost at once. But the point to be made here is that the movements of the two Moesian legions from the Danube to the east, though no details of their routes are recorded, must have been by way of Byzantion and the crossing of the Bosporos.

Thrace had been annexed by Claudius in AD 46 (using V Macedonica) and roads through the new province were presumably developed. When it moved from Oescus (its base on the Danube) to Armenia, the passage through Byzantion was the obvious route, as it had been for IV Scythica. When in AD 66 Vespasian had to travel (overland) to Syria, he went by way of the Sestos-Abydos crossing and through the Cilician Gates. The two routes were thus both now in use. When XV Apollinaris went from Carnuntum on the Danube to the Armenian frontier, it no doubt went through Byzantion again. In his last year Nero ordered VII Claudia to move from Syria to Moesia; its route was presumably through Byzantion.

After his accession, Vespasian removed Byzantion's free status (along with a series of other Greek cities); the reason is not known, but it may have had something to do with the unusual frequency and size of the Roman forces which had been passing through the city; it is unlikely that they behaved well while present, and the free city may well have reacted badly, at least from the Roman government's point of view. In that case, the city was behaving like Kyzikos in disciplining Roman citizens; Byzantion's punishment by Vespasian would thus have been the same as Kyzikos' by Augustus – and like Kyzikos its free city status was restored soon afterwards.

The Bosporos route was therefore available, even necessary, for the Roman army by the 50s AD, and was used by legions with some frequency between AD 55 and AD 70. The new Parthian war launched by Trajan in AD 114 required a similar movement of soldiers, though since the main fighting took place by an invasion of Mesopotamia out of Syria, the Hellespont-Cilician Gates route was also no doubt in use. The same may be said of the Parthian wars of Lucius Verus and Septimius Severus. But the return of the legions to Europe put them usually into Dacia, and the Byzantine route would be the shorter. For a traveller from Italy or Greece heading for Syria the Hellespont route was clearly the shorter, but the Bosporos route was now available for travel to and from the Balkans.

The obscurity of the Straits region in the second century, in which little seems to have happened in the cities, was therefore only relative. It may not have been mentioned much in the sources, but it was in use as a transport node all through the century, and in that time the importance of the Bosporos route, and Chalkedon and Byzantion as ferry ports, will have become strategically of increasing importance. The cities of the Straits, of course, went on building when they could afford it, or when an emperor decided they needed a new facility. Hadrian financed an aqueduct for Byzantion,[42] for example, perhaps as a mark of the city's new importance in the imperial road system, as revealed in Trajan's eastern war and Hadrian's own travels. Ilion went on adding buildings and holding its festivals; from the Flavians to Hadrian it saw 'the largest number of construction projects in the city' of the Roman period.[43] Hadrian's travels no doubt emphasised to him the usefulness and condition of the imperial road network. He was in the Straits area for about a year after his assumption of power in AD 117, directing the military measures needed to recover control of the frontiers in the Balkans, and in Egypt and Palestine. He had travelled by the Byzantine route on his initial journey, leading to suggestions that he had stayed in Nikomedia and Byzantion, both of which are very likely to have hosted him, though a lengthy stay in either place seems unlikely.[44] He was accompanied by the praetorian guard and by some of the legionary troops, which would be a heavy burden for any city, and they would be more easily accommodated in a temporary camp in open country.

Hadrian visited Bithynia, Thrace, and the Troad again during his empire tour in AD 124–125. He arrived shortly after a major earthquake which had damaged many of the cities. It has been suggested again that he stayed at Nikomedia for the winter of AD 124/125. The damage from the earthquake proved to be an ideal opportunity for the display of imperial largesse, and the Emperor was commemorated as the city's 'restorer' on a civic coin; other coins, and inscriptions over the gates of Nikaia, also call him the 'restorer' of the province.[45]

He can be traced, either by the formal record or by a reasonable presumption, into Thrace, at Perinthos, Apri, and Hadrianopolis (renamed for him on this occasion), and in the Chersonese at Coela, which he promoted to the status of a *municipium*.[46] Then he went back across the Propontis to Kyzikos, where he was extravagantly greeted and financed the continued building of an old but still unfinished temple.[47] He seems to have visited Miletopolis and Apollonia-on-Rhyndakos inland of Kyzikos,[48] then travelled along the Propontis coast by Parion and Alexandria Troas, and a visit to Ilion was, of course, a necessity. Then he moved south into Ionia. And everywhere he was expected to distribute promises and financial support.

It may also be that his travels had developed in the Emperor an eye for country, or maybe some local geographer had pointed out to him the curious social configuration of the region south of Kyzikos which had dominated its history for the past centuries. In Bithynia he had twice arrived from the east, using the two main routes which had long existed and were now officially maintained by the Roman state as imperial roads leading from the Bosporos crossing to the Armenian frontier. One ran along parallel to the Black Sea coast, but somewhat inland, and that was the way he had arrived in AD 124. The second came from the Anatolian interior by way of Ankyra and then turned west through Bithynia, keeping to the north of the intermittent mountains, of which Mount Olympos was the most prominent. These mountains separated Bithynia from the region called Phrygia Epiktetos to the south, and from Mysia to the south-west. It was this area which I have been calling a no-man's-land, the old frontier area between Bithynia and the Seleukid and Attalid kingdoms, where Antiochos II give his estranged wife a large estate next to Zeleia. The Bithynian kings had moved their power south to the mountain line, which then became their defence line; Kyzikos had dominated the land to the south of the city; the coastal Greek cities controlled the Propontis coast; the interior which all these territories faced continued as a land of villages and peasants, as it had been as far back as the Lydian kingdom.

It was Hadrian who finally saw that here was a region which could be developed by imperial decree and finance. Three more cities were founded in his name to occupy the fertile region which was available, one on this visit, the others on his return visit in AD 131. The political organization of the region had remained tribal all through the Akhaimenid and Hellenistic times, with chieftains occupying strong points – M'. Aquillius had campaigned here, with difficulty, in the early AD 120s.[49] The three cities were Hadrianutherae, Hadriani, and Hadriana, and they neatly occupied the hinterland of Kyzikos.[50] In a way, this was a continuation of the work of the Bithynian kings – Hadriani was south of Mount Olympos, as Prousa was to the north. The other towns were on rivers flowing north towards the Propontis, that is, within the drainage area south of Kyzikos, with Apollonia and Miletopolis to their north. Hadrian's work at last brought urban life to this frontier land and incorporated it finally into the empire.

At Parion, the city celebrated Hadrian's visit by adopting the surname Hadriani; and he was called founder, or perhaps second or third founder (after the original Greeks, and Julius Caesar, who planted a veteran colony there); what imperial generosity stimulated this honour for the Emperor is not recorded.[51] Alexandria Troas called him *restitutor*, presumably thanking him for helping to rebuild the city after the earthquake. The area had suffered a series of earthquakes, in AD 93, AD 105, and about 120 BC, spread out at just the right time distances to destroy any restorations which had been undertaken.[52] Several buildings in Ilion's Lower City had collapsed at about this period. A determined effort to rebuild there began in Trajan's reign and was no doubt assisted by Hadrian; the Lower City had largely recovered by about AD 140. Hadrian also organised the restoration of the Tumulus of Ajax, which had been eroded by the sea, by rebuilding it on a new site inland. The Odeon and a bath-cum-gymnasium were built or repaired in Hadrian's time, possibly stimulated by his visit – an imperial statue was put up – but the major finance came, in the Odeon's case, from a wealthy woman called Aristonoe. A new aqueduct to supply the city, necessary if the baths were to be of use, may be of Hadrian's date. He shared the cost of another aqueduct for Alexandria Troas with the hugely wealthy Greek Herodes Atticus.[53]

These buildings certainly enhanced the facilities of the cities, and the founding of new cities will have enabled local notables to enjoy privileged official positions in local government, while the long slow process of construction will have afforded employment opportunities for the poorest inhabitants, though it was the wealthy, as usual, who principally benefited from the work of the poor. Yet the whole scheme was not sustainable over the longer term. One reason why Hadrian could be so generous was that the empire was mainly at peace during his reign, but that condition did not significantly reduce the tax burden. Instead, the taxes collected were recycled into imperial grants and subventions. When wars began again, under Marcus Aurelius, finances would be directed into defence and the military, and the cities of the empire would lose their grants. The vaunted peace of the second century and its presumed prosperity were based on this recycling of monetary resources, which could only be temporary; the distortion of the financial system led directly to the wider failure of the third century.

Chapter 12

The New City (AD 180–330)

C hanges in the Straits area were slow to develop when it was part of the Roman Empire. Once the Roman Civil Wars were over and Augustus had vented his annoyance at some victims, there were few events which affected the region. The Civil War of 69 only brought men and armies through the region, not any fighting within it; damage was no more than could be expected from a passing army; earthquakes were far more lethal. The visits of emperors and their families, occasions when change might be forced, were few and well spaced – there were none between Germanicus in AD 17–19 and Hadrian in AD 117 (though three visits by Hadrian in fifteen years might be a case of making up for lost time). But change nonetheless did take place. Some cities failed, some were founded, as by Hadrian, all were supported by financial subventions. Pliny's inspection perhaps led to some changes, but the Bithynian cities still required imperial inspections again afterwards.[1] Hadrian urbanized the no-man's-land in Mysia, but in AD 190, when the next imperial crisis was looming, the country was recognisably that which Augustus had seen in 21–19 BC.

One of the major changes which did take place was the role of the roads, and with it the new imperial importance of Byzantion, which Trajan pointed out to Pliny was a busy town 'with crowds of travellers pouring from all sides'.[2] This importance also emerged in the crisis of the imperial succession in AD 193. The Emperor Commodus was murdered on the last day of AD 192, and for several months the crisis was confined to Rome, with rather too many new emperors being emplaced and then swiftly overthrown. But, like the preceding crisis in AD 69, this one then spilled over into the rest of the empire. In late March, the Emperor Pertinax was killed and Didius Julianus, the surviving consul, persuaded the Guard to appoint him as the new emperor rather than Flavius Sulpicianus, the Prefect of the City, who was the other possibility at that moment.

But then, as the news of what had gone on spread, and the weakness of Julianus' position as Emperor was understood, the crisis came to the frontiers, and three men claimed the post of Emperor in his place.[3]

The governor of Britannia, Clodius Albinus, had three legions at his back; the governor of Syria, Pescennius Niger, had six; the governor of Pannonia, Septimius Severus, had three in his own province, but he was in the prime geographical position with regard to Rome and was able to gather support from neighbouring governors and their legions to the extent of a total of sixteen legions. He bought off Clodius Albinus and reached Rome, first of the three.[4] Possession of the city gave him a certain legitimacy, he intimidated the Senate into accepting him and his success brought further support; soon he held all Europe and North Africa, except Britannia, while Niger held the eastern provinces. It seemed like a replay of the situation in AD 69, and Niger marched his forces westwards, but could gain no new support. He established a precarious control over Asia Minor, gathered support from neighbouring governors – again precariously, for they did not have any significant armed forces. He crossed the Bosporos into Thrace. Byzantion was garrisoned.

But there was not to be a replay of the imperial crisis of 69.

Niger found that there was a Severan army commanded by L. Fabius Cilo already in the neighbourhood in Thrace, having probably arrived from his governorship of Illyricum by sea, and the two forces clashed in rival attempts to seize the city of Perinthos. According to Dio Cassius, Niger advanced towards Perinthos but then retired on the perception of unlucky omens. He does not mention the battle itself, but it is referred to by the *Historia Augusta*, and by Herodian; Niger claimed it as a victory and celebrated it on a coin issue. His commander was Asellius Aemilianus, the governor of Asia, who had perhaps crossed to Thrace before Niger arrived and had fought the battle.[5]

The arrival of further Severan forces compelled Niger to relinquish whatever land in Thrace he had seized, except for Byzantion. An army of three legions under L. Marius Maximus, the governor of Moesia, laid siege to Byzantion while a second army commanded by Claudius Candidus crossed from Thrace into the land south of the Propontis. Although no historian says so, it is obvious that the army crossed by way of the Hellespont, though since Kyzikos had apparently declared for Severus some troops may have been shipped directly from Perinthos into the city.

(One notes Kyzikos' canny recognition of the locus of power, once again.) The appearance of these Severan forces, in the Troad and advancing towards Kyzikos, brought Niger's army under Aemilianus to face the invader; it had presumably been stationed in the Bithynian peninsula to support the Byzantines and to block a crossing by the Bosporos. Nikomedia, with Niger's army on one side, and the Severan on the other, declared for Severus and was reinforced by a Severan detachment. Its early defection from Niger was partly the result of rivalry with Nikaia,[6] and partly a recogition of the fragility of Niger's political position.

A battle of sorts was fought near Kyzikos, and another, more serious, at the approaches to Nikaia, with archers shooting from the lake, and Niger's forces occupying defences in the hills south of the city. The battle was a hard fight and Candidus had to personally intervene at one point to rally his defeated and retreating troops when Niger himself arrived to inspire his own men. Candidus' victory led to Nikomedia's confirmation as the chief city of Bithynia, whereas until then Nikaia, as the wealthier of the two, had seemed the more important.

Aemilianus was captured and executed; Niger and the survivors of the army 'fled' eastwards, though the term seems inaccurate since the army moved across Asia Minor in relatively good order and made a stand in the Taurus passes; dislodged from that position, it retreated again and gathered at Issos on the borders of Cilicia and Syria, where, after a stubborn fight, it was finally defeated.

This campaign was, in some ways, a reprise of the campaign of Alexander the Great five centuries earlier: his first victory had been in the Troad, not far from Kyzikos, and the decisive victory which opened up the Persian Empire for him was at Issos – a function of the military geography of Asia Minor; it is clear that once a victorious army had crossed the Straits – both armies crossed over at the Hellespont – and defeated the defender, the whole of Asia Minor was open to it. The Kyzikos-Nikaia fighting was equivalent to the Granikos battle; Issos was the last place on the route east at which Syria could be defended.

The evacuation of the Syrian army did not include the forces holding Byzantion. The siege went on for another two years, described with some detail by Dio Cassius and Herodian.[7] How hard the besiegers tried to capture the city is not obvious, but it is clear that they failed. At the same time, the citizens soon appreciated that, with Niger dead, Fabius

Cilo as governor of Bithynia, and Marius Maximus commanding the besieging army, they were going to lose. Another aspect which is not clear is just how committed the citizens were to Niger's cause; the city had been occupied by Niger's army before it was called on to decide, so it seems probable that, in keeping with its earlier history, the city would have opted for neutrality had it had the choice. Probably the forces put in the city by Niger compelled the resistance to continue.

There was a steady flow of deserters, or refugees, leaving the city by boat during the siege, and the remainder were reduced to starvation. A final attempt at evacuation failed when the boats, overloaded and sailing badly, were intercepted by Severus' fleet and sunk with great execution. The survivors in the city then surrendered. The soldiers and the city magistrates were killed at once, and the rest appear to have been left alone (though possibly enslaved). The city was destroyed, at least to the extent that it was no longer physically defensible. The walls, widely and justly admired, and correctly so judging by the length of the siege, were dismantled. The city was also destroyed in the sense of being deprived of its civic status; the ruins were awarded as a village to Perinthos.[8]

The city's status was restored soon enough. The story is that Severus' son, later called Caracalla, requested this, but the work that was done implies that the Emperor was fully aware of the importance of the place.[9] He had gone on to a Parthian war after defeating Niger and marched his army back through Byzantion when he had made peace. He had a soldier's eye for strategic positions, and since the might of Roman military strength was now divided between the Danube frontier (with which he was already very familiar) and the eastern frontier, the Byzantion crossing was a vital point he cannot have missed. Hence the rebuilding and refortification.

The city was rebuilt, with a new wall, hippodrome, agora, baths and basilica, all the normal equipment of a Roman city (though the hippodrome inside the walls was an extravagance). But the city was not in the same place as before. The former city was on the higher part, occupying the point overlooking the Bosporos, which is now occupied by the Ottoman Palace. This was left in ruins, a stark reminder of the cost of defying an emperor. The new city was on the lower ground to the west of the old. Theoretically its new walls enclosed twice the area of the former city, which was included in the site, but the occupied area was about the same. Two harbours were also constructed on the Golden Horn side, one for warships, one for commerce – an imitation of other cities with notable ports, notably Carthage and Alexandria. A military base and headquarters, the Strategeion, was rebuilt nearby, and warehouses were constructed. A colonnaded street in the latest architectural fashion was laid from the centre of the new city to a gate in the new walls, to connect with the Via Egnatia, which by now extended from Kypsela to the Bosporos.[10]

The Parthian War of Severus inflicted severe damage on the Parthian monarchy and in the AD 220s it succumbed to an internal rebellion, being replaced by a new and much more vigorous dynasty, the Sassanids. Meanwhile the Roman Empire went through a series of coups, rebellions, and divisions. Repeated wars with the Sassanids called for repeated expeditionary forces heading west; repeated coups saw new emperors passing through; all used the Byzantion route. The Severan city was a much busier place than the earlier version.

The collapse of the administration of the Roman Empire in the AD 250s, with emperors following one another after only brief reigns, attracted the attentions of outsiders, not just the Sassanid emperors, but the old Roman enemies north of the European frontier. For the people of the Straits region, the enemy came from the Ukraine and beyond the Danube, raiding first into Thrace and the eastern lands along the Black Sea, and then in AD 257 directly into Asia Minor. These were Goths, who prepared their expedition very carefully, building their own ships, and sailing their fleet along the western coast of the Black Sea, and keeping pace with their army as it marched. At Byzantion, which they did not attack, no doubt because it was apparently well defended, they crossed the Bosporos and seized Chalkedon, where it is said the soldiers fled at the barbarians' approach.[11]

The city was sacked and the raiders went on to do the same at the Nikomedia, Nikaia, Kios, Apameia, and Prusa. They did not reach Kysikos only because the Rhyndakos River was in flood, and perhaps because they were by now heavily burdened with plenty of loot. They returned the same way that they had come, burning Nikaia and Nikomedia on the way.[12] There were supposed to be soldiers in Nikomedia, but they are not referred to. (These city garrisons were usually fairly small, commanded by a centurion and with perhaps no more than a dozen or twenty soldiers.) Zosimus claims that the Emperor Valerian did nothing except send a commander, Felix, to Byzantion to take command. He fails to note that this was the one city which effectively defended itself.[13]

A second raid later in the AD 260s again sacked Chalkedon and Nikomedia, cities which could be easily reached from the sea. They sailed on through the Hellespont, apparently without stopping, and then raided in Ionia and on into Greece. Once again Byzantion was ignored, as were Kyzikos and the cities along both sides of the Hellespont. Kyzikos, however, was certainly raided in AD 267, but probably only on its island; it was as well defended as Byzantion, or better, and even survived a siege, according to Ammianus Marcellinus.[14] One historian suggested that the strong current drove the Goths' and Herulean ships through the Strait too quickly for them to do more than go with the flow, but it is unlikely that he (Zosimos) knew much about ships or the sea.[15]

The domination of the upstart Palmyrenes out of Syria in the early AD 270s extended as far as Ankyra, and was being stretched further by intrigues. Chalkedon was the scene of internal disputes about whether to accept Palmyrene authority, but as soon as the news of Emperor Aurelian's approach was known, the 'Palmyrene faction', as Zosimus calls it, faded away.[16] Palmyrene control of the rest of Asia Minor faded in much the same way as soon as Aurelian's army began marching through. How far the Chalkedon situation was repeated in other cities is not actually known, but it seems likely that many others held 'Palmyrene factions'. It is perhaps one of the signs of the instability of the empire that cities were undecided as to who was Emperor and who was to be supported.

Roman armies repeatedly marched through the city and across into Asia, or in reverse, from Asia through Byzantion to deal with European problems. This was the route followed by the Emperor Aurelian in AD 272 in his campaign to quench the pretensions of the Palmyrenes under Zenobia. His army included a series of future emperors – Carus and his sons, Probus, perhaps Tacitus, Diocletian – who could thus have become as familiar with the Straits region as Aurelian and his imperial predecessors.

One of the major changes in the whole perception of the empire between the times of Elagabalus (AD 218–222), who came from Syria to Rome by way of Byzantion in a long, slow, leisurely journey,[17] and that of Carus and his sons and Diocletian in the AD 280s, was that Rome was demoted from the necessary imperial centre to the status of an historical monument.

Aurelian (AD 270–275) organised the building of a wall around the city in a gesture of defence, but neither he nor his predecessors for fifty years had spent much time there, and some none at all. With the frontiers in Britain, in Germany, on the Danube, and in the East liable to burst into flame at any moment, the centre of the empire was now wherever the Emperor was, and the emperors had necessarily become warriors.

So Alexander Severus (AD 222–235) spent much time, and was killed at, Colonia Agrippina in Germany, Gallienus (AD 253–268) marched about campaigning in the Balkans and Italy, expelling invaders and suppressing rivals, and meanwhile Gaul detached itself into a rival, stable, imperial regime for over a decade, and so on. By the time Diocletian's fist of iron gripped the empire for two decades (AD 284–305) – the longest rule of an emperor since Antoninus Pius and Hadrian – Rome had ceased to be the capital of the empire in all but name, and the Senate, which had often determined the choice of Emperor during the preceding anarchy, was reduced to impotence.

With the return of political stability, which may be dated from the reign of Aurelius, if not from that of his predecessor Claudius Gothicus, who had defeated the Gothic invasion of AD 268, though the new condition was one only by comparison with the preceding chaos, there could be a return to a less frenetic imperial journeying. Diocletian's curious experiment in government, the 'Tetrarchy', in which the empire was in effect divided into four sections, each of which had its own emperor – 'Augustus' or 'Caesar' – virtually insisted that each Emperor establish himself and his administration in one place, inevitably in a city which was already populous and well-established where the imperial personnel could be supported, fed, entertained, and could find accommodation. In some areas the choice was inevitable – Antioch in Syria, for example, was the only possible choice in the east – but elsewhere it was less clear. In Italy, several cities – Milan, Ravenna, Rome – were used, and in the west also. In that section of the empire which Diocletian himself ruled, the Balkans and Asia Minor, with Syria and the East, there was a choice of several places, and he resided at several places in his campaigns, but he chose to build his new capital at Nikomedia.

There were certain constraints to be observed in choosing an imperial capital. Given the constant threats of barbarian invasion, it had to be within relatively easy reach of the frontiers; at the same time, it could not be actually on the frontier, except for a relatively brief period while the Emperor was campaigning in the area. It could not be far from the action or potential action – this was why Rome had been abandoned as the imperial centre, because it was a march of a week or more from the action in northern Italy, and then there were the Alps to pass to reach the frontier itself. In the east Antioch was ideally placed, some distance back from the frontier, in a fertile and populous country, well established as a major city, and as a governing centre. The emperors could live in the governor's palace, which had been an imperial palace in the time of the Seleukid kings – a city which had been a capital for six centuries. In Italy, Milan was close to the Alpine passes if the barbarians penetrated so far, and in a rich and populous region where the army could be fed and supplied, and as well the imperial administration could operate. In Gaul, one of the cities on the frontier – Moguntiacum or Colonia Agrippina – might be used, but it was soon realised it was better to settle the administration in Trier, a little back from the active frontier, and later one of the cities of southern Gaul, such as Nemausus or Arelate, was also used. From there, a constant contact could be kept with the emperors in Italy and the east by sea and the German frontier was not too far off; the British frontier was less important, but the danger did provoke a usurpation by Carausius in AD 286.

The German frontier, with that along the upper Danube, was a unit, and could be watched from Trier and Milan; the frontiers in the east were separate, in that penetration across the Danube brought the invaders into the Balkans, whereas the eastern frontier had to be guarded against Sassanid attacks, which were likely to be much more predictable and organized. In the section of the empire comprising the Balkans and Asia Minor, therefore, the geopolitical problem was greater than elsewhere, since there were two frontiers to be watched, that on the Danube and that from Persia. This meant that the imperial administrative centre had to be at a convenient route centre, as well as in a fertile and productive land which was populous and within reach of both frontiers in a relatively short time. This dictated a city somewhere in the Straits region.

So, after a thousand or more years of Greek settlement and occupation, the region around the Propontis and its maritime connections had finally become the centre of power for a wide region. It was not, of course, actually the first time this had come about. Apart from the existence of

Troy for a couple of thousand years, there had been moments when some king or empire who had lingered in the region had governed from it. But could Troy be considered any sort of a capital, when it was the only place of any size in the area? It had been attended, or surrounded, by villages on both sides of the Hellespont, but there had been, so far as we know, no other urban centre for tens of miles in all directions, and the place itself had normally been small. It had been, that is, an isolated minor city state. Troy had been alone, and it may be reckoned a kingdom with the surrounding territory, but hardly any sort of capital centre – that lay far to the east at Hittite Hattusas, or south by water at one of the Mycenaean palaces for a short time, or perhaps in Crete.

The Greek colonial cities had held their territories, large or small, notably Byzantion, Kyzikos, and Alexandria Troas but they had never shown any sign of an ambition for anything greater than owning an island or dominating a nearby city. It appears that Pompey had organized the territories of some of the cities, so that most of the old Bithynian kingdom was partitioned between them, but the royal estates would no doubt have passed the Roman state.[18]

Lysimachos had founded his city of Lysimacheia at a nodal point on the Hellespontine Chersonese, an equivalent of Troy as a local centre on the other side of the water, but he had hardly used his new city as a capital centre. It was in a very useful position when he held both Asia Minor and Thrace (and later Macedon), but he preferred the more comfortable Ephesos as a residence to the still new city of Lysimacheia, still with builders' dust blowing in the cold winds from the Black Sea. A century and a half later, another king ruled in Asia Minor and (at least part of) Thrace, a replication of Lysimachos' kingdom; Antiochos Hierax had chosen the same geographical area for his imperial centre. He had used Alexandria Troas as his capital, though he cannot have been there for long given his constant need to defend his kingdom. No doubt the name of Alexandria was attractive as an imperial capital and as a claim to sovereignty, and the nearby presence of Troy/Ilion provided him with a ready-made imperial shrine. He certainly spent money on enhancing the locality, but he lasted as king only a dozen years; his status as a Seleukid rebel and as an Attalid enemy in a sense contaminated the area for his successors. But it had been a better try than Lysimachos'.

It may in fact be partly accidental that the new imperial capital was selected to be Nikomedia in the Straits area. In AD 283 the Emperor Carus died, and his two sons inherited the empire jointly, Numerian in the east, Carinus in the west. This was hardly the first time the empire had been divided or had come under the rule of young men; if they could have time enough to grow up, establish their power, and remain in harmony, there was hope for a long joint reign and a stable recovery. But Carinus was much disliked, and Numerian died on the journey across Asia Minor. This may not have mattered, but Numerian's praetorian prefect, Lucius Aper, concealed the death and, claiming that he was ill, issued orders in his name. Eventually some of the soldiers became suspicious, opened the curtains of the litter he was in and found the truth. At least that is one version of the events; Numerian certainly died on the way and Aper certainly aimed for the throne. Aper was arrested. The army halted to consider what to do. It was at that time not far from Nikomedia.[19]

To most it was clear that Aper was attempting to become Emperor; he had a claim of sorts, being Carus' brother-in-law. But now he was counted out. A council of officers met. It had a number of options to consider – accept Carus' surviving son as sole emperor, choose a new emperor to rule with him, sit and wait, reject Carinus and find a new emperor to rule alone, even accept Aper. The leading man in the council was Diocles, indeed he may have organised it in order to present the solution as one which had been carefully considered, rather than a coup, though it is clear that he himself was aiming to be chosen. With a bit of manoeuvring, the decision arrived at was that Diocles should be the new emperor. He took the name Diocletian and at a meeting with the army, publicly murdered Aper. Carinus, of course, objected. The two emperors' armies fought a sanguinary battle at the River Margus near the border of Italy and Illyricum. Carinus, repeatedly betrayed and deserted by his chief colleagues, and widely disliked for his brutality, was murdered during the battle by his own soldiers. Diocletian, a relatively junior commander before the army council meeting, emerged as sole emperor.[20]

The crucial meeting was thus at or near Nikomedia, and it may be that the superstitious Diocletian chose it as his seat of government because of its association with his election. Emperors have certainly been known to make decisions on such a basis, but he may also have found more rational reasons. The city was in a way a blank sheet, having been raided three times, and wrecked a quarter of a century before by Gothic raiders. How extensive the damage had been is not known, but they had first sacked it and then returned and burned it. It is probable that a good deal of the city survived, but the experience would have been harrowing, and probably some of the public buildings had not been rebuilt, for lack of money at a time of stress and in the public finances. In a similar situation, the burnt areas at Ilion remained uncleared for a century or so. There was probably an area of ruins which was available for the new imperial palace.

The city had suffered in a third attack in the 260s because the Goths and Heruli raiders were in ships this time, and they could reach the city from the sea. This had been a misfortune at the time, but for developing, or redeveloping, a major city easy access to the sea, and the ability of ships to reach the city, was a major benefit. Imperial palaces demanded the best, and Proconnesian marble could be brought easily by sea from the island where it was mined; the island, of course, belonged to Kyzikos. The city was also in a useful position with regard to the eastern and Danube frontiers, and being a port it could house a fleet, which would have access to the Black Sea (whence had come the raiders) and the Aegean, and thus to the rest of the empire. It was also situated on the main imperial road from the Bosporos to the legionary base at Satala, facing Armenia. Whether or not Diocletian had superstitious reasons for choosing the city as his new capital, he had plenty of good practical reasons as well. The Roman army was by this time fully familiar with the usefulness of such a base in Bithynia; it is doubtful that Diocletian needed to be very persuasive.

The city was rebuilt, but in a style suited to an autocracy, that is, with a strong concentration on a large palace, together with the foundation of one of Diocletian's *fabricate*, for manufacturing military equipment. He also is said to have built a palace for his wife, and one for his daughter – they will certainly have had separate establishments and courts.[21] The city already hosted some military units, as Pliny had noted eighty years before, but now there would be a much larger contingent of soldiers as Imperial guards and as an emergency field force under the emperor's own hand. The city also already had several aqueducts, perhaps including the one which Trajan had insisted that Pliny saw was finished.[22] There will have been new walls, perhaps – the old one had maybe been damaged in the raids – and certainly new villas for the wealthy and the senior officials. There was presumably also an incoming of a new population which would serve the rich and powerful in their several ways. It all reputedly cost a great deal of money, but that is hardly surprising. If the required workmen were found quickly enough the buildings would have been completed fairly quickly. (The short-reigned Emperor Elagabalus had a great new temple built in Rome, probably in less than a year.) It was all designed to impress, and to proclaim that here was a new, permanent, imperial regime.

The half century between Elagabalus' weird and self-defeating religious exhibitionism and the grim regime instituted by Diocletian, was a time of imperial collapse and retreat. It was also a time of wasting wealth, so that resources for every city were much reduced. The investigations at Ilion illustrate the problem.[23] In the AD 260s there was considerable damage caused in the Lower City, occasioned possibly by a barbarian raid in AD 262 (probably not the one which raided Nikaia and Nikomedia) or an earthquake (or possibly both), that constant explanation for damage in this area.[24] The damaged buildings were left in ruins, as had happened before, and the reduced population retreated to a smaller part of the Lower City.

A reference to a 'New Panathenaia' suggests that the celebration of the festivals in the city had been interrupted or intermittent and, along with the absence of imperial largesse ever since Caracalla's visit in AD 217, this will have sharply reduced the receipts from tourism. No doubt the same lack was felt at Alexandria Troas, since one of that city's main economic activities was in forwarding tourists from its port to Ilion and back again. Constantine visited Ilion in AD 324, only to dismiss the possibility of using either of the two cities as his new capital. But the surviving citizens at Ilion, perhaps reviving somewhat by that time, seem to have put up a quartet of statues to the four emperors of the Tetrarchy at some point in the AD 290s (though only the bases remain). In the AD 360s the Emperor Julian was honoured for his revival of paganism, which implies that the city, not at all surprisingly, remained staunchly loyal to the Greek and Roman gods, a generation after the imperial administration became officially Christian.

This change had taken time to be effected. The empire had become increasingly concerned at the possible sedition of Christians, the new sect which, with the promise of salvation in heaven, had spread particularly widely during the troubled times in the third century AD.[25] Attempts had been made to suppress this new religion, which distinguished itself from the other beliefs which had spread in the empire – Mithraism, worship of Jupiter Dolichenus, Judaism, and others. It was different, from the Roman government's point of view, in that it refused to acknowledge any supervening authority other than its own god. This meant that its adherents might refuse to accept Roman civil (and military) authority, following the example of the sect's prophet, Jesus Christ, who had been executed as a criminal and seditious agitator by the governor of Judaea, an example likely to be followed by its later adherents. The problem for the government was that its automatic reaction was to imprison and/or execute these disobedient subjects, but this was something many of them welcomed as martyrdom, providing them with a swift passage to their heaven. That is, force was unsuccessful.

This, of course, made Christianity even more obnoxious to the Roman system, and efforts at suppression redoubled. The religion was especially prominent in the eastern half of the empire, perhaps in part because it fed on the resentment which many groups in that part of the empire felt at Roman suppression. But the governmental effort involved in the persecutions was so great, and the results so meagre, that each bout of persecution lasted only a year or so before being abandoned, an abandonment greeted by the Christians as a victory, while they celebrated those who had been killed as martyrs. The empire could not win this contest.[26]

Diocletian, inevitably, was a persecutor, though not eagerly so. His overall policy was to fasten imperial control over all aspects of life in the empire even more strongly than ever before. Cities' independence was no longer to be tolerated, civil coinages were replaced by uniform imperial issues, the population was to be directed, above all into imperial service, individuals were to follow their fathers into the same work, and so on, even down to dictating the prices for goods throughout the empire – all in all, a good attempt at a totalitarian state. The gods were to be enlisted also, and prayers, worship, and sacrifice were to be offered to them; and those gods included the emperors, Diocletian as the personification of Jupiter, Maximian as that of Hercules.[27] Needless to say, the Christians would not fit in, though many actually did as they were told – martyrdoms were only for the few and the fanatical.

But the Christians were a seditious group and were persecuted once Diocletian understood their recalcitrance. On the other hand, as Pliny had found when he discovered that Bithynia held many professing to be Christians, it did not take much pressure for the majority of Christians to cease to practice the religion; in other words, it was often more a social movement than an affair of belief.[28]

Diocletian and his fellow Emperor Maximian were shocked to find that the oracle of Apollo at Didyma was blaming the prevalence of Christians for its inability to reply effectively to the emperors.[29] Diocletian had already attempted to remove Christians from the army, and a decree of persecution had been directed at Manichaeans, so that this existed as a model for a carefully directed persecution of Christians, at first aimed at bishops, churches, and documents – the essential elements of the religion as an institution.[30] It soon became more violent, however, but much of the pressure still remained social – prominent men discovered as Christians were to lose their social status, imperial freedmen who were Christians were to be returned to slavery, slaves were to be forbidden manumission.[31] Of course, Christian propagandists emphasised the suffering and the deaths, which were no doubt considerable and numerous, though the chroniclers' accounts are clearly exaggerated, even invented, and they do tend to dwell rather sickeningly on the suffering involved. The whole proceeding was, however, as before, futile, and in AD 305, when Diocletian and Maximian retired from their offices, the persecution ended; it was quickly revived by one of their successors, Galerius, until 311, but only in the east of the empire.

Diocletian's imperial scheme of government suffered a serious blow within the year after his retirement. In Britannia, on the death of Constantius Chlorus in AD 306, his son Constantine was proclaimed, or proclaimed himself, Emperor. This was quite against the scheme which Diocletian had devised. Constantine proved to be more capable than any of his competitors (who were several) until by AD 312 he had gained control of all the western half of the empire and was pressing eastwards. His main competitor was Licinius (Galerius died in AD 311), and the two of them eliminated other Emperor-claimants to share the empire between them. Constantine initiated a tolerant regime in his area, and Licinius, one of whose main centres was Nikomedia, is accused of being a persecutor by Christian sources, though this was mainly an artefact of the Christian historians to justify their support for Constantine. The differences between the two men were in fact more personal and political than religious, though Licinius did remain loyal to the old Roman religion.

Nikomedia had remained Diocletian's capital until his retirement, then it was Galerius' city for a time and then Licinius'. By the time the final break between Licinius and Constantine occurred in AD 324, Nikomedia had been the imperial capital for forty years, certainly long enough for its status to be widely understood and accepted, and for the imperial administration to be fully founded there. Constantine, on the other hand, had been on the move all during his reign, partly because he had only gradually acquired the various parts of the empire from Britannia eastwards and each additional territory became, at least for a while, his residence. As a result, his capital had shifted frequently from York, to Trier, to Arles, to Milan, to Rome, to Sofia in Moesia. Furthermore, he was a man who was personally familiar with much of the empire. He had grown up in Diocletian's Nikomedia, where he had experienced the anti-Christian measures taken when the Emperor found that a number of the people working in the palace were Christians and had to be expelled in the same way that soldier-Christians were removed from the army. He was therefore able during his life to appreciate the usefulness of a permanent residence for the imperial administration, which, since Diocletian's reforms, had become steadily more elaborate. He could also evaluate the usefulness of the various cities he had used, many of which he had stayed in, or used, for long enough to appreciate their advantages and deficiencies.

The partnership of Constantine and Licinius, if that is anything like an accurate description, was never stable, and they were easily able to find causes for enmity. Above all, Constantine, with his string of victories and conquests behind him, was ambitious to become the sole emperor. Since neither Constantine nor Licinius appointed Caesar-deputies, it is evident that both harboured the same ambition. A first war between the two in AD 316–317 resulted in Constantine's conquest of most of the Balkans, though Licinius held on to Thrace. In AD 324 they fell into a further conflict, and again Constantine, better prepared, more militant, and more capable than Licinius, attacked. Licinius was driven out of Thrace after a defeat at Hadrianopolis. He stood a siege at Byzantion, but Constantine's son Crispus gained control of the Propontis and the

Straits with a large fleet. Licinius evacuated Byzantion and crossed with all his forces to Chalkedon. Byzantion, abandoned, therefore surrendered to Constantine, who then used his fleet to move his own army across the Bosporos. The two armies met at Chrysopolis, beside Chalkedon, on the southern tip of the Bithynian peninsula, where the Byzantines had long had a customs post. Licinius once again lost the fight and retired to Nikomedia, while much of his army disintegrated. He surrendered on the promise of his life to be spared and spent in retirement at Thessalonica, a promise which lasted only a year.[32]

Constantine's ambition had been realised, and in the process he had used yet another city, Thessalonica, as his residence during his last war. He now decreed an end to all persecution in the empire. He therefore permitted Christians to worship in their own way, but clearly expected loyalty to the empire – and to him personally – in return. This was one of the reforms he enacted in this period of victory, but it may not be the most important. There is evidence that he counted himself as a Christian, but as Emperor he clearly had difficulty in subordinating himself to any god, still less to a bishop. In many ways he followed Diocletian's practice in emphasising the unity of the empire, and set about reconciling, or at least bringing together in some way, the various Christian factions and practices. The council he convened at Nikaia in AD 325 in Bithynia had that purpose, not so much for the benefit of the Christian participants, as for the benefit of the empire and to promote internal peace. The Christian participants proved even more disputatious, even quarrelsome, than the previous imperial rivals. Christian unity proved to be very difficult, indeed impossible, to achieve; Diocletian's emphasis on unity and uniformity carried on through until the Christians resorted to persecuting each other.

The location of the council, at Bithynian Nikaia, is another mark of the imperial centrality which the Straits region had acquired since the reconstruction of imperial unity by Diocletian, and by the victory of Constantine. It was preceded by provincial councils, and it had been intended to meet at Ankyra; Constantine enlarged it in size and membership and shifted it to Nikaia, explaining that this was more convenient for bishops from the west to reach, its climate was better than that of Ankyra, and he wanted to participate himself. This last is surely the crucial point; he wanted the meeting close by and under his hand; that is, he was still using Nikomedia as his capital.[33]

It is probable that Constantine's familiarity with Nikomedia, the presence of the council at Nikaia, and the need to remain in the area to see to the establishment of his authority in the eastern half of the empire, brought the centrality of the Straits region to his full attention. He had already rejected Rome as his preferred centre, despite the popularity he had earned by the overthrow of Maxentius and the 'liberation' of the city from that emperor's rule.[34] None of the other places he had used were apparently attractive for various reasons – too small, too remote, too difficult to supply, and so on. Some were, now that the empire was under one man's rule, far too marginal geographically for anything but a brief visit or as a campaign headquarters. This would rule out anything west of Rome, though Milan remained a possibility, though from there communications with the East would be difficult. Anything east of Nikomedia was also too remote for Western problems. Constantine travelled to Syria while considering this problem and must have realized his isolation from the west once he was in Antioch. Whether he formulated the matter in these terms is not known, but it is clear that he concentrated his attention on the Balkans and Asia Minor.

Nikomedia may have beckoned. It was fully established as a major governmental city, it had the palace, and the imperial administration was already there, and he stayed there after the overthrow of Licinius. Nikaia might have been considered, given that it could host all those quarreling clerics. It is possible that he considered Chalkedon, but there is only a late story that he did so, and by comparison there were obviously better sites in the Straits area. He must have considered Kyzikos also, which had become a local government centre for half of Asia Minor in Diocletian's scheme, and the station of a legion. To the west in the Straits region was the site of Lysimacheia; this was now desolate, but if he wanted a clear site on which to build a new city this might do. And across the Hellespont there was Ilion.

Further away there was Thessalonica which, like the others under consideration, was a substantial city, on the coast, and had been used as an imperial administrative centre already. It had good communications northwards into the Balkans and towards the Danube frontier, and was in fact somewhat closer to that frontier than any of the others. Serdica (Sofia) was a possibility, in a fertile region and closer still to the Danube frontier, but it did not have the good communications nor any access to the sea of the other cities, being well inland. These landward and peripheral cities were probably listed only to be rejected, if they were actively considered. If Constantine was going to be establish a new capital and if Rome was to be rejected, it would have to be in the Straits area.

That finding a site for his new city was on Constantine's mind is shown by the story of his visit to Ilion during AD 324. He sailed from, probably, Nikomedia or Nikaia, going the length of the Propontis, no doubt viewing Kyzikos and Lysimacheia on the way, and perhaps Perinthos and Parion as well. But his destination was the site of Troy, legendary home of the origin of the Romans. This legend was clearly the notion which inspired both the visit and the thought that the place might become Constantine's new city. It was also, as a bonus, a place of renown, or holiness, to the Greeks because of the Trojan War, which they claimed to have won. Constantine could see the city which had flourished with its festivals for the past three centuries on the basis of being a major tourist attraction. It had probably become rather age-worn and less prosperous than before along with all the other cities of the empire because of the troubles of the past century, and the rise of Christianity. But its spiritual resonance for Romans and Greeks were strong enough to bring the busy Emperor on the two-day voyage.[35]

But when he came to examine the site Constantine would have seen also that it was quite unsuitable for a major city. The current through the Hellespont was difficult, the winds would similarly hinder communications, the anchorages were inconvenient, the productivity of the surrounding land was only average, the water supply was inadequate even for the existing cities and its land communications were poor. And, on consideration, those spiritual resources were of the past, the past of the old gods which he was renouncing. He had probably by now accepted Christianity wholeheartedly; a new city redolent with tales of Aeneas and Ajax and Hector and Helen, and whose most prominent buildings were the temple of Athena and a great statue of Zeus, was an unsuitable place for his new city. The new city would have to be distinctively Christian.

Considering other candidates for the site of the new city, many could be eliminated for geographical reasons, but others for the same reason Constantine could give for eliminating Ilion. He claimed that God pointed out the difficulty of Troy in a dream, but this fiction was no doubt largely to avoid argument, for no Christian could argue against God's nocturnal message to the emperor. But it equally ruled out Nikomedia from the possibilities, since that had been the seat of the Great Persecutor, where Diocletian as Jupiter had reigned – and it simultaneously eliminated Rome. And so, by process of elimination, because it had good sea and land communications and had no previous overwhelming pagan atmosphere, and despite its less than fertile and productive hinterland, Byzantion ended being the Emperor's choice. His dream had named it, so it had been under consideration along with the rest, and had gradually floated to the top of the list as the others were serially eliminated. Therefore, the choice was sanctified. But it was Constantine's decision, since Troy had been dismissed along with Nikomedia. And yet it was not a city which had been the obvious choice until the very end; Byzantion was the least bad option.

Once the decision was made, the work proceeded swiftly. The Severan city had a number of the necessary buildings already in place, but Constantine, with a greater vision for his city, enlarged the hippodrome and the great baths, removed the enclosing wall and built a new one to defend a much larger area. This also included the junction of the two great roads from the interior, so that whereas the Severan wall had just one gate – the 'Old Gate', a name suggesting that the built gate survived for some time – Constantine's wall had three. The new wall was four kilometres in advance of the old – the city was planned to be one of the largest in the Roman world from the start. (This, of course, would necessitate a much larger garrison.)

These walls were later superseded by the present Theodosian Wall, even further in advance of the city centre, and their form can only be conjectured from the general understanding of military architecture of the time. One of the elements in Constantine's choice of this site for development and enlargement was the military history of the old city of Byzantion. It had stood a siege for nearly three years against Severus' army when defended only by an old Hellenistic wall and it had been held by Licinius, again under siege, until he evacuated it. And that was when it was only a relatively small place. Now bigger, and better equipped with fortifications and soldiers, it could well be invulnerable – a major consideration in a time of invasions and civil wars.

The basic equipment of the city was thus already present, but for two major items. A new imperial palace was built. It was placed beside the hippodrome. The two were in fact a single imperial unit, for the hippodrome was not only a racetrack, but was also an integral part of the imperial system, the place where the Emperor appeared to his assembled subjects, visibly; there was a special imperial box from which he could see the races and where he was visible to the crowd. That box, the *Kathisma*, led directly back into the Palace, which was built alongside the hippodrome, occupying a large part of the south-eastern corner of the city site. Appearances in the hippodrome were the nearest thing the new totalitarian empire possessed for any sort of popular participation or approval, all that was left of the elections and politics of the old Rome. Eventually, of course, the emperors realised that appearing in the *Kathisma* could be dangerous if the population was sufficiently roused against them – popular approval included displays of disapproval – and the most detested Emperors suffered overthrow.

Then it was necessary to equip the city with churches. No doubt there had been some in the city before Constantine, though it was a small city and the record is deficient; where they were is not clear, other than that they must have been within the walls of the Severan city. (Any which had been established in the old Greek city had no doubt been wrecked in the destruction by Severus' army.) The only church built at Constantine's instructions and finished in his lifetime was that of the Holy Apostles, intended to be his mausoleum. It was built on the highest point of the city, inside the walls, and it dominated the city (as its successor the Fatih Mosque also does today). To be buried inside the walls of an ancient city was the privilege of a founder, a *ktistes*, which, of course, Constantine was. (Non-founders had to be buried outside the walls.) Other churches were apparently intended to be built as they became required by the increasing Christian, or increasingly Christian, population. Constantine ordered the production of a set of fifty Bibles in preparation for the church-building which was to take place in the future.

The essentials, the wall, the Palace and the hippodrome were finished, the ports, the warehouses, the garrison, the military headquarters were all pre-existent though, no doubt, like other buildings, they had to be refurbished and enlarged. For new buildings, construction at least was far enough advanced for them to be used by 328 for a ceremony of civic dedication. The cathedral of Hagia Sophia had been founded in AD 326, but it took over thirty years to build, and so was not a priority. By AD 330 the city walls were ready and the city was officially consecrated – that is, it was formally constituted as a new city, a *polis*. It was possible to build a defensive wall about 2.5 kilometres long in six years, whereas the cathedral took six times that; the priority was clearly to establish the city as a political and defended entity; the cathedral was evidently not seen as an essential element, particularly since many people would probably worship in small local churches or even house churches.[36]

The empty spaces between the buildings and between centre of the city and the walls were to be filled by private residences, plus the necessary shops, workshops, markets and roads which make up the city. Only these last were laid out in advance; subventions were available for villas to attract the wealthy, whose presence would provide employment for others and markets for workmen and shopkeepers. This scheme, if it was actually thought out, worked only to a degree. The later Theodosian walls were built in order to enclose an area where these villas had been built outside Constantine's walls, but each one would have occupied a large area, and there were always sections within the walls devoted to horticulture or even pasture. Constantine had planned for a corn dole sufficient for 80,000 recipients, the corn to be imported from Egypt (diverted from the supply originally destined for Rome) but this was never fully taken up and was halved in the next reign. The city's population remained well below the planned number for the next thousand years; in 1927 there were 200,000 people living in the area of the Theodosian city, and that area was then full. Like Rome, extravagant estimates of the city's population have long been made.[37]

Conclusion

From the time of Troy, about 3000 BC, until AD 330, the region of the Ancient Straits was the domain of a large number of relatively small cities, none of whom had made much of a mark in history, except Troy as the inspiration for a great poem; other places as victims of greater external powers.

The founding of Constantinople, on the site of the defunct city of Byzantion, was the decisive change in the political geography of the region. The immense city, the rival of Rome not merely in renown but in size, inevitably dominated its surroundings for dozens of miles in all directions. Some of the earlier cities of the region did survive, but inevitably much of their life was drained from them by the existence of 'the Great City'. Only in the recent past, with the growth of population, have places such as Izmid and Iznik revived in size; even so most of the other cities which existed before Constantinople are little more than villages even now.

The choice of Constantinople as the new imperial capital was partly by chance, partly by rational decision, partly by superstition but mainly as a result of geopolitical developments within the Roman Empire. Those considerations compelled the city to remain large, important and imperial even when it had been captured by its enemies and dethroned from its status as a capital city in favour of a cold and windy city in the middle of Anatolia. Once founded, of course, the city then embarked on an extraordinary history which separated it largely from its surroundings. In the next 1600 years it survived at least forty sieges and succumbed to only three. No other city in the world has such an extraordinary record.

The region of the Straits is therefore now centred on Constantinople in a way it never had been before the city was founded. The beginning of the human settlement in the area saw the region holding just one city, if it could be called such, at Troy. These two places are located at the furthest extremes of the Straits in two senses, chronologically and geographically. In all senses therefore the Straits stretch from Troy to Constantinople.

Notes

Chapter 1

1. Strabo 39.4–6.
2. Admiralty, *Turkey*, London 1942, 92.
3. Gunther A. Wagner *et al.*, *Troia and the Troad, Scientific Approaches,* Berlin 2003; a further examination is by Mehmet Ozdogan, based on archaeological surveys – see note 5 below.
4. This was found by British submariners who entered the Propontis by way of the Hellespont in the Great War, for the waters also provided them with unexpected buoyancy and accelerated their progress; see also David Jean Shirley and Christine Blenpied, 'Late Quaternary Water Exchange Between the Mediterranean and the Black Seas', *Nature* 285, 1980, 537–541, for a detailed explanation; the existence of the reverse flow was also known to sailors in the ancient world, and was always known to and exploited by local fishermen; it even had a local name – Kanal: John Freely, *The Bosphorus*, Istanbul 1993, 3; Dionysios of Byzantion 53.
5. M. Ozdogan, 'A Surface Survey for Prehistoric and Early Historic Sites in North-western Turkey', *National Geographic Society research Reports, 1979 Projects*, 1985, 519–541.
6. Ibid, 522, and map on 521.
7. Fikirtepe: M. Ozdogan, 'Neolithic Cultures in North-western Turkey', *Varia Archaeologicae Hungarica*, 1989 Budapest, 201–206; Pendik: M. Ozdogan, 'Pendik: a Neolithic site of the Fikirtepe Culture in the Marmara Region', in N. Hauptmann *et al.*, *Festschrift fur Kurt Bittel*, Mainz 1983, 401–411.
8. J.J. Roodenberg *et al.*, 'Preliminary Report on the Archaeological Investigation at Ilipinar in North-west Anatolia', *Anatolica* 16, 1989–1990, 61–144, and M. Ozdogan, *Neolithic in Turkey, New Discoveries*, Istanbul 1991.
9. A brief resume of these finds is in Bettany Hughes, *Istanbul, A Tale of Three Cities*, London 2017, chs 1 and 2.
10. M. Ozdogan, 'Prehistoric Sites in the Gelibolu Peninsula', *Anadolu* 10, 1988, 51– 66, at 57.
11. M. Buitenheis, 'Note on Archaeozoological research around the Sea of Marmara', *Anatolica* 20, 1994, 141–144.
12. Ozdogan, 'Neolithic cultures'.
13. Ozdogan, 'Surface Survey'.
14. J.W. Sperling, 'Kum Tepe in the Troad, Trial Excavations 1934', *Hesperia* 45, 1976, 305–364; also Jak Yakar, *Prehistoric Anatolia, the Neolithic Transformation and the Early Chalcolithic Period*, Tel Aviv, 1991.
15. Sperling, 'Kum Tepe', 355–357.
16. Ozdogan, 'Prehistoric Sites', 54; R. Demangel, 'Le Tumulus dit de Protesilaos', *Fouilles du Corps d'Occupation Francaises de Constantinople*, fascicule I, Paris 1926.

17. Sperling, 'Kum Tepe', 356.
18. Ozdogan, 'Prehistoric Sites'.
19. David Trump, *The Prehistory of the Mediterranean*, Harmondsworth 1980, 71–72.
20. Ozdogen, 'Neolithic Cultures'.
21. Trevor Bryce, *The Trojans and their Neighbours*, London 2006, 39–40; he claims the diameter is 100 metres, but the plan in the *Guide to Troy* by the staff measures it at only eighty metres; the difference does not affect the conclusion.
22. Ozdogan, 'Surface Survey', and 'Prehistoric Sites'; Sperling, 'Kum Tepe'.
23. M. Ozdogan, 'The Black Sea, the Sea of Marmara, and Bronze Age Archaeology: an Archaeological Predicament', in Wagner *et al.*, *Troia and Troad*, 105–120.
24. Map in several editions of *Studia Troia*, reproduced in the *Guide to Troy*.
25. Ozdogan, 'Black Sea'.
26. This is the conclusion reached by Carl W. Blegen as a result of his 1930s excavations at Troy: C.W. Blegen, *Troy and the Trojans*, London 1963.
27. Stefan Hiller, 'The missing Mycenaeans and the Black Sea', in R. Lauffiere *et al.*, (eds), *Thalassa L'Egee Prehistorique et la Mer*, Liege 1991, 207–216; a survey by Peter Jablonka, 'The Link' (note 2) mainly reports the same evidence.

Chapter 2
1. A convenient explanation of the latest evidence is in the *Guide to Troia*, compiled by Manfred Kaufmann *et al.*, (Istanbul 2001); later findings can be located in the successive volumes of *Studia Troia*.
2. The state of the argument on Indo-European migration was well summed up by G. Steiner, 'The Immigration of the first Indo-Europeans into Anatolia Reconsidered', *Journal of Indo-European Studies* 18, 1990, 185–214; the argument has not really moved on since then.
3. G.G. Aperghis, *The Seleukid Royal Economy*, Cambridge 2004, 13–14, put forward a convincing theory that village population densities varied from 150 to 250 per hectare, with the figure lower the larger the site (because of the presence of more public buildings). The estimate of Troy VI's population of 7,000 is by Kaufmann in his *Guide to Troy* (38). By Aperghis' criteria the population would be less than half that.
4. Mehmet Ozdogan, 'A Surface Survey from Prehistoric and Early Historic Sites in North-eastern Turkey', *National Geographic Society Research Report*, 1979 Projects, 1985, 517–541, and emphasised in his 'The Black Sea, the Sea of Marmara, and Bronze Age Archaeology: an Archaeological Predicament', in Gunther A. Wagner *et al.*, *Troia and the Troad, Scientific Approaches*, Berlin 2003. The point is also made by Jak Yakar, *Ethnoarchaeology of Anatolia*, ch. 7.
5. M. Ozdogan, 'Prehistoric Sites in the Gelibolu Peninsula', *Anadolu* 10, 1988, 51–65.
6. Trevor Bryce, *The Trojans and Their Neighbours*, London 2006, 122; Bryce then makes reference to Bronze Age shipwrecks off the southern Turkish coast, but these are not relevant to the cultural situation at Troy.
7. *Studia Troia* 12, 2002.
8. Bryce, *Trojans*, 125; David Trump, *The Prehistory of the Mediterranean*, Harmondsworth 1980, 118, refers to 'tolls' on passing ships.
9. Manfred Kaufmann, 'Besik-Tepe, Vorbericht uber die Ergebrisse der Grabugun vor 1984, Grabungen dem Besik-Yepr, Besik-Sivritepe und Besik Graberfeld', *Archaeologischer Anzieger* 1986, 303–363.

10. Identified by J. Garstang and O.R. Gurney, *The geography of the Hittite Empire*, London 1959, and not really altered since.
11. Gary Beckman *et al.*, *The Ahhiyawa Texts*, Atlanta 2011, AhT4.
12. Discussed in Trevor Bryce, *The Kingdom of the Hittites*, Oxford 2005, 321–323.
13. The only writing from the site is on a seal inscribed with two names in Luwian, found in VIIb/2, and so after the end of the city, and clearly imported.
14. Carl W. Blegen, *Troy and the Trojans*, London 1963, supported by George Rapp, Jr, 'Earthquake in the Troad', in G. Rapp and J.A. Giffard (eds), *Troy, the Archaeological Geology*, Princeton NJ 1982.
15. Manfred Kaufmann, 'Troia – Ausgrabungen 1995', *Studia Troia* 6, 1996, 7, and 'Die Arbeiten in Troia/Wilusa 2003', *Studia Troia* 14, 2004, 15.
16. Summary table in Eric H. Cline, *The Trojan War, a Very Short Introduction*, Oxford 2013, 94.
17. G. Beckman, *Hittite Diplomatic Texts*, Atlanta 1999, 87–93.
18. Beckman *et al.*, *Ahhiyawa Texts*, AhT4.
19. Ibid, AhT5.
20. Millman Parry, *The Making of Homeric Verse*, Oxford 1971.
21. Nancy Sanders, *The Sea Peoples*, London 1985.
22. It was probably the long-standing Hittite enemies from the north of Anatolia, the Kaska, who finally triumphed and destroyed the Hittite capital at Hattusa – cf Bryce, *Kingdom of the Hittites*, ch. 13, for a summary of the suggested causes; sub-Hittite kingdoms continued to exist in south central Anatolia and north Syria for several centuries after the destruction of Hattusa.

Chapter 3
1. There were, according to Kaufmann (*Studia Troia* 6, 1996) no 'architectural remains in the south and north cities'; R.W.V. Catling, 'The Typology of the Protogeometric and Sub-geometric Pottery from Troia and its Aegean context', *Studia Troia* 8, 1998, 151, recognised a 'gap' dating to c.950–c.800.
2. Strabo 10.3.16 and 12.4.6.
3. M. Ozdogan, 'Prehistoric Sites in the Gelibolu Peninsula', *Anadolu* 10, 1988, 51–66.
4. Strabo 7.6.1; Stephanos, 'Ainos'; B. Isaac, *The Greek Settlements in Thrace until the Macedonian Conquest*, Leiden 1986, 146–147.
5. Homer, *Iliad* 836; I assume all through this chapter that Homer's political geography reflects the situation as in the late eighth century, when he probably lived, modified by his imagination, of course.
6. Apollonios 'of Rhodes', *Argonautica* 1.956–1153; the king was 'King Kyzikos'; Apollonios claimed to have based himself on two local historians, Deiochos of Prokonnesos and Neanthea of Kyzikos, but the main source of the poem we have was his own imagination and modern (that is, third century BC) conditions. He cannot be used as an historical source.
7. Isaac, *Greek Settlements*, 218.
8. Vladimir Popov, 'Les Thraces en Asie Mineure', *Congres Internationale de Thracologie*, Vol I, 121–125.
9. The study of DNA evidence from skeletons is the source of the revival of the mass migration theory.
10. Strabo 7.6.1.
11. Stephen Mitchell, *Anatolia*, Vol. 1, Oxford 1993, 174–175.

12. See note 2.
13. Note 6.
14. A.R. Burn, *The Lyric Age of Greece*, London 1960, 50–51.
15. Strabo 1.61; Burn, *Lyric Age*, 101–102.
16. Herodotos 1.14; Burn, *Lyric Age*, 57–58.
17. Herodotos 2.44 and 6.47; Pausanias 5.2 5.12.
18. Elias K. Petropoulos, *Hellenic Colonists in Euxeinos Pontos*, Oxford, BAR S 1394, 2005, 15–24, for a discussion of the discussions.
19. R. M. Cook, *The Troad*, Oxford 1973, 92–103.
20. Ibid, 360–363.
21. Isaac, *Greek Settlements*, 189–191.
22. Herodotos 1.8–10; Nicholas of Damascus fr. 49.
23. Summary at O. Murray, *Early Greece*, London 1980, 222; Burn, Lyric Age, 102–106.
24. J. Hind, 'Megarian Colonisation in the Western half of the Black Sea', in G.R. Tsetskhladze, *The Greek Colonisation of the Black Sea Area, Historia* Einzelschriften 121, Stuttgart 1998, 131–152.
25. G. R. Tsetskhladze, 'Greek Penetration of the Black Sea', in Tsetskhladze and de Angelis, *The Archaeology of Greek Colonisation*, Oxford 2009, 111–136.
26. R. Osborne, *Greece in the Making, 1200–479 BC*, London 1996, table 5, pages 121–125, lists colonies and ponders the dates; Boardman, *Greeks Overseas*, 235, 240–241; Isaac, *Greek Settlements*, 198–199.
27. F.W. Hasluck, *Cyzicus*, Cambridge 1910, reprinted 2010, 157–164.
28. Homer, *Iliad*, 2.836.
29. Strabo 13.1.22.
30. Cook, *Troad*, 57–61.
31. Hasluck, *Cyzicus*, 68–87.
32. Plutarch, *Brave Deeds of Women* 18; Strabo 13.1.8; Burn, *Lyric Age*, 108–111; P. Frisch, *Die Inschriften von Lampsakos*, Bonn 1976, 107–110.
33. Strabo 13.1.18.
34. Isaac, *Greek Settlements*, 187–189.
35. Strabo 13.1.19 and 14.1.6
36. Pliny *NH* 5.32/144; Strabo 12.563.
37. Ibidem.
38. Nicholas of Damascus, fr. 49.
39. Strabo 12.4.2, 7.6.1–2; Herodotos 4.144; Hind, 'Megarian Colonisation'; Isaac, *Greek Settlements*, 208–211, 218–222; Burn, *Lyric Age*, 113–114.
40. Strabo 7, fr. 52; Isaac, *Greek Settlements*, 187–189; Demosthenes 23.182.
41. Isaac, *Greek Settlements*, 140–148.
42. Strabo 13.1.22, fr. 55–56; Isaac, *Greek Settlements*, 194–196.

Chapter 4

1. Strabo 7.56; Synkellos, p. 298; Plutarch, *Greek Questions* 57.
2. Strabo 7.41; Herodotos 5.12–16.
3. Colin McEvedy, *Cities of the Classical World*, London 2011, 258, for a sketch plan.
4. Admiralty, *Turkey*, 67.
5. Strabo 13.1.2.
6. Ibid.
7. Hasluck, *Cyzicus*, 55–58, listed possible sites but omitted that which is now accepted for the main city, though discussing that to the east.

8. Charles B. Rose, *The Archaeology of Greek and Roman Troy*, Cambridge 2014, 72–74.

9. Ibid, 73.

10. Herodotos 1.70–86, who appends a romance about Croesus surviving to become Cyrus' adviser; J.M. Cook, *The Persian Empire*, London 1983, 28–29; George Cawkwell, *The Greek Wars, the Failure of Persia*, Oxford 2003, 30–31.

11. Pausanias 1.44; Strabo 8.6.22, 9.1.1; Burn, *Lyric Age* 88–89.

12. Herodotos 1.15–22.

13. Strabo 13.1.39; Cook, *Troad*, 178–186.

14. Herodotos I.61–62; Aristotle, *Atheneion Politeia* 15.

15. Herodotos 1.154–159.

16. Teos: Herodotos 1.168; Phokaia: Herodotos 1.164; when it became clear that the Phokaians would have to sail to the western Mediterranean considerable numbers of them returned to their former city, which therefore survived.

17. Herodotos 1.168–170, does not give details.

18. Rose, *Greek and Roman Troy*, 101–102; Hasluck, *Kyzikos*, 164.

19. Herodotos 5.94.

20. J. Boardman, *The Greeks Overseas*, Harmondsworth 1973, 264, referring to French Excavations in 1919–1921.

21. Herodotos 6.37.

22. Herodotos 6.36.

23. Herodotos 6.38.

24. Described by Herodotos 2.90–94; see also Cook, *Persian Empire*, Ch. 8.

25. Ktesias (from Photios) 17.

26. Herodotos 4.93.

27. Herodotos 4.88.

28. Herodotos 4.90; Ktesias F 13, 21.

29. Herodotos 4.137–138; Cawkwell, *Greek Wars*, 47–48.

30. Herodotos 5.10.

31. Herodotos 6.33.

32. Herodotos 5.26.

33. Ibid; Cook, *Troad*, 264 notes that their treatment is 'peculiar'.

34. Herodotos 5.27.

35. Herodotos 4.138; he mentions four more tyrants, but none from the Straits cities.

36. Herodotos 5.1.

37. Herodotos 4.143; Megabazos was the Persian to whom the remark was attributed that the Chalkedonians must have been blind when they chose not to settle at Byzantion.

38. Herodotos 5.26; Strabo 13.1 .22.

39. Herodotos 5.18.

40. Herodotos 5.12–17.

41. Herodotos 6.41.

42. Herodotos 7.137.

43. Herodotos 5.94.

44. Herodotos 5.30–33; this failure is odd, since the Persians had proved themselves masters at siege warfare; the expedition would therefore seem to have been almost exclusively Greek, and the real problem for them at Naxos was shortage of food.

45. Cawkwell, *Greek Wars*, 71–74.

46. Herodotos 5.34–38.

47. Herodotos 5.103.
48. Herodotos 5.117.
49. Herodotos 5.122.
50. Herodotos 6.40; 6.140; A.E. Burn, *Persia and the Greeks*, 2nd ed., London 1984, 218–220.
51. Herodotos 6.39.
52. Herodotos 6.140.
53. Herodotos 6.33.
54. Herodotos 6.5; 26–30.
55. Herodotos 6.40.
56. Peter Green, *The Greco-Persian Wars*, Berkeley and Los Angeles 1996, 24–25.
57. Herodotos 6.43.
58. Herodotos 7.105.
59. Herodotos 6.43.
60. Herodotos 6.44–46.
61. Herodotos 5.98.
62. Herodotus 6.46.
63. Herodotos 7.106.
64. Herodotos 7.34–36.
65. Herodotos 7.25.
66. Herodotos.
67. Herodotos 7.21–24.
68. Herodotos 7.111–112.
69. Herodotos 8.116.
70. Herodotos 7.111.
71. Herodotos 8.115–116.
72. Herodotos 8.107.
73. Herodotos 9.120.

Chapter 5
1. Nepos, *Pausanias* 3.1; Athenaios 13.50.
2. A detailed consideration of Byzantium's condition from 498 does not really concern modern historians: Russell, *Byzantion the Bosporus* ignores the issue, as does Freely, *Istanbul*, Madden, *Istanbul, and Hughes, Istanbul.*
3. Justin 9.1.3; *Oxyrhynchus Papyri* 13.1610 F 6.3; Thucydides 1.94.
4. Herodotos 6.33.
5. Herodotos 6.44.
6. Herodotos 7.96.
7. Herodotos 7.147.
8. See Alonso Moreno, *Feeding the Democracy, the Athens Grain Supply in the Fifth and Fourth Centuries BC*, Oxford 2007, 153–161.
9. Herodotos 6.56.
10. See Russell, *Byzantium*, 56–574, for the possibilities and references.
11. Ibid; Thomas N. Noonan, 'The Grain Trade of the Northern Black Sea in Antiquity', *American Journal of Philology* 94, 1975, 231–242.
12. Thucydides 1.95.
13. Thucydides 1.129.
14. Thucydides 1.128.

15. Plutarch, *Aristeides* 23, 4–5; on the foundation of the League, see Russell Meiggs, *The Athenian Empire*, Oxford 1975, ch. 3.
16. The sending of heralds to invite participation is not actually recorded, but in the founding of the Second Athenian Confederacy in 377 this was the procedure followed (Tod, *GHI*, 2.123) and indeed there seems to be no other feasible method.
17. Thucydides 1.96–97; for the early membership see Meiggs, *Athenian Empire*, 50–60.
18. Meiggs, *Athenian Empire* 52–53.
19. Thucydides 1.98; Herodotos 7.107; Plutarch, *Kimon* 7–8.
20. Herodotos 7.106.
21. Thucydides 1.98.
22. Plutarch, *Kimon* 9; Pausanias' conduct is much discussed, the details being agreeably complex; for a list of useful sources see Russell, *Byzantium* 58, note 16.
23. Thucydides 1.131.
24. Aristotle, *Athenaion Politeia* 23.5; Plutarch, *Aristeides* 25.1.
25. Thucydides 1.98; Meiggs, *Athenian Empire* 70–71.
26. Thucydides 1.100–101.
27. Thucydides 1.98; Plutarch, *Kimon* 8.3–7.
28. Thucydides 1.98; Meiggs, *Athenian Empire* 69–70.
29. Thucydides 1.96.
30. Ibid; Meiggs, *Athenian Empire*, 234–236.
31. The records are published and discussed in B.D. Merritt, H.T. Wade-Gery and M.F. McGregor, *The Athenian Tribute Lists*, 4 vols, Cambridge MA and Princeton, 1939–1953; summary lists are in Meiggs, *Athenian Empire*, appendix 14, with useful discussions in appendices 12 and 13. Here, references to individual contribution records will not be given; they can be found in these publications.
32. This is in fact an inference from the coincidence of the defeat of the allied expeditionary force in Egypt and the appearance of the inscribed lists in Athens.
33. The problem is, of course, that this was a special occasion; on the other hand, it appears clear that it was the responsibility of the member cities to transfer the money to Athens, and not that the *hellenotamiai* went out to the cities themselves. The decree setting up the extraordinary 425 BC reassessment is at Tod, *GHI* 1.66, and Fornara 136, as well as ATL.
34. Meiggs, *Athenian Empire*, 153–155.
35. Ibid, 158, referring to *Athenian Tribute Lists* 3.39–52.
36. Plutarch, *Perikles* 19.
37. Meiggs, *Athenian Empire*, appendix 11.
38. Thucydides 1.113–114; Plutarch, *Perikles* 23; Meiggs, *Athenian Empire*, 177–179.
39. Meiggs and Lewis 58; the date of this inscription is disputed; it may be c.440 BC.
40. For details of these places, sizes, sites, and territories, see Cook, *Troad*.
41. Thucydides 1.115–117.
42. Meiggs, *Athenian Empire* 189, 192.
43. Plutarch, *Perikles* 20; the expedition in the context of the Black Sea is discussed at length by David Braund, 'Pericles, Cleon, and the Pontus; the Black Sea in Athens c.440–421', in David Braund (ed.), *Scythians and Greeks: Cultural Interaction in Scythia, Athens, and the early Roman Empire (Sixth Century BC – First Century AD)*, Exeter 2005, 80–89.
44. Plutarch, *Perikles* 20.
45. Strabo 12.3.14 (quoting Theopompos, F 389).

46. Diodoros 12.31; Moreno, *Feeding the Democracy*, 155, rejects any direct connection between the Athenian expedition, the accession of Spartokos I and the grain supply, but the establishment of Athenian influence in the Black Sea and the stability brought by the Spartokid dynasty certainly facilitated the trade.
47. Diodoros 12.34.5.

Chapter 6

1. Moreno, *Feeding the Democracy*, ch. 4.
2. Xenophon, *Hellenica* 1.1.22.
3. Russell, *Byzantium and the Bosphorus*, 81–83.
4. E.g., Xenophon, *Hellenica* 2.2.
5. Ibid, 2.2.18–19.
6. Rose, *Greek and Roman Troy*, 143–152.
7. Diodoros, 14.10.1–2 and 13.1; Plutarch, *Lysander*, 13.3–5.
8. Xenophon, *Hellenica*, 1.3.16–17.
9. Diodoros 14.10.1–2; Xenophon, *Hellenica* 3.4.2.
10. Hasluck, *Cyzicus*, 168, citing Xenophon, *Hellenica* 3.4.10–11 and *Anabasis* 7.3.
11. *British Museum Catalogue, Ionia*, 325, 12; Xenophon, *Hellenica* 4.1.29; Plutarch, *Agesilaos*, 12.
12. Xenophon, *Hellenica* 3.1.3–4.
13. Ibid, 3.1.13–16; Cook, *Troad*, 322 (note 1), 330–331.
14. Xenophon, *Hellenica* 3.4.3–4.
15. Ibid, 3.2.2–3.
16. Ibid, 3.2.18–19.
17. Ibid, 4.8.1–4.
18. Xenophon, *Hellenica* 4.4.25–28; Tod 2.118.
19. For the route, well used at the time, cf Cook, *Troad*, 289.
20. Xenophon, *Hellenica*, 4.8.34–38.
21. Ibid 5.1.25–28.
22. The terms are detailed at Xenophon, *Hellenica* 5.1.25–34; Crawford/Whitehead 263; cf also G.L. Cawkwell, 'The King's Peace', *Classical Quarterly* 31, 1981, 69–83; T.T.B. Ryder, *Koine Eirene, General Peace and Local Independence in Ancient Greece*, Oxford 1965, 34–36.
23. Tod 2.118.
24. Tod 2.121.
25. Diodoros 15.28.2–5.
26. An example is Methymna in Lesbos, allied to Athens before 377 bc; Tod 2.122.
27. Tod 2.123; Crawford/Whitehead 269 B; G.L. Cawkwell, 'The Foundation of the Second Athenian League', *Classical Quarterly* 23, 1973, 46–60; Ryder, *Koine Eirene*, 55–57.
28. Diodoros 15.34.3–6.
29. Xenophon, *Hellenica* 6.5.23.
30. Ibid 15.79.1; Isokrates, Philip, 53.
31. Isocrates, *On the Exchange*, 115 and 119.
32. Diodoros 15.81; Cornelius Nepos, *Timotheos* 1.
33. Demosthenes, *Against Aristokrates* 663.
34. Ibid, 570.
35. Ryder, *Koine Eirene* 89.
36. Tod *GHI*, 141 and 142.

37. Simon Hornblower, *Mausolus*, Oxford 1982, 125–126.
38. Diodoros 16.7.3 and 21.2; Tod *GHI* 152 and 156; Ryder, *Koine Eirene* 89–90.
39. Arrian, *Anabasis* 1.11; British Museum Catalogue, *Troas* xxxii – xxxiv, 86–88; Rose, *Greek and Roman Troy*, 152.
40. Hornblower, *Mausolus*, 127.
41. Demosthenes, *For the Liberty of the Rhodians*, 3, 26; Nepos, *Chabrias* 4, *Timotheos* 3, *Iphikrates* 3; Plutarch, *Chabrias* 6.1; Polyainos I 3.9.28.
42. Demosthenes, *Against Meidias*.
43. Diodoros 16.36–37; Justin 8.28.
44. Diodoros 16.3 1.5–6; Demosthenes, *Third Philippic* 26.
45. Diodoros 16.34.3.
46. Diodoros 16.34.4; Demosthenes, *Against Aristokrates* 103.
47. Demosthenes, *Third Olynthiac*, 4–5.
48. Aischines, 2.90 and 3.22; Strabo 7 F 47; J.R. Ellis, *Philip II and Macedonian Imperialism*, London 1976, 204 and note 61.
49. Aischines 2.90–91; Demosthenes, *De Falsa Legatione* 156, 158.
50. Diodoros 16.60; Demosthenes, *On the Peace* 24–25; C.L. Cawkwell, 'Aeschines and the Peace of Philocrates', *Revue des etudes grecques* 79, 1960, 416–438; Ryder, *Koine Eirene* 145–150.
51. Ellis, *Philip II*, 169, for details and references.
52. Diodoros 16.1 7.1–2; Justin 9.1.
53. Demosthenes, *On Halonessos* 39–41.
54. Demosthenes, *On the Chersonese* 6 and 9; ib., *Letter of Philip* 11.
55. Demosthenes, *Letter of Philip*, passim.
56. Ellis, Philip II, 166–171; G.L. Cawkwell, *Philip of Macedonia*, London 1978, 116–117; Nicolas Hammond, *Philip of Macedon*, London 1994, 122–125,
57. Demosthenes, *On the Crown*, 244 and 302; Hypereides, frags 5–6.
58. Pausanias 4.3 1.5; Diodoros 16.74; Plutarch, *Alexander* 70.5; Ellis, *Philip II*, 174–175; E.W. Marsden, *Greek and Roman Artillery, Historical Development*, Oxford 1969, 100–101; W.W. Tarn, *Hellenistic Naval and Military Developments*, Cambridge 1930, 103.
59. Demosthenes, *Answer to Philip's Letter*, 5; Arrian, *Anabasis* 2.14.5; Polybios 1.29.10.
60. Ellis, *Philip II*, 176–177; other moderns apparently see nothing remarkable in this exploit, and rarely discuss it.
61. [Demosthenes], *Letter of Philip*.
62. Justin 9.1.5–6; Demosthenes, *On the Crown* 139; Didymus, *In Demosthenes* 10.45–47; Ellis, *Philip II*, 179 and note 101.
63. Demosthenes 50.18–19; Arrian, *Anabasis* 2.14.4.
64. Diodoros 16.7 7.2; Plutarch, *Phokion* 14; Frontinus, *Stratagems* 1.4.13; Justin 9.1.7; Ellis, *Philip II*, 162–164.

Chapter 7
1. Diodoros 17.7.2 and 8.
2. Diodoros 17.7.8.
3. Numbers are as ever uncertain; I take those used by N.G.L. Hammond, *Alexander the Great*, London 1981, 68–70, though I suspect him of adopting the largest possible figures for the Persian forces.
4. Arrian, *Anabasis* 1.11.9–12.1; Strabo 594; Plutarch, *Alexander* 15.7.7; Diodoros 17.17.3; Justin 42.5.12.

5. Suggested by Rose, *Greek and Roman Troy*, 73.
6. Arrian, *Anabasis* 1.14.11–16.4; Plutarch, *Alexander* 11.8–16; Diodoros 17.20.5–7; Curtius Rufus 8.1.20.
7. Arrian, *Anabasis* 1.16.3
8. Arrian, *Anabasis* 1.17.2.
9. C.B. Welles, *Royal Correspondence of the Hellenistic Period*, New Haven, 1936, no 18–20.
10. R.A. Billows, *Kings and Colonists, Aspects of Macedonian Imperialism*, Leiden 1995, 82–84.
11. Rose, *Greek and Roman Troy*, 142.
12. Polyainos 4.3.15; Strabo 13.587.
13. Arrian, *Anabasis* 3.4.1; Curtius Rufus 3.1.22.
14. Curtius Rufus 4.1 .34–35; R.A. Billows, *Antigonos the One-Eyed and the Creation of the Hellenistic State*, Los Angeles and Berkeley CA 1990, 43–45.
15. Memnon, *FGrH* 434 F 1 12.4.
16. Arrian, *Met' Alex* 1.26.
17. Diodoros 18.5 1.1–52.5.
18. Diodoros 18.52.5–6.
19. Diodoros 19.60.3.
20. Diodoros 19.61.1–5.
21. Diodoros 19.62.7; Billows, *Antigonos* 112.
22. Diodoros 19.68.3.
23. Diodoros 19.75.6.
24. Diodoros 19.77.7.
25. Diodoros 19.73.6.
26. This annoyed Antigonos and was one of the factors behind his proclamation at Tyre promising autonomy (Diodoros 19.61.2–3).
27. Diodoros 20.19.3.
28. Diodoros 20.108.1.
29. Getzel M. Cohen, *The Hellenistic Dettlements in Europe, the Islands, and Asia Minor*, Berkeley and Los Angeles 1985, 398–400.
30. Billows, *Antigonos*, 296–297, 301–305: Cohen, *Europe*, 391–392.
31. Stephanos of Byzantion, 'Antigoneia'; Billows, *Antigonos*, 298–299.
32. Billows, *Antigonos*, 218–220; Rose, *Greek and Roman Troy*, 159.
33. Diodoros 20.111.4; Billows, *Kings and Colonists*, 84.
34. Billows, *Antigonos*, 295: Rose, *Greek and Roman Troy*, 168–170.
35. Cook, Troad, 202.
36. Rose, *Greek and Roman Troy*, 160–170.
37. Diodoros 20.19.2, 5; Billows, *Antigonos*, 305.
38. Cohen, *Europe*, 82–87.
39. Diodoros 20.106.1–5.
40. The campaign of Ipsos has been discussed frequently; a clear version is in Billows, *Antigonos*, 174–185.
41. Diodoros 20.111.3.
42. Diodoros 20.111.3l Polyainos 4.12.1.
43. Diodoros 20.112.2–3.
44. Diodoros 20.113.4–5, 21.1.1–4b; B. Bar-Kochva, *The Seleucid Army, Organisation and Tactics in the Great Campaigns*, Cambridge 1977, 106–110.

Chapter 8

1. Plutarch, *Demetrios*, 31–32.
2. Ibid, 31; Memnon, *FGrH* 224b – 225a.
3. John D. Grainger, *The Cities of Seleukid Syria*, Oxford 1990, part 1.
4. Cohen, *Hellenistic Settlements*, 143–148, 391–392, 398–400.
5. Strabo 13.1.26.
6. Strabo 13.1.27.
7. Diodoros 19.60.
8. Strabo 12.4.2, blaming Lysimachos: Pausanias 5.12.7, blaming the Bithynian King Zipoetes.
9. Appian, *Syrian Wars*, 62; Helen S. Lund, *Lysimachos, a Study in Hellenistic Kingship*, London 1992.
10. John D. Grainger, *Seleukos Nikator*, London 1991, 187–189.
11. Appian, *Syrian Wars* 63; Grainger, *Seleukos Nikator*, 194; it was the duty of the next king to carry through the funerary rites for his dead predecessor, and this could constitute a claim on the throne.
12. Memnon, *FGrH* 227a, 28–34: Justin 24.1.
13. Plutarch, *Demetrios*, 50–52.
14. Grainger, *Seleukos Nikator*, 195–196.
15. Memnon 226b, 29–37: Justin 17.2.
16. G. Nachtergael, *Les Galates en Grece at Les Soteria de Delphes*, Brussels 1977.
17. John D. Grainger, *The Galatians*, Barnsley 2020, 67–76.
18. Memnon *FGrH* 227a, 28–38 and 227b 3–40; Livy 38.16.1–10.
19. Memnon *FGrH* 228a 1–4; Strabo 12.5.1–2.
20. A.H.M. Jones, *The Cities of the Eastern Roman Provinces*, 2nd ed., Oxford 1971, 151–152; Henri-Louis Furneaux, *Nobles et elites dans les cutes de Bithynie aux epoques hellenistique et romaine*, Brussels 2004, ch. 1.
21. *OGIS* 748; Austin 225.
22. Rose, *Greek and Roman Troy*, 170–172, and the references there.
23. Strabo 13.1 .26–27, mixing up Alexandria and Ilion.
24. Cook, Troad, 338–344; Cohen, *Hellenistic Settlements*, 147–151; it has to be said that the basis for this theory is a single coin, but it is well argued both by Cohen and by Louis Robert, and it is the sort of thing to be expected in a war between Ptolemies and Seleukids.
25. Grainger, *Galatians*, 100–104.
26. I. Ilion 25.
27. Strabo 13.1.26.
28. Rose, *Greek and Roman Troy*, ch. 8, passim.
29. Russell, *Byzantium*, 104–113, and references there to Robert, Robu, and Gabelko.
30. Pausanias 8.46; Rose, *Greek and Roman Troy*, 156.
31. B.L. McGing, *The Foreign Policy of Mithridates Eupator, King of Pontus*, Leiden 1986, 14–15.
32. Russell, *Byzantium*, 165–167.
33. Ibid, 106, referring to Dionysios of Byzantion 41.
34. *I. Didyma*, II, 492; Welles, *Royal Correspondence*, 18–20; *OGIS* 225; Austin 173.
35. Polybios 4.50.3; Russell, *Byzantium*, 108–110.
36. Strabo 12.8.11; Jones, *Cities*, 87; this extent overlaps with Antiochos II's gift to his wife in 253 BC; possibly Kyzikos acquired the estate later; Hasluck, *Cyzicus* 101–103.

37. Cohen, *Hellenistic Settlements*, 400–401.
38. Ibid, 171–172.
39. Memnon *FGrH* 434 F 15; Russell, *Byzantium*, 98–104 and 113–128; Cohen, *Hellenistic Settlements*, 82–86 (on Lysimacheia).
40. Austin 173.
41. Cohen, *Hellenistic Settlements*, 150–151; Jones, Cities, 36, 87–88.
42. Austin 266–268; G. Holbl, *The Ptolemaic Empire*, London 2001, 48–50.
43. E.T. Newell, *The Coinage of the Western Seleucid Mints from Seleucus I to Antiochus III*, New York, 1941 319–358; O. Morkholm, *Early Hellenistic Coinage from the Accession of Alexander to the Peace of Apamea*, Cambridge 1991, 123–127.
44. Rose, *Greek and Roman Troy*, 174.
45. *I. Ilion* 5.
46. Rose, *Greek and Roman Troy*, 172.
47. Diodoros 20.107.2; Rose, *Greek and Roman Troy*, 162.
48. Rose, *Greek and Roman Troy* 160–164 (the Panathenaia), 170–172 (the Seleukeia), 173–174 (the Ilieia).
49. Ibid, 175.
50. Ibid, 175–182.
51. Ibid, 176–177, with comparisons with other nearby cities.
52. H. G. Jansen and N. Blindow, 'The Geophysical Mapping of the Lower City of Troia/Ilion' in G.A. Wagner *et al.*, (eds), *Troy and the Troad: Scientific Approaches*, Berlin 2003, 325–340.
53. Austin 269; R.S. Bagnall, *The Administration of the Ptolemaic Possessions outside Egypt*, Leiden 1976, 159–168.
54. Cohen, *Hellenistic Settlements*, 157–158.
55. L. Basch, 'The Isis of Ptolemy II Philadelphus', *The Mariner's Mirror* 71, 1985, 129–151; W.M. Murray, *The Age of Titans, the Rise and Fall of the Great Hellenistic Navies*, Oxford 2012, 197.

Chapter 9

1. Polybios 5.74.4.
2. Polybios 4.45–46.
3. The main source for this crisis and war is Polybios 4.47–52; recent modern treatments are Russell, *Byzantium*, 95–97, and N. Jefrenow, 'Der rhodisch-byzantinisch Krieg con 220 c. Chr.: Ein Handeskrieg in Hellenismus?', *MBAH* 24, 2005, 51–98.
4. Polybios 8.2 2.1–3; Grainger, *Galatians*, 72–76.
5. Polybios 5.111.3; Cohen, *Hellenistic Settlements*, 145.
6. Polybios 7.15.1–18.3; and 8.20.8–21.9.
7. Polybios 5.7 7.2–78.6; R.E. Allen, *The Attalid Kingdom, a Constitutional History*, Oxford 1983, 39–50.
8. Polybios 5.111.3.
9. Polybios 22.20.1–8; *OGIS* 308.
10. Livy 28.7.7–8.
11. Livy 28.7.10; Cassius Dio 17, frags 57–58.
12. Justin 30.2.6; Polybios 15.2 5.3–12; Holbl, *Ptolemaic Empire*, 134–136.
13. John Ma, *Antiochos III and the Cities of Western Asia Minor*, Oxford 1999, 63–74.
14. Polybios 15.25.13.
15. Polybios 15.2 5.20–33.12.

16. Polybios 15.20.1–8; Livy 31.14.5; Appian, *Macedonian Wars* 4.1; Justin 38.2.8.
17. Polybios 15.2 2.4–23.10; Strabo 12.4.3; F.W. Walbank, *Philip V of Macedon*, Cambridge 1940 reprinted 1967, 114–115.
18. Polybios 15.22.4–23.6.
19. Appian, *Macedonian Wars* 4.1; Polybios 16.2.4; Livy 31.3 1.4; Walbank, *Philip V*, 117–119; R.B. McShane, *The Foreign Policy of the Attalids of Pergamon*, Urbana IL 1964, 119–121.
20. Polybios 16.1.7.
21. Polybios 16.1.8–9; this was the only mark of an alliance between Philip and Antiochos – that is, they were not allies in any real sense.
22. Polybios 16.2.1–7.13.
23. Karia: Polybios 16.11.1–6, 18.2.3 and 8.9; Livy 30.18.1–7, 19–22; Polyainos 4.18.1; Frontinus, *Stratagems* 3.8.1; Bargylia: Polybios 16.2 4.1–9; Philip's escape: Polyainos 4.18.2.
24. Polybios 16.2 5.3–26.10; Livy 31.14.11–15.8.
25. Polybios 60.2 7.1–5; Walbank, *Philip V*, 131.
26. Livy 31.16.3–6.
27. Polybios 16.30.1–33.5; Livy 31.16.6–17.11.
28. Polybios 16.3 4.1; Livy 31.18.1; Diodoros 28.6.1; Appian, *Macedonian Wars* 4.1.
29. Livy 31.18.8.
30. Polybios 18.4.5–6; Livy 22.5.8.
31. Polybios 18.1.10–2.6; Livy 32.33.1–8.
32. Livy 32.34.6; Polybios 18.4.6.
33. John D. Grainger, *The Roman War of Antiochos the Great*, Leiden 2002, chapter 2.
34. John D. Grainger, 'Antiochos III in Thrace', *Historia* 15, 1996, 329–343.
35. Polybios 18.5 2.1–2.
36. Livy 33.38.6–7.
37. Polybios 18.5 2.2; Grainger, 'Antiochos III in Thrace'.
38. Appian, *Syrian Wars* 6.
39. Grainger, *Roman War*, 98–162.
40. Livy 37.33.1–3.
41. Livy 37.37.2.
42. Livy 3.40.4–41.8; Appian, *Syrian Wars* 43.
43. Polybios 21.24.2–3; Livy 38.39.14–15.
44. Strabo 13.1.13–14; Rose, *Greek and Roman Troy*, 193.
45. Strabo 13.1.28.
46. Ancient sources are few and scattered for this war. Allen, *Attalid Kingdom*, 79, asserts that the causes of the war are unknown, but it is obvious that it grew from the award of land claimed by Prusias in the Apameia judgement. McShane, *Foreign Policy*, 159–161, attempts an account.
47. Cohen, *Hellenistic Settlements*, 406–407.
48. Ibid, 392–393 (Apameia Myrleia), 405–406 (Prusias-by-the-Sea).
49. Arrian, *FGrH* 156 F 29; Pliny *NH* 5.148; Cohen, *Hellenistic Settlements* 401–402.
50. Polybios 23.5.1; Livy 39.5 1.1–12; Plutarch, *Flamininus* 20–21.
51. Polybios 25.2.1–15.
52. Cohen, *Hellenistic Settlements* 87; Strabo 13.4.2; *OGIS* 301.
53. Livy 42.13.8, 40.6, 42.7
54. Polybios 26.1.10.

55. Polybios 32.15.1–16.14; 33.13.5–9; McShane, *Foreign Policy*, 188–189.
56. Zonaras 9.28.2–5; Diodoros 32.15.5–7; Polybios 36.10.4–5; R. Kallet-Marx, *Hegemony to Empire, the Development of the Roman Imperium in the East from 148–62 BC*, Berkeley and Los Angeles 1995, 31–37 and 345–346; John D. Grainger, *Rome, Parthia, India, the Violent Emergence of a New World Order 150–140 BC*, Barnsley 2013, chapter 3.
57. Diodoros 32.15.6.
58. Polybios 36.14–15; Livy, *Per.* 50; Diodoros 32.20–21; Appian, *Mithridatic Wars* 4–7.

Chapter 10
1. *IGRR* IV.134; Hasluck, *Cyzicus* 180; there may have been an attack by Thracians in c.135 BC, occasioning a call to the Macedonian governor for help, but he could surely not do so, being involved in a war in the northern Balkans, and Kyzikos being outside his province.
2. Aulus Gellius, *Noctes Atticae* 11.10.
3. Rose, *Greek and Roman Troy*, 219.
4. Sherk 36 (Via Egnatia), 42, (via Aquillia).
5. Strabo 7.7.4 and 8, for the name; Polybios 34.12.2–8; Walbank, *Commentary* III, 622–628; Kellet-Marx, *Hegemony to Empire*, 347–349.
6. D.H. French, 'The Roman Road System in Asia Minor', *ANRW* 7.2, 698–729.
7. Appian, *Syrian Wars* 69.
8. Sherk 1 is an example, a Roman employed as a mercenary commander in Crete for Ptolemy IV.
9. The basic study is J. Hatzfelt, *Les Trafiquants Italiens dans L'Orient Hellenique*, Paris, 1919; a later treatment is by A.J.N. Wilson, *Emigration from Italy in the Republican Age of Rome*, Manchester 1966.
10. Diodoros 36.3; E. Badian, *Publicans and Sinners, Private Enterprise in the Service of the Roman Republic*, Oxford 1972, 87.
11. *I. Ilion* 71 and 72.
12. W.V. Harris, *War and Imperialism in Republican Rome*, Oxford 1971.
13. The sources for this are usefully collected in A.H.J. Greenidge and A.M. Clay, *Sources for Roman History 133–70 BC*, 2nd ed., Oxford 1961 1–48, and in translation in D.L. Stockton (ed.) *From the Gracchi to Sulla*, London 1981.
14. The *lex de provincia Asia*, Appian, *Civil Wars* 5.4; Diodoros 35.25 Cicero, *in Verram* 3.6.16.
15. McGing, *Foreign Policy*, 68–88.
16. Appian, *Mithradatic Wars* 11; McGing, *Foreign Policy*, 108–109.
17. Livy, *Per.* 76; Appian, *Mithradatic Wars* 22.
18. Justin 3.3.9; Appian, *Mithradatic Wars* 22.
19. Appian, *Mithradatic Wars*, 51.
20. Ibid, 53; Dio Cassius, frag. 104.1; Strabo 13.1.27.
21. Appian, *Mithradatic Wars*, 52–53; Plutarch, *Lucullus* 4.
22. Appian, *Mithradatic Wars*, 53; Rose, *Greek and Roman Troy*, 219–221.
23. Frontinus 3.17.5; *CIG* 6855; Diodoros 38.8 .3; Hasluck, *Cyzicus* 178.
24. Plutarch, *Sulla* 22; Appian, *Mithradatic Wars,* 55; Memnon *FGrH* 434 F 25.2.
25. Appian, *Mithradatic Wars*, 59.
26. *I. Ilion* 10; Rose, *Greek and Roman Troy*, 219.

27. Kellet-Marx, *Hegemony to Empire*, 264–267.
28. Ibid, 275.
29. Cicero, *In Verram* 2.1.63–85.
30. McGing, *Foreign Policy*, 133–135.
31. Eutropius 6.6.1; Appian, *Mithradatic Wars*, 71; Sallust, *Histories* 2.71.
32. Appian, *Mithradatic Wars*, 69; One may justifiably be sceptical of such a number.
33. McGing, *Foreign Policy*, 144–145.
34. Appian, *Mithradatic Wars*, 72.
35. Ibid 71; Hasluck, *Cyzicus*, 178–179.
36. Appian, *Mithradatic Wars*, 72.
37. Ibid.
38. Plutarch, *Lucullus* 14.1.
39. Appian, *Mithradatic Wars*, 72.
40. Ibid, 73–75.
41. Suetonius, *Julius* 4.2 (Karia); *OGIS* 445 (Mysia); Appian, *Mithradatic Wars*, 75 (Phrygia and Pisidia).
42. Appian, *Mithradatic Wars*, 75.
43. Ibid, 76.
44. Appian, *Mithradatic Wars*, 76; Plutarch, *Lucullus* 11.6; Memnon *FGrH* 434 F 28.4.
45. Appian, *Mithradatic Wars*, 76.
46. Ibid, 77.
47. Memnon *FGrH* 434 F 29.5.
48. Rose, *Greek and Roman Troy*, 221–222.
49. *I. Ilion* 73; H.A. Ormerod, *Piracy in the Ancient World*, Liverpool 1928; Nicholas K. Rauh, *Merchants, Sailors, and Pirates in the Roman World*, Stroud, 2003, chapter 6.
50. Memnon, *FGrH* 434 F 27.5–6; discussed by Kellet-Marx, *Hegemony to Empire*, 302.
51. Dio Cassius 51.20.6.
52. Fernoux, *Notables et elites*, 146–161.
53. Rose, *Greek and Roman Troy*, 221–234, on the city's slow recovery.
54. Sherk 75 C.
55. Rose, *Greek and Roman Troy*, 223.
56. Ibid, 223–224, 234–235.

Chapter 11

1. M.L. Clarke, *The Noblest Roman, Marcus Brutus and his Reputation*, London 1981, 17–19.
2. Lucan, *Pharsalia* 9.964–979.
3. Rose, *Greek and Roman Troy*, 222–223.
4. Strabo 12.4.3.
5. It had the *ius Italica*, like Apameia, which is a sign that it was a Caesarean foundation: Jones, *Cities*, 86 and note 98.
6. Rose, *Greek and Roman Troy*, 222–226.
7. Pliny, *NH* 5.124; Strabo 13.1 .26.
8. Pliny, *NH* 5.141; Strabo 13.1.14.
9. Appian, *Mithradatic Wars* 117; Jones, *Cities*, 163 and note 30.
10. Pliny *NH* 4.48; Diodoros 33.14.
11. Dio Cassius 54.29.

12. Pliny *NH* 4.49; *CIL* 3.7380.
13. Jones, *Cities* 17.
14. Pliny *NH* 4.47; *CIL* 3.726.
15. Pliny *NH* 4.45; *CIL* 3.386.
16. Jones, *Cities* 25.
17. Ibid.
18. Ibid, 14–15.
19. Suetonius, *Vespasian* 8.4.
20. Jones, *Cities*, 164–165.
21. Dio Cassius 54.7; Suetonius, *Augustus*; Zonaras 10.34.
22. *CIG* 3665; Plutarch, *Brutus* 28; Appian, *Civil Wars* 4.75.
23. Appian, *Civil Wars* 5.137.
24. Rose, *Greek and Roman Troy* 222–226.
25. Dio Cassius 54.23–24; Tacitus, *Annals* 4.36; Suetonius, *Tiberius* 37.
26. Honours for the imperial family are discussed by Rose, *Greek and Roman Troy*, 226–230, and Hasluck, *Cyzicus*, 184–185.
27. Hasluck, *Cyzicus*, 184, note 3, with references.
28. Nicholas of Damascus, frag. 134; Josephus, *Antiquitates Judaicae* 16.26; Rose, *Greek and Roman Troy*, 226.
29. *CIL* 3.335 and supplement 6991 and 14188, quoted in Fernoux, *Notables et elites*, 416.
30. Jones, *Cities*, 160.
31. Rose, *Greek and Roman Troy*, 226–234.
32. Dio Cassius 51.20.6.
33. Such was the advice said to have been given to Augustus by Maecenas in 29 BC – Dio Cassius 52.37.10 – so that they would be divided and would then more readily submit to Rome.
34. It was this experience which appears to have led to his selection by Trajan for the task: Jesper Mayborn Madsen, *Eager to be Roman, Greek response to Roman Rule in Pontus and Bithynia*, London 2009, 11–12; Roy K. Gibson, *Man of the Empire, the Life of Pliny the Younger*, Oxford 2020, ch 8.
35. Pliny 10.48 and 33.
36. Plutarch could see this – *Moralia* 814E – 815A; Madsen, *Eager* 56–57; no doubt many others understood what was happening as well.
37. Dio Cassius 57.24.6.
38. *PIR* L 309; these names are usefully collected in Fernoux, *Notables et elites*, 416–489 for all Bithynia; here I select those in the west of the province, close to the Straits.
39. *PIR* C 558, 556 and 557.
40. Arriani – *PIR* F 219 and *IG* II/III 2054 and 4251–4253; R. Syme, 'The Career of Arrian', *Roman Papers* IV, 27–28; Cassii, *CIL* II 2212; *PIR* C 481, 492; F. Millar, *A Study of Cassius Dio*, Oxford 1964.
41. Fernoux, *Notables et elites*, 416–428.
42. J. Crow, J. Bardill, and R. Bayliss, *The Water Supply of Byzantine Constantinople*, Journal of Roman Archaeology, monograph 11, London 2008.
43. Rose, *Greek and Roman Troy*, 236–246; the quote is from 238.
44. Anthony R. Birley, *Hadrian, the Restless Emperor*, London 1997, 84–85.
45. Pliny, *Letters* 10.37, 39 and 41; *Historia Augusta, Hadrian* 1.5; *BMC* III 490, 520–521, 524; *IGRRP* III 77; J.M.C. Toynbee, *The Hadrianic School, a Chapter in the History of Greek Art*, Cambridge 1934, 51–52 and 126.

46. G.W. Bowersock, *Greek Sophists of the Roman Empire*, Oxford 1969, 120–122: Birley, *Hadrian*, 159–161.
47. Birley, *Hadrian*, 162–164; A. Schultz and E. Winter, 'Zum Hadrianstempel von Kyzikos', *Asia Minor Studien* 1, Bonn 1990, 33–81.
48. *IGRRP* IV 120–121, 128–129; it is not certain he actually visited these two places
49. *OGIS* 445, 446; Strabo 12.8.11; J. and L. Robert, *Claros* I, Paris 1989, 31–34.
50. *Historia Augusta, Hadrian* 20.13; Dio Cassius 69.10.2; E. Schwertheim, *Inschriften greichisshe Stadte aus Kleinasien: Hadrianoi und Hadrianeia*, Cologne 1987, 56 and 129; id., 'Zu Hadriens Reisen und Stadtgrundungen in Keinasien', *Epigrafica Anatolica* 6, 1985, 37–42.
51. *CIL* III 374.
52. *CIL* III 7282; Rose, *Greek and Roman Troy*, 246.
53. Rose, *Greek and Roman Troy*, 246–254; *I. Ilion* 158; Philostratos, *Lives of the Sophists* 2.1; M.T. Boatwright, *Hadrian and the Cities of the Roman Empire*, Princeton NJ, 2000, 114–116.

Chapter 12
1. Hadrian visited the province several times.
2. Ibid, 10.77; translation by Betty Radice.
3. A.R. Birley, *Septimius Severus, the African Emperor*, London 1988, 94–97; David S. Potter, *The Roman Empire at Bay 180–395*, London 2004, 93–96.
4. Birley, *Septimius Severus*, 97–102; Potter, *Roman Empire*, 103–104.
5. *Historia Augusta, Severus* 8.13; Dio Cassius 74.6.3–6; *ILS* 1141.
6. Herodian 3.2.9; L. Robert, 'La titulature de Nicee et de Nicomedee: la gloire et la haine', *HSCP* 81, 1977, 1–39.
7. Dio Cassius 75.10.1–14.6; Herodian 3.6.9.
8. Dio Cassius 75.14.1–3.
9. *Historia Augusta, Caracalla* 1.7.
10. John Freely, *Istanbul, the Imperial City*, London 1996, 27–28, quoting Dionysios of Byzantion and the *Chronicon Pasquale*.
11. Zosimus 1.34.
12. Zosimus 1.35.
13. Zosimus 1.36.
14. Ammianus Marcellinus 31.5 and 16 and 16.8; Hasluck, Kyzikos 190–191.
15. Zosimus 1.40 and 43; on the chronological problems see Potter, *Roman Empire* 263, note 3; George C. Brauer Jr, *The Age of the Soldier Emperors*, Park Ridge NJ 1975, 268.
16. Zosimus 1.50.
17. Potter, Roman Empire at Bay, 153, and notes; his imperial predecessor, Macrinus, had fled as far as Chalkedon, where he was captured and executed; Macrinus' praetorian prefect was executed at Nikomedia. No one in the area could be in any doubt as to who the new emperor was.
18. Fernoux, *Notables et elites*, 133–135.
19. *Historia Augusta, Numerian*; Aurelius Victor 39; Eutropius 9.18.
20. *Historia Augusta, Carus* 13; Aurelius Victor 39; Eutropius 9.20; Zosimus 1.73; T.C. Skeet, *Papyri from Panopolis*, Dublin 1964; T.H. Barnes, *The New Empire of Diocletian and Constantine*, Cambridge MA 1982, chapter 4.
21. Lactantius, *De Mortibus Persecutorum*, 7.

22. Pliny, *Letters*, 10

23. Rose, *Greek and Roman Troy*, 260–265.

24. Jordanes, *Getica* 20.108 (not altogether convincing or reliable); R. Tybout, 'Barbarians in Phrygia: a New Grave Stele', *Epigraphica Anatolica* 20, 1992, 35–41.

25. Discussed in *The Cambridge History of Christianity*, vol. 1, ed. Margaret M. Mitchell and Frances M. Young, in Part IV.

26. Pliny *Letters*, 10.46, 47; W.H.C. Frend, 'Persecution: Genesis and Legacy', in the *Cambridge History*, 503–523; no estimate is made of the results of the persecutions; also Herbert B. Workman, *Persecution in the Early Church*, London 1906, paperback edition, Oxford 1980.

27. Barnes, *New Empire*; Stephen Williams, *Diocletian and the Roman Recovery*, London 1985, Part 3.

28. As Pliny's experience in Bithynia suggested.

29. Lactantius, *De Mortibus*, 10.7–9.

30. Ibid, 10; J. Stevenson and W.H.C. Frend, *A New Eusebius, Documents Illustrating the History of the Church to A.D. 337*, London 1987, no 236.

31. Frend, 'Persecution', 517–522.

32. Potter, *Roman Empire*, 377–380, with sources.

33. T.D. Barnes, *Constantine and Eusebius*, Cambridge MA 1981, 214.

34. Nazarius, *Panegyricus* 4; ILS 694 (the dedication on the Arch of Constantine in Rome); Potter, *Roman Empire*, 359–363; Iain Ferris, *The Arch of Constantine, Inspired by the Divine*, London 2013.

35. Zosimus 2.23; Sozomen 2.3.2 (the source of the story about Chalkedon); Cook, *Troad*, 158–159; Gilbert Dagron, *Naissance d'une capitale: Constantinople*, Paris 1974; Richard Krautheimer, *Three Christian Capitals: Topography and Politics, Rome, Constantinople*, Milan, Berkeley and Los Angeles 1983.

36. Krautheimer, *Three Christian Capitals*, 41–67, is a clear account of the foundation process.

37. Colin McEvedy, *Cities of the Classical World*, London 2011, 100–115.

Abbreviations

ANRW – *Aufstieg und Niedergang der romischen Welt*

Austin – Michel Austin, *The Hellenistic World from Alexander to the Roman Conquest*, 2nd Ed.

BAR – *British Archaeological Reports*

BMC – *British Museum Catalogue*

CIG – *Corpus Inscriptionum Graecarum*

CIL – *Corpus Inscriptionum Latinarum*

FGrH – *Die Fragmente der greichischen Historiker*

Fornara – Charles W. Fornara, *Archaic Times to the End of the Peloponnesian War.*

HSCP – *Harvard Studies in Classical Philology*

I Didyma – T. Wiegand, *Didyma*, vol. II, *Die Inschriften*

IG – *Inscriptiones Graecae*

IGRRP – *Inscriptiones Graecae ad res Romanas pertientes*

I Ilion – P. Frisch, *Die Inschriften von Ilion*

ILS – *Inscriptiones Latinae Selectae*

Meiggs and Lewis – R. Meiggs and D. M. Lewis, *A Selection of Greek Historical Inscriptions*

OGIS – *Orientis Graecae Inscriptiones Selectae*

PIR – *Prosopographia Imperii Romanae*

Pliny, *NH* – Pliny, *Natural History*

Sherk – R.K. Sherk, *Rome and the Greek East to the Death of Augustus*

Tod, *GHI* – M.N. Tod, *Greek Historical Inscriptions*

Bibliography

Admiralty, *Turkey*, London 1942.

R.E. Allen, *The Attalid Kingdom, a Constitutional History*, Oxford 1983.

G.G. Aperghis, *The Seleukid Royal Economy*, Cambridge 2004.

E. Badian, *Publicans and Sinners, Private Enterprise in the Service of the Roman Republic*, Oxford 1972.

R.S. Bagnall, *The Administration of the Ptolemaic Possessions outside Egypt*, Leiden 1976.

T.D. Barnes, *Constantine and Eusebius*, Cambridge MA 1981.

T.H. Barnes, *The New Empire of Diocletian and Constantine*, Cambridge MA 1982.

L. Basch, 'The Isis of Ptolemy II Philadelphus', *The Mariner's Mirror* 71, 1985, 129–151.

Gary Beckman *et al.*, *The Ahhiyawa Texts*, Atlanta 2011.

G. Beckman, *Hittite Diplomatic Texts*, Atlanta 1999.

R.A. Billows, *Kings and Colonists, Aspects of Macedonian Imperialism*, Leiden 1995.

R.A. Billows, *Antigonos the One-Eyed and the Creation of the Hellenistic State*, Los Angeles and Berkeley CA 1990.

Anthony R. Birley, *Hadrian, the Restless Emperor*, London 1997, 84–85.

A.R. Birley, *Septimius Severus, the African Emperor*, London 1988.

C.W. Blegen, *Troy and the Trojans*, London 1963.

J. Boardman, *The Greeks Overseas*, Harmondsworth 1973.

M.T. Boatwright, *Hadrian and the Cities of the Roman Empire*, Princeton NJ, 2000.

G.W. Bowersock, *Greek Sophists of the Roman Empire*, Oxford 1969.

George C. Brauer Jr, *The Age of the Soldier Emperors*, Park Ridge NJ 1975.

David Braund, 'Pericles, Cleon, and the Pontus; the Black Sea in Athens c.440–421', in David Braund (ed.), *Scythians and Greeks: Cultural Interaction in Scythia, Athens, and the early Roman Empire (Sixth Century BC – First Century A.D.)* , Exeter 2005, 80–89.

Trevor Bryce, *The Kingdom of the Hittites*, Oxford 2005.

Trevor Bryce, *The Trojans and their Neighbours*, London 2006.

M. Buitenheis, 'Note on Archaeozoological research around the Sea of Marmara', *Anatolica* 20, 1994, 141–144.

A.R. Burn, *The Lyric Age of Greece*, London 1960.

A.R. Burn, *Persia and the Greeks*, 2nd ed., London 1984.

R.W.V. Catling, 'The Typology of the Protogeometric and Sub-geometric Pottery from Troia and its Aegean context', *Studia Troia* 8, 1998.

C.L. Cawkwell, 'Aeschines and the Peace of Philocrates', *Revue des etudes grecques* 79, 1960, 416–438.

G.L. Cawkwell, 'The Foundation of the Second Athenian League', *Classical Quarterly* 23, 1973, 46–60.

G.L. Cawkwell, 'The King's Peace', *Classical Quarterly* 31, 1981, 69–83.

G.L. Cawkwell, *Philip of Macedonia*, London 1978.

George Cawkwell, *The Greek Wars, the Failure of Persia*, Oxford 2003.

M.L. Clarke, *The Noblest Roman, Marcus Brutus and his Reputation*, London 1981.

Eric H. Cline, *The Trojan War, a Very Short Introduction*, Oxford 2013.

Getzel M. Cohen, *The Hellenistic Dettlements in Europe, the Islands, and Asia Minor*, Berkeley and Los Angeles 1985.

J.M. Cook, *The Persian Empire*, London 1983.

R.M. Cook, *The Troad*, Oxford 1973,

J. Crow, J. Bardill, and R. Bayliss, *The Water Supply of Byzantine Constantinople*, Journal of Roman Archaeology, monograph 11, London 2008.

Gilbert Dagron, *Naissance d'une capitale: Constantinople*, Paris 1974.

R. Demangel, 'Le Tumulus dit de Protesilaos', *Fouilles du Corps d'Occupation Francaises de Constantinople*, fascicule I, Paris 1926.

J.R. Ellis, *Philip II and Macedonian Imperialism*, London 1976.

Iain Ferris, *The Arch of Constantine, Inspired by the Divine*, London 2013.

John Freely, *The Bosphorus*, Istanbul 1993.

John Freely, *Istanbul, the Imperial City*, London 1996.

D.H. French, 'The Roman Road System in Asia Minor', *ANRW* 7.2, 698–729.

P. Frisch, *Die Inschriften von Lampsakos*, Bonn 1976.

Henri-Louis Furneaux, *Nobles et elites dans les cutes de Bithynie aux epoques hellenistique et romaine*, Brussels 2004.

J. Garstang and O.R. Gurney, *The Geography of the Hittite Empire*, London 1959.

Roy K. Gibson, *Man of the Empire, the Life of Pliny the Younger*, Oxford 2020.

John D. Grainger, *The Cities of Seleukid Syria*, Oxford 1990.

John D. Grainger, *Seleukos Nikator*, London 1991.

John D. Grainger, *The Galatians*, Barnsley 2020.

John D. Grainger, *The Roman War of Antiochos the Great*, Leiden 2002.

John D. Grainger, 'Antiochos III in Thrace', *Historia* 15, 1996, 329–343.

J.D. Grainger, *Rome, Parthia, India, the Violent Emergence of a New World Order 150–140 BC*, Barnsley 2013.

Peter Green, *The Greco-Persian Wars*, Berkeley and Los Angeles 1996.

A.H.J. Greenidge and A.M. Clay, *Sources for Roman History 133–70 BC*, 2nd ed., Oxford 1961.

Nicolas Hammond, *Philip of Macedon*, London 1994.

N.G.L. Hammond, *Alexander the Great*, London 1981

W.V. Harris, *War and Imperialism in Republican Rome*, Oxford 1971.

F.W. Hasluck, *Cyzicus*, Cambridge 1910, reprinted 2010.

J. Hatzfelt, *Les Trafiquants Italiens dans L'Orient Hellenique*, Paris, 1919.

Stefan Hiller, 'The missing Mycenaeans and the Black Sea', in R. Lauffiere *et al.* (eds), *Thalassa L'Egee Prehistorique et la Mer'*, Liege 1991, 207–216.

J. Hind, 'Megarian Colonisation in the Western half of the Black Sea', in G.R. Tsetskhladze, *The Greek Colonisation of the Black Sea Area*, Historia Einzelschriften 121, Stuttgart 1998, 131–152.

G. Holbl, *The Ptolemaic Empire*, London 2001.

Simon Hornblower, *Mausolus*, Oxford 1982.

Bettany Hughes, *Istanbul, A Tale of Three Cities*, London 2017.

B. Isaac, *The Greek Settlements in Thrace until the Macedonian Conquest*, Leiden 1986, 146–147.

H.G. Jansen and N. Blindow, 'The Geophysical Mapping of the Lower City of Troia/Ilion, in Wagner *et al.*, *Troy and the Troad*

N. Jefrenow, 'Der rhodisch-byzantinisch Krieg con 220 c.Chr.: Ein Handeskrieg in Hellenismus?', *MBAH* 24, 2005, 51–98.

A.H.M. Jones, *The Cities of the Eastern Roman Provinces*, 2nd ed., Oxford 1971.

R.B. Kallet-Marx, *Hegemony to Empire, the Development of the Roman Imperium in the East from 148–62 BC*, Berkeley and Los Angeles 1995.

Manfred Kaufmann *et al.*, *Guide to Troia*, compiled by Istanbul 2001.

Manfred Kaufmann, 'Besik-Tepe, Vorbericht uber die Ergebrisse der Grabugun vor 1984, Grabungen dem Besik-Yepr, Besik-Sivritepe und Besik Graberfeld', *Archaeologischer Anzieger* 1986, 303–363.

Manfred Kaufmann, 'Troia – Ausgrabungen 1995', *Studia Troia* 6, 1996.

Manfred Kaufmann, 'Die Arbeiten in Troia/Wilusa 2003', *Studia Troia* 14, 2004.

Richard Krautheimer, *Three Christian Capitals: Topography and Politics, Rome, Constantinople, Milan*, Berkeley and Los Angeles 1983.

Helen S. Lund, *Lysimachus, a Study in Hellenistic Kingship*, London 1992.

John Ma, *Antiochos III and the Cities of Western Asia Minor*, Oxford 1999.

Colin McEvedy, *Cities of the Classical World*, London 2011.

B.L. McGing, *The Foreign Policy of Mithridates Eupator*, King of Pontus, Leiden 1986.

R.B. McShane, *The Foreign Policy of the Attalids of Pergamon*, Urbana IL 1964.

Thomas F. Madden, *Istanbul, City of Majesty at the Crossroads of the World*, New York 2016.

Jesper Mayborn Madsen, *Eager to be Roman, Greek response to Roman Rule in Pontus and Bithynia*, London 2009.

E.W. Marsden, *Greek and Roman Artillery, Historical Development*, Oxford 1969.

Russell Meiggs, *The Athenian Empire*, Oxford 1975.

B.D. Merritt, H.T. Wade-Gery and M.F. McGregor, *The Athenian Tribute Lists*, 4 vols, Cambridge MA and Princeton, 1939–1953.

F. Millar, *A Study of Cassius Dio*, Oxford 1964.

Margaret M. Mitchell and Frances M. Young, (eds), *The Cambridge History of Christianity*, vol. 1,

Stephen Mitchell, *Anatolia*, 2 vols, Oxford 1993.

Alonso Moreno, *Feeding the Democracy, the Athens Grain Supply in the Fifth and Fourth Centuries BC*, Oxford 2007, 153–161.

O. Morkholm, *Early Hellenistic Coinage from the Accession of Alexander to the Peace of Apamea*, Cambridge 1991.

O. Murray, *Early Greece*, London 1980.

W.M. Murray, *The Age of Titans, the Rise and Fall of the Great Hellenistic Navies*, Oxford 2012.

G. Nachtergael, *Les Galates en Grece at Les Soteria de Delphes*, Brussels 1977

E.T. Newell, *The Coinage of the Western Seleucid Mints from Seleucus I to Antiochus III*, New York, 1941.

Thomas N. Noonan, 'The Grain Trade of the Northern Black Sea in Antiquity', *American Journal of Philology* 94, 1975, 231–242.

H.A. Ormerod, *Piracy in the Ancient World*, Liverpool 1928.

R. Osborne, *Greece in the Making, 1200–479 BC*, London 1996.

M. Ozdogan, 'A Surface Survey for Prehistoric and Early Historic Sites in North-western Turkey', *National Geographic Society research Reports, 1979 Projects*, 1985, 519–541.

M. Ozdogan, 'Neolithic Cultures in North-western Turkey', *Varia Archaeologicae Hungarica*, Budapest, 1989, 201–206.

M. Ozdogan, 'Pendik: a Neolithic site of the Fikirtepe Culture in the Marmara Region', in N. Hauptmann *et al.*, *Festschrift fur Kurt Bittel*, Mainz 1983, 401–411.

M. Ozdogan, *Neolithic in Turkey, New Discoveries*, Istanbul 1991.

M. Ozdogan, 'Prehistoric Sites in the Gelibolu Peninsula', *Anadolu* 10, 1988.

M. Ozdogan, 'The Black Sea, the Sea of Marmara, and Bronze Age Archaeology: an Archaeological Predicament', in Wagner *et al.*, *Troia and Troad*, 105–12.

Millman Parry, *The Making of Homeric Verse*, Oxford 1971.

Elias K. Petropoulos, *Hellenic Colonists in Euxeinos Pontos*, Oxford, BAR S 1394, 2005, 15–24.

Vladimir Popov, 'Les Thraces en Asie Mineure', *Congres Internationale de Thracologie*, Vol I, 121–125.

David S. Potter, *The Roman Empire at Bay* 180–395, London 2004.

George Rapp, Jr, 'Earthquake in the Troad', in G. Rapp and J.A. Giffard (eds), *Troy, the Archaeological Geology*, Princeton NJ 1982.

Nicholas K. Rauh, *Merchants, Sailors, and Pirates in the Roman World*, Stroud, 2003.

J. and L. Robert, *Claros I*, Paris 1989.

L. Robert, 'La titulature de Nicee et de Nicomedee: la gloire et la haine', *HSCP* 81, 1977, 1–39.

J.J. Roodenberg *et al.*, 'Preliminary Report on the Archaeological Investigation at Ilipinar in North-west Anatolia', *Anatolica* 16, 1989–1990, 61–144.

Charles B. Rose, *The Archaeology of Greek and Roman Troy*, Cambridge 2014.

T. Russell, *Byzantium and the Bosphorus*, Oxford 2016.

T.T.B. Ryder, *Koine Eirene, General Peace and Local Independence in Ancient Greece*, Oxford 1965.

Nancy Sanders, *The Sea Peoples*, London 1985.

A. Schultz and E. Winter, 'Zum Hadrianstempel von Kyzikos', *Asia Minor Studien* 1, Bonn 1990, 33–81.

E. Schwertheim, *Inschriften greichisshe Stadte aus Kleinasien: Hadrianoi und Hadrianeia*, Cologne 1987.

E. Schwertheim, 'Zu Hadriens Reisen und Stadtgrundungen in Keinasien', *Epigrafica Anatolica* 6, 1985, 37–42.

David Jean Shirley and Christine Blenpied, 'Late Quaternary Water Exchange Between the Mediterranean and the Black Seas', *Nature* 285, 1980, 537–541.

T.C. Skeet, *Papyri from Panopolis*, Dublin 1964.

J.W. Sperling, 'Kum Tepe in the Troad, Trial Excavations 1934', *Hesperia* 45, 1976, 305–364.

G. Steiner, 'The Immigration of the first Indo-Europeans into Anatolia Reconsidered', *Journal of Indo-European Studies* 18, 1990, 185–214.

J. Stevenson and W.H.C. Frend, *A New Eusebius, Documents Illustrating the History of the Church to A.D. 337*, London 1987.

D.L. Stockton (ed.) *From the Gracchi to Sulla*, London 1981.

R. Syme, 'The Career of Arrian', *Roman Papers* IV, 27–28.

W.W. Tarn, *Hellenistic Naval and Military Developments*, Cambridge 1930.

J.M.C. Toynbee, *The Hadrianic School, a Chapter in the History of Greek Art*, Cambridge 1934.

David Trump, *The Prehistory of the Mediterranean*, Harmondsworth 1980.

G. R. Tsetskhladze, 'Greek Penetration of the Black Sea', in Tsetskhladze and de Angelis, *The Archaeology of Greek Colonisation*, Oxford 2009, 111–136.

R. Tybout, 'Barbarians in Phrygia: a New Grave Stele', *Epigraphica Anatolica* 20, 1992, 35–41.

Gunther A. Wagner *et al.*, *Troia and the Troad, Scientific Approaches*, Berlin 2003.

F.W. Walbank, *Philip V of Macedon*, Cambridge 1940 reprinted 1967.

C.B. Welles, *Royal Correspondnce of the Hellenistic Period*, New Haven, 1936.

Stephen Williams, *Diocletian and the Roman Recovery*, London 1985.

A.J.N. Wilson, *Emigration from Italy in the Republican Age of Rome*, Manchester 1966.

Herbert B. Workman, *Persecution in the Early Church*, London 1906, paperback edition, Oxford 1980.

Jak Yakar, *Prehistoric Anatolia, the Neolithic Transformation and the Early Chalcolithic Period*, Tel Aviv, 1991.

Index

The waterways noted in the title – Dardanelles/Hellespont, Sea of Marmar/
Propontis and Bosporos, together with the Black Sea – are omitted from
this index; all three appear on almost every page so to index them would be
meaningless.